£65-00

143097

BCFTCS

KT-460-661

FLYING TOO CLOSE TO THE SUN

B.C.F.T.C.S.
143097

To Snorri Arnar

Flying too Close to the Sun

The Success and Failure of the New-entrant Airlines

SVEINN VIDAR GUDMUNDSSON
Assistant Professor Transport and Logistics
Faculty of Economics and Business Administration
Maastricht University, The Netherlands

Ashgate

Aldershot • Burlington USA • Singapore • Sydney

© Sveinn Vidar Gudmundsson 1998

All rights reserved. No part of this publication may be reproduced, stored in a retrieval system, or transmitted in any form or by any means, electronic, mechanical, photocopying, recording or otherwise without the prior permission of the publisher.

Published by
Ashgate Publishing Limited
Gower House
Croft Road
Aldershot
Hants GU11 3HR
England

Ashgate Publishing Company
131 Main Street
Burlington, VT 05401-5600 USA

Reprinted 2001 (twice)

Ashgate website: http://www.ashgate.com

British Library Cataloguing-in-Publication Data
Gudmundsson, Sveinn Vidar
Flying too close to the sun : the success and failure of new-entrant airlines. - (Ashgate studies in aviation economics and management)
1. Airlines - Management 2. Aeronautics, Commercial-Deregulation
I. Title
387.7'068

Library of Congress Cataloging-in-Publication Data
Gudmundsson, Sveinn Vidar
Flying too close to the sun : the success and failure of the new-entrant airlines / Sveinn Vidar Gudmundsson.
p. cm.
Includes bibliographical references and index.
ISBN 1-84014-366-5 (hb)
1. Airlines--United States--Management. 2. Airlines--United States--Finance. 3. Aeronautics, Commercial--United States--Management. 4. Business failures--United States. I. Title.
HE9803.A4G83 1998
385.7'0973--dc21 98-40396
CIP

ISBN 1 84014 366 5

Printed and bound in Great Britain by Biddles Limited, Guildford and King's Lynn.

Contents

List of Tables

List of Figures

Preface

In 1984 at the height of the new-entrant airlines' successes, Meyer and Oster published a book titled *Deregulation and the New Airline Entrepreneurs* (MIT Press, 1984). Only three years later the whole industry had concentrated and many new-entrants gone out of business. Observing these developments, one can call the eighties the period of 'first wave' new-entrants, and the nineties the period of 'second wave' new-entrants. This book is an attempt to explain the complex issues that led to the almost total failure rate of the 'first wave' new-entrant airlines.

The book covers the new-entrants' structure and strategies and then the identification of critical factors through distress/failure prediction models. It can easily be said that the coverage is too broad and that the conclusions not prescriptive enough. However, working on this project the practice of explaining an airline failure based on one or few factors was rejected and the need for a more complex and dynamic framework of explanations suggested. The reader will, therefore, not find a simple prescription for success or how to avoid failure. However, it is hoped that the reader will recognise the adaptability of incumbent airlines, past mistakes of new airlines and gain some insights into new airline strategies. Furthermore, the reader will be able to recognise some of the underlying management emphasis that distinguish between the distressed airlines and those that have secured better fortunes.

By having managers of airlines rate various factors selected from the literature and previous studies on company failures, the study sought to identify the factors that were the most important in the mind of the manager during a period of non-distress as well as distress. The study was organised into two main parts. The first part is a literature review, whose purpose was to establish what sort of an environment the new-entrants encountered, how the new-entrants organised them selves and behaved within the constraints they had. The second part starts with a literature review to establish what research has been performed on success and failure in general and failure prediction models specifically. Then the design, implementation and results of the survey research is covered, whose purpose was to gain direct insight into management priorities and organisation characteristics at new-entrant airlines and their linkages with good and poor performance. Following from this a database containing financial and traffic data on new-entrants is explained, as well as the development of failure/distress prediction models. The failure prediction models were based on three data sources questionnaire Part I, Part II and the database. The final aspect of the analysis was the comparison of the models in order to investigate whether such comparison increased the information content for prediction enhancement. The final chapter brings together the various parts of the book and covers an inventory of new-entrants' critical factors and a concept of *Critical Performance Factor* and *Performance Indicators*.

Acknowledgements

I would like to begin with extending my acknowledgement to those many people who have vested so much in the new airlines, some of whom were so kind to spend time on the questionnaire on which large part of this book is based.

Furthermore, I wish to express my gratitude to the numerous people who directly or indirectly contributed to this book. The School of Aeronautics and the School of Management at Florida Institute of Technology, equipped me with the foundation knowledge on which I have built through the years, while the College of Aeronautics, Cranfield University provided me with a stimulating environment through its excellent staff, while working on this project.

The book is the outgrowth of my DPhil thesis, completed at Cranfield University in 1995. The thesis work was supported by a Scholarship from the Cranfield College of Aeronautics and the Overseas Research Students Awards Scheme (ORSA). Special thanks are due to Prof. Rigas Doganis and Dr. Fariba Alamdari, who supervised my thesis work. Of the many people who gave advice and encouragement, I wish to mention, Peter Morrell, Dr. Rafael Echevarne, Ian Stockman, Paul Jackson and Doris Corbett the public reference assistant at the U.S. Department of Transport, who all contributed knowingly and unknowingly to this work. I am especially indebted to my partner, Vala Jónsdóttir, for her continuing support and numerous suggestions that helped improve the organisation and readability of the book. I also want to thank Michael Levine, John R. Meyer and Clinton V. Oster that inspired academic interest in new-entrant airlines through their publications.

I have had the fortune of meeting people that have had much positive impact on me, providing assistance and encouragement when most needed. I would like to mention the late Agnar Kofoed-Hansen, who regardless of being a busy head of Civil Aviation was always ready and willing to assist and inspire aviation enthusiasts of all ages, Pétur Einarsson former head of Civil Aviation who got me first involved in serious air transport research and Prof. Stefán Ólafsson who trusted me with a much needed project.

List of Abbreviations

CAB	Civil Aeronautics Board (USA)
DoT	Department of Transportation (USA)
CAA	Civil Aviation Authority (UK)
PSA	Pacific Southwest Airlines
CRS	Computer Reservation System
TA	Travel Agent
DoJ	Department of Justice (USA)
CPI	Consumer Price Index
ASK	Available Seat Kilometers
PIMS	Profit Impact of Strategy
ROI	Return on Investment
TWA	Trans World Airways
FAA	Federal Aviation Administration
HHI	Herfindahl-Hirschman Index
DIP	Debtor in Possession
EU	European Union
EEA	European Economic Area
SWA	Sabena World Airways
BA	British Airways
EC	European Commission
RPK	Revenue Passenger Kilometers
AEA	Association of European Airlines
TFP	Total Factor Productivity
BM	British Midland
FFP	Frequent Flyer Program
ILG	International Leisure Group
ATW	Air Transport World
AOM	Air Outre Mer
YMS	Yield Management System
GAO	Government Accounting Office (USA)
MII	Majority in Interest

JWA	John Wayne Airport
ADD	Average Daily Departures
HBA	Harvard Business School
CEO	Chief Executive Officer
US	United States of America
EPS	Earnings Per Share
ASM	Available Seat Miles
CPF	Critical Performance Factor
PI	Performance Indicator
LRA	Logistic Regression Analysis
MDA	Multiple Discrimination Analysis
CT	Catastrophe Theory
ATC	Air Traffic Control
IC	Indifference Contour
LC	Loyalty Contour
AC	Avoidance Contour
PC	Positive Contour
NC	Negative Contour
UoS	Units of Satisfaction
GPFI	General Passenger Fare Investigation (USA)
SW	Southwest Airlines
USP	Unique Selling Point
SLD	Strategic Leadership Dimensions
D	Distressed
ND	Non-Distressed
F	Failed
NF	Non-Failed
NN	Neural Networks
LL	Log of the Likelihood
BSTEP	Backward Stepwise
FSTEP	Forward Stepwise
ATK	Available Ton Kilometres
GDP	Gross Domestic Product
QI	Questionnaire Part I
QII	Questionnaire Part II

'Dollars' ($) refer to United States dollars, unless otherwise stated.

All tons are metric tons, unless otherwise stated.

PART I

NEW-ENTRANT AIR-LINES' SUCCESS AND FAILURE: THEORY, STRATEGY AND POLICY

1 The new-entrants

Introduction

At the dawn of deregulation it was believed that the threat of entry by a new airline with new ideas and low cost structure would cause the incumbents to strive to fulfil customers' needs and wants at a price they are willing to pay, producing the highest obtainable total utility for the users. New-entrants started to appear soon after deregulation stimulating exciting changes in the market. Soon it became apparent, however, that the new-entrants had problems surviving as the post deregulation years passed. From 1978 to 1989 about 88 jet-operating airlines were formed (scheduled, charter and cargo) of which 83 failed, the survivors (scheduled and charter/scheduled passenger) being Southwest Airlines (*est.* 1967), Midwest Express (*est.* 1984), America West (*est.* 1981), Tower Air (*est.* 1982) and World Airways (*est.* 1948/scheduled services 1979). Another important fact is that of the scheduled and mixed (charter/scheduled) carriers only 26 operated for three or more years. Some of the failed airlines operated for much shorter period of time than three years and others under more than one name following stints of reorganisation attempts.

There have been numerous explanations to this failure phenomena provided by industry analysts and ex-managers of new-entrant airlines, explanations such as: (i) poor management; (ii) unfavourable regulatory environment (route rights, etc.); (iii) inadequate infrastructure (slots, etc.); (iv) poor financial foundation; (v) over-expansion; (vi) poor service standards; (vii) inadequate distribution systems; (viii) poor marketing strategy; (ix) lack of protection against predatory pricing; (x) brand image conflict due to evolutionary change in the product or strategy (the problems of growth, etc.); (xi) conspiracy to undermine the new-entrant by incumbents; and (xii) unfavourable economic climate (recession, etc.).

Of course, each downfall has its unique explanation in the eyes of the stakeholder, but is there perhaps similar factors to blame in new-entrant airlines' failures? Can it be that factors that are assumed to be important for survival are actually not the ones that make or break an airline? Can the downfall of a new-entrant be foretold prior to failure? Can a financial distress model prevent failure if used timely enough by the carrier's management? How does the change in various factors affect the well-being of new-entrants? Are new-entrants being discriminated against by authorities in terms of infrastructure barriers? In the book it is hoped that answers will be found to some of the questions stated here.

Classification of new-entrants

The book is based on a classification of new-entrant airlines that may be less than straightforward to the reader. The general definition of a new-entrant in the book became therefore

> A domestic or international airline established after deregulation or liberalisation of a domestic market or bilateral route; or a regional, intrastate, charter or cargo carrier that expands to scheduled operations after a regulatory change.

The main groups of new-entrants resulting from the definition, were: (i) start-up new-entrants; (ii) intrastate new-entrants; (iii) regional based new-entrants; and (iv) charter or cargo based new-entrants. In addition, it must be clarified that the airlines covered in the study are only jet-operating airlines that emphasised scheduled passenger operations and existed for more than one full year of operations.

New entry is characterised by advancement from a lower revenue class to a larger class with the exception of charters and cargo carriers that are classified as such regardless of size. The thin lines in Figure 1.1 show from left to right the direction of new-entry and the thick lines to the far right, the possible development path of the new-entrant. The reason for including the whole development path from relatively small size to large size is the fact that these are all carriers that derive their existence or ability to expand on deregulation or liberalisation.

New-entrant's problems

Most jet-operating new-entrants have been characterised by exceptionally fast growth in their first years of operation. Such fast growth shows clearly that consumer markets develop extreme demand if the price is right. In fact, new-entrants have a common advantage of lower costs than the incumbents (Bailey and Williams, 1988), allowing the offering of lower fares for comparable product. This seems to be a secure ticket to success with the failure record proving otherwise.

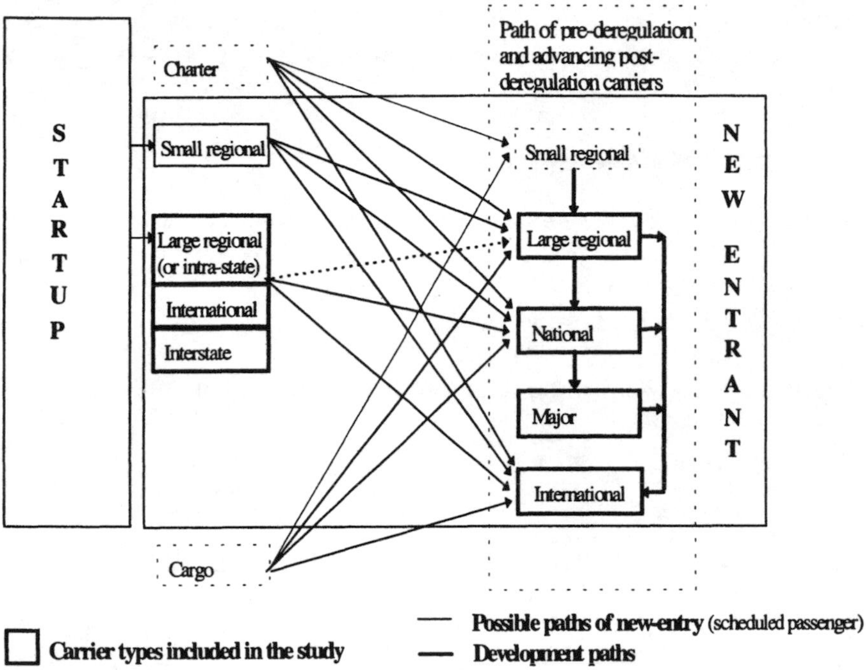

Figure 1.1 The new-entrants' classification model

New-entrant airlines' problems can be divided into three main categories: (i) managerial problems; (ii) industry barriers; and (iii) adverse environment conditions. The managerial problems are extremely hard to address as one can look at management as an art rather than science. What one must accept is that management has alternatives in any decision and those decisions shape the company's ability to deal with the environment. For example, an airline enters a competitor's hub airport and fails as a result. It can claim that the incumbent used predation to hinder the financial viability of the entry decision. The reason for the failure, though, was the management decision to enter the hub airport in the face of poor legal protection against predation.[1] Hence, the airline took a risk, and high risk can cause failure, success or everything in-between. Thus the operating disadvantages are a nuisance and a focus of removal, while decision-making must reckon with the associated risks. Similar issue is industry barriers, which obviously limit the new-entrants' options, although, it is management decision whether to go ahead or not while a specific barrier is not yet overcome. Cyclical economy can now be assumed as certainty influencing decisions concerning long-term debt and revenue generation. A common fallacy is to assume a favourable economic climate, but encounter a storm. When the airline's resources are exceeded it can only survive in a favourable climate, however finding the equilibrium is no simple task as many managers are only too willing to attest to.

Characteristics of new-entrants

As can be expected, the new-entrants have had difficulty reaching large size, primarily because of high exit rates rather than slow or early growth maturity. To show the new-entrants' size progression, Table 1.1 was constructed, having four revenue categories or steps.

Table 1.1 New-entrant airline's advancement through life-cycle 1980 – 1990

Revenue-band (000.000)	$0-99 *(1)*	$100-499 *(2)*	$500-999 *(3)*	$1000 + *(4)*
New-entrants				
America West	*t*	*t*+1	*t*+4	*t*+7
People Express	*t*	*t*+1	*t*+3	
Midway Airlines	*t*	*t*+3	*t*+10	
New York Air	*t*	*t*+2		
Muse Air	*t*	*t*+3		
Jet America	*t*	*t*+3		
Braniff II		*t*		
Florida Express	*t*			
Air Atlanta	*t*			
Empire Airlines[1]	*t*			
Presidential Airways	*t*			
Former Intra-States				
Air California		*t*		
Air Florida		*t*		
PSA		*t*	*t*+4	
Southwest Airlines[2]		*t*	*t*+4	*t*+9
Charter-Based				
Carnival	*t*			
Tower Air				
Arrow Airways		*t*		
Capitol Air		*t*		
World Airways		*t*		

Initial size at *t* as of 1980 or later. [1] Granted air carrier status in 1979. [2] The only airline listed in the table that is still operating and not having gone through Chapter 11 proceedings.

Time (*t*) shows in what year the carrier reached a particular stage as well as the entry stage reached in the first year of operations or 1980 if the carrier existed before that year.

Most new-entrant carriers start operations in the first revenue band during the first year of operations, with few notable exceptions, namely the former intrastate and charter based carriers. Only one carrier Braniff (II), classified as a start-up new-entrant, entered at a higher stage, unusual in terms of its large scale operations right from the beginning. Carriers reach the second stage during the first to fourth year of operations, with three start-ups entering in their fourth year, one in the third year and two in the second year and one in the first year.[2] There is considerable difference when carriers enter the third stage ranging from the fourth year of operations to the eleventh year as in the case of Midway Airlines. Of the six carriers entering the third stage, three did so during the fifth year of operations. Only two carriers enter the fourth stage, America West in the eighth year and Southwest Airlines in the tenth year (base year 1980).

Regional airlines

The regional new-entrants took advantage of deregulation at a slower phase and less grandiose scale than the intrastate and start-up carriers, perhaps due to their existing experience of operating next to the large carriers. All the airlines listed in Table 1.2 entered jet operations and all failed with Air Wisconsin being the last casualty of the airlines listed in the table, acquired and dismantled by United in 1992-1993.

Under increased pressure in the early forties to provide increased service to smaller communities the CAB created a level of scheduled service called 'local service'. The resulting 'local carriers' were then subsidised to provide 'essential' service to these communities. In the late fifties, there was a substantial pressure to cut these subsidies in order to reduce the government deficit. To accomplish this the local carriers were allowed to serve the higher density routes in order to cross-subsidise the thinner routes. This, however, shifted the carriers' focus into the more profitable markets leaving the small communities with the minimum government required service of two flights a day (Feldman, 1987).[3]

As the local carriers started to abandon some of the most unprofitable markets a gap was left for 'air taxis' operating small aircraft. These carriers were not regulated by the CAB and did not receive subsidies from the government. As a result, the CAB recognised air taxis as 'third level commuter carriers' in 1969. Consequently, they were allowed to make agreements with the local carriers to take over the most unprofitable routes on the terms of receiving part or all of the subsidy payments meant for the local carrier. To further facilitate the commuter service the CAB gradually reduced the restrictions in terms of aircraft size until the passing of the Airline Deregulation Act when these carriers were allowed to fly aircraft of up to 60 seats. After the passage of the Act these carriers increased the number of exclusively subsidised routes served, from 112 to 266 out of 316 subsidy points. This shift in commuter carriers' importance governed the change in the name from 'commuters' to 'regionals' in the early 1980's (Feldman, 1987).

The deregulators recognised that it was not enough to increase competition between existing carriers but there had to be ample scope for entry of new carriers. This was accomplished through the Loan Guarantee Program.[4] Another no less important aspect was the guarantee of service to small communities for ten years (Bailey, Graham & Kaplan, 1985). On the basis of 'essential air service' scheme airlines serving small communities would receive subsidies until 1988. However, in the bill it was made possible for a carrier to bump out another carrier receiving subsidies, if it could provide the same level of service without the subsidy payments.

Some of the regionals did not make any major changes in their strategy immediately following deregulation. Air Wisconsin for example kept its initial strategy of serving short-haul routes between medium sized communities and major hubs (O'Hare). What changed for Air Wisconsin was the increased competition and faster growth than anticipated. The reason for the accelerated growth was primarily the reduction or suppression of service by United and Republic following deregulation. This development at Air Wisconsin characterises many of the regionals during the early deregulation years. Not only in terms of picking up routes abandoned by the majors but also in starting jet operations with small jets such as the BAe146, BAC-111 or F28, as Air Wisconsin did on short-haul hubroutes to communities with population of 100 thousand inhabitants or more (ATW, 1982).

Table 1.2 Regional based new-entrants

	Entered service[a]	Ended service	
Air Wisconsin	1982[b]	1992	Acquired by United Airlines
Empire	1980[c]	1986	Acquired by Piedmont
Horizon	1981	1986	Acquired by Alaska

[a] Included are only carriers that operated jets to some extent. The table is based on the starting year of jet-operations. [b]Started service as Oneida Aviation in 1975, but began F28 jet operations in 1980. [c] Began operations in 1965 and jet operations in 1982.

Another strategy of the regionals was to become a fully independent jet operator, such as Empire Airlines that began operations in 1975 with small propeller aircraft. Deregulation led its founder Paul Quackenbush to steer his regional airline into filling gaps left by the majors in New York State, acquiring Fokker F28's, 85 passenger jets in 1980, becaming a fully fledged jet operator focusing on hub strategy out of Syracuse to the immediate surrounding area, including Canada. Conversely, Horizon Air and Air Wisconsin, selected a strategy in-between, operating a mixed fleet of turboprops and jets.

An important aspect of deregulation for regionals was their changing status in the CRS and the resulting shift from interlining to code-sharing with the majors. Many regionals lost their separate image and independence as they secured closer ties with the incumbents, effectively turning some regionals into an extension of the major's image, by becoming a feeder carrier under the major's name, such as: United Express, Continental Express and so forth. Under such a scheme the carriers loose control as one can see from the fact that many of these carriers have sold-out to the majors or failed, Air Wisconsin being the latest fatality in terms of the carriers listed in the table.

Charter based airlines

Shortly after the enactment of the Civil Aeronautics Act of 1938 the CAB issued an exempt order authorising non-scheduled operations. After World War II, this type of operations received a boost with the availability of large surplus war aircraft. As a result of increased activity the Board changed the exemption regulation to divide the irregulars into two groups, large- and small irregulars. The change in the regulation prohibited the large irregulars to operate regularly, that is more than 12 flights per month between any two points. In 1962 supplemental carriers were granted certificates to provide non-scheduled charter services.[5] Due to increased fare competition in the seventies with the trunks, the supplementals entered their decline period that reached its height with the advent of deregulation in 1978.

Charter airlines are heavily depended on tour operators, meaning that the decision to start scheduled operations involves setting up basically all the necessary infrastructure, except flight operations. This has placed the charters in a similar situation as any start-up carrier except that the charter has fully operational flight department from the outset. The downside is, however, that the flight equipment is usually long-range wide-body aircraft suitable for long-haul domestic or international routes.

Following deregulation the scheduled incumbents exited many unprofitable short-haul routes and increased their emphasis on medium to long-haul domestic routes, limiting the charters' options even further. As the domestic passenger growth levelled off the incumbents then increased the stress on international routes increasing even further the constraints on the charter based new-entrants.

With deregulation the charters lost a large portion of their market to the scheduled carriers due to reduction in fares on scheduled routes. The logical answer seemed therefore be to enter the scheduled market such as done by many charter carriers. The charters that did not performed poorly and most failed, such as: McCulloch, ONA and Saturn. Evergreen, on the other hand, turned to cargo operations and became successful there.

Carriers such as Capitol, World, TIA, TransAmerica, Tower and American Trans Air, entered scheduled operations and had different stories to tell (*see* Figure 1.2 and Figure 1.3). Capitol, TIA, TransAmerica went soon out of business, while World closed down its scheduled operations. Tower with a clear-cut niche market and American Trans Air with sophisticated structure of peripheral businesses have succeeded so far. All of the carriers that entered scheduled operations struggled to maintain their charter base by mixing it with scheduled and cargo operations. Even that strategy did not secure success for the former supplementals, although it can not be said to be the cause of their troubles.

Table 1.3 Charter based new-entrants

	Entered scheduled service[a]	Ended scheduled service	
American Trans Air	1992[b]		Still operating
Capitol	1979	1984	Bankruptcy
Carnival	1988[c]		Acquired by Pan Am (II) '97
Morris Air	1992[d]	1994	Acquired by Southwest Airl.
National Airlines	1993[e]		Still operating ('94)
Tower	1983		Still operating
World	1979	1985	Bankruptcy

[a] The table is based on the starting year and ending year of scheduled operations only. [b] Limited scheduled operations, mostly charter. The carrier did not gain scheduled authority on its own until the date specified in the table. [c] Established from the assets of Pacific Interstate Airlines. [d] Started as a charter carrier in 1984. [e] Started service in 1988 as Private Jet Expeditions.

It is noteworthy that consumer complaints are high for charter-based new-entrant airlines. One possible explanation is the vulnerability of long distance route system to extensive delays throughout the network in the case of mechanical delay, acts of god and ad-hoc charters that are sometimes given priority over poorly booked scheduled flights. Furthermore, these airlines tend to operate both scheduled and charter flights with the same equipment increasing aircraft utilisation but also increasing the possibility of delays.

All in all, the charters lacked customer recognition and were, therefore, just as any other new airline starting operations in a new market. Furthermore, the charter carriers in the United States were prohibited to integrate vertically and operate tour-operating companies. Thus, the advantage of charters over new carriers seems to have been limited to easier access to capital, less preparation time in terms of fulfilling operating regulation as the operation was licensed and ready. In other aspects the charters ran into similar problems as other new-entrants, for example in securing an effective distribution system and carving out a niche and protecting it.

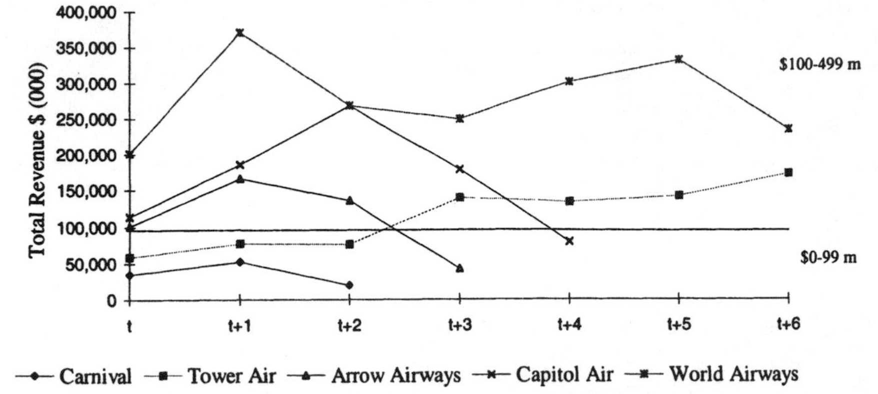

Figure 1.2 Total revenue: charter-based new-entrant airlines

Source: Data compiled from DoT, Form 41.

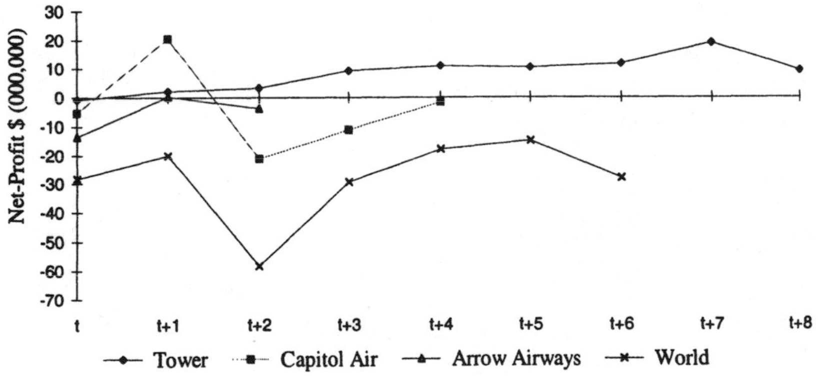

Figure 1.3 Net profit: charter-based new-entrant airlines

Source: Data compiled from DoT, Form 41.

Intrastate airlines

As early as 1946 the state of California had liberal view towards entry of new airlines in its intrastate market. This lead to 18 new-entrants until 1975 but only 3 remained in service at the end of the period. In 1965, one of the proponents of deregulation, Levine (1965) reported that the deregulated market between Los Angeles and San Francisco was benefiting the consumers by the provision of the lowest 'overland' fares in the world and 300 percent increase in passengers over the period from 1959 until 1965.

Table 1.4 Former intrastate carriers

	Entered service	Ended service	
Alaska*	pre-1978		Still operating
Air California	pre-1978	1987	Acquired by American
Air Florida	pre-1978	1984	Bankruptcy/acquired by Midway
PSA	pre-1978	1987	Acquired by USAir
Southwest Airlines	pre-1978		Still operating

* Is not included in the analysis in the following chapters.

The state of Texas had similar liberated views, although, the state controlled entry, but not fares. Southwest Airlines had therefore, a substantial advantage in 1978 with the advent of interstate deregulation by having experience with differential pricing, specifically 'off-peak' and 'peak-pricing.' Southwest Airlines's advantage was also substantial having experience in low-fare operations, while the competition transferred its emphasis to fare-competition from service-competition after 1978. The idea of Southwest Airlines's operations was, nevertheless, not unique as Pacific Southwest Airlines (PSA) began operations in 1949, initiating the low-fare, no-frills concept (Meyer and Oster, 1984).

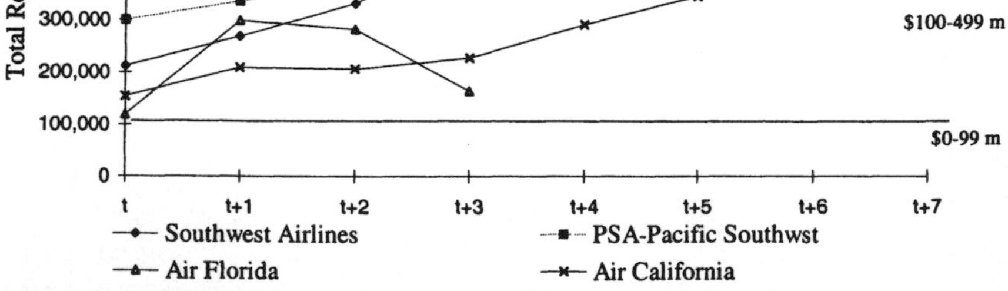

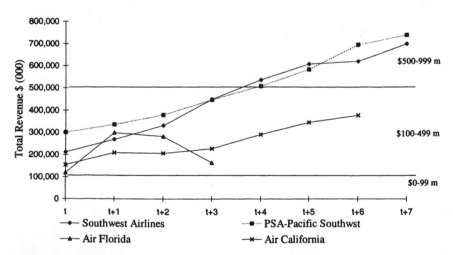

Figure 1.4 Total revenue: former intrastate airlines

Source: Data compiled from DoT, Form 41.

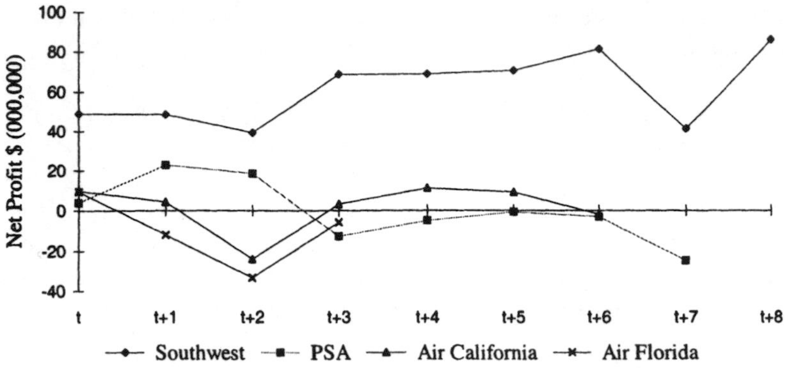

Figure 1.5 Net profit: former intrastate airlines

Source: Data compiled from DoT, Form 41.

As deregulation came into effect these carriers expanded their services into the adjacent states. The most aggressive in terms of such expansion was Air Florida, that actually cut off its intrastate operations, focusing on domestic and international routes until bankruptcy in 1984.

The operating environment prior to deregulation had diverse effect on intrastate carrier's strategy at the beginning of deregulation. The intrastate carriers had more experience operating in a competitive environment prior to deregulation than the incumbents. Although, PSA and Air California had monopoly status on some intrastate routes that were not served by the interstate carriers, they were in competition with the interstate carriers on many intrastate routes. PSA had experienced success against the CAB regulated trunks in California, but with the advent of Air California its success dissipated. The California Public Utilities Commission had been inclined to approve rates considered to provide only 'reasonable' rate of return. Moreover, the Commission divided the markets between PSA and Air California on routes not served by the interstate carriers. These developments just prior to deregulation, may have affected PSA's experience of full fledged competition as can be hypothesised by high increase in operating cost between 1978 and 1980.

PSA, strangely enough, was therefore forced by the Public Utilites Commission to maintain its low fare structure prior to deregulation but needed to raise fares due to costs that were higher than the fares could sustain. Thus, PSA saw deregulation primarily as an instrument for raising fares and a way to abandon its 'forced' fare strategy. Southwest Airlines, on the other hand, kept its fare strategy, as its operation philosophy and cost structure was in line with it (Lloyd's Aviation Economist, 1984a, p. 29)

> The battle [with Braniff] provided a case study in airline marketing and the lessons learnt have stood Southwest Airlines in good stead not only in its intra-state expansion but, post-1978 in its operations outside Texas.

Both PSA and Southwest Airlines had similar growth levels (*see* Figure 1.4), while profit levels were markedly different for those airlines. Air Florida had faster initial growth (base year 1980) than the other carriers, but unlike them it had a two year period of rapid revenue decline before its demise. Of the former intrastate carriers only Alaska Airlines and Southwest Airlines are still operating. Air California and PSA were acquired by American and USAir respectively, while Air Florida was acquired by Midway Airlines.

Table 1.5 Start-up jet-operating new-entrants 1979 - 1986

	Entered service*	Ended service	
Air Atlanta	1984	1986	Bankruptcy
Air Chicago	1980	1982	Bankruptcy
Air One	1983	1984	Bankruptcy
America West	1983	1994	Chapter 11 (re-emerged)
American Internat.	1982	1984	Bankruptcy
Florida Express	1984	1988	Acquired by Braniff
Frontier Horizon	1984	1985	Bankruptcy
Hawaii Express	1982	1983	Bankruptcy
Jet America	1982	1986	Acquired by Alaska
McClain Airlines	1986	1987	Bankruptcy
MGM Grand Air	1987	1993	Became charter only, then folded
Midway	1979	1991	Bankruptcy
Midwest Express	1984		Still operating
Muse (TranStar)	1981	1985	Acquired by Southwest Airlines
New York Air	1980	1985	Acquired by Continental
Northeastern	1982	1984	Bankruptcy
Pacific East	1982	1984	Bankruptcy
Pacific Express	1982	1984	Bankruptcy
PeoplExpress	1981	1986	Acquired by Continental
Presidential	1985	1989	Bankruptcy
Sunworld	1983	1988	Bankruptcy

* Note that this table is not fully exhaustive of new-entrant jet carriers as some carriers entered bankruptcy very soon after initiation of operations and are beyond the scope of this study, which covers only carriers operating for more than one year.

New airlines

Start-up airlines entered usually on the basis of much lower costs than the incumbents, being able to offer lower fares. Their entry strategies have been varied but fall basically into four categories: (i) low-fare, no-frills service (PeoplExpress, Southwest Airlines); (ii) low fare, full service (Muse Air); (iii) standard fare, premium service (Air Atlanta, Presdential, Air One); standard to first class fares, luxury service (MGM Grand Air).

In addition to these there was, of course, a difference in route strategies such as hub operation, point to point or feeding. It is apparent that the start-up carriers selecting to operate hub service from an under-served metropolitan airport at the dawn of deregulation experienced explosive growth, with PeoplExpress, Midway and America West falling into this category. Other carriers experienced less success with premium and luxury service carriers having the greatest difficulties.

The greatest number of new start-ups occurred from 1979 to 1981 when 55 new carriers started operations and from 1983 to 1985 when other 55 carriers started operations. As the book is only concerned with jet-operating carriers the record is even worse, as Table 1.5 shows. Of the 21 airlines listed 13 went bankrupt, 5 were acquired, 2 are still operating and one became a charter carrier solely. Only America West has re-emerged from Chapter 11 bankruptcy.

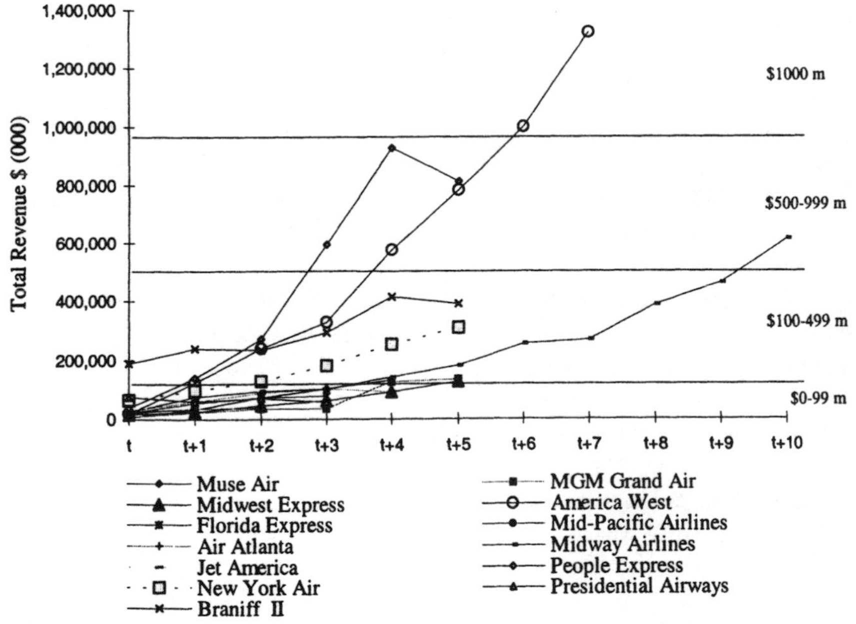

Figure 1.6 Total revenue: start-up new-entrant airlines

Source: Data compiled from DoT, Form 41.

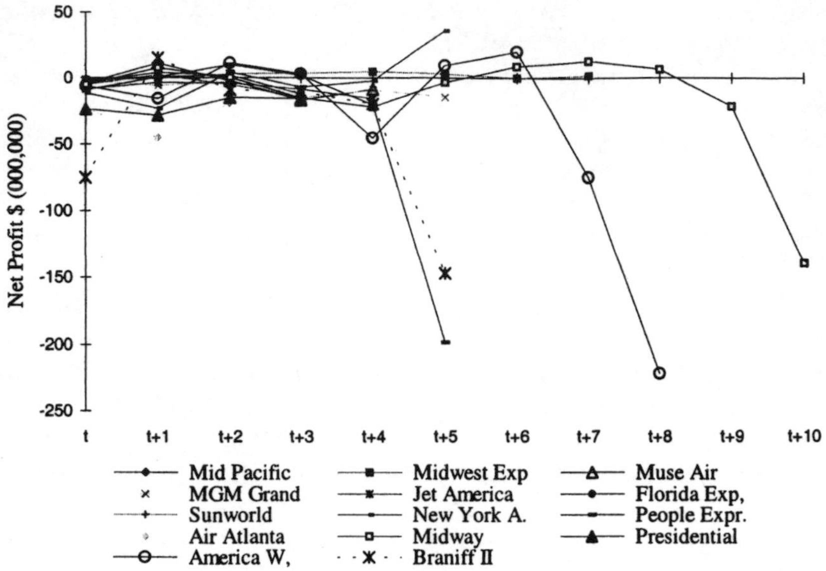

Figure 1.7 Net profit: start-up new-entrant airlines

Source: Data compiled from DoT, Form 41.

A substantial reduction occurred in new start-ups from 1985 until 1991, as only 77 airlines entered operations compared to 110 in the period from 1979 until 1985. The year 1992 there was an increase in start-ups again, with 15 new airlines appearing in that year alone, marking the start of the 'second' wave of new-entry.

The market-share of new-entrants increased from 1978 to 1985 by 346 percent or from 3 to 10.4 percent overall market-share in the US domestic market. During the same period the former local carriers gained 30.5 percent increase, or from 9.1 overall market-share in 1978 to 13.1 percent in 1985.The start-up new entrants experienced the fastest growth levels of all new-entrants' groups (*see* Figure 1.6), with America West being the first to reach the one billion dollar mark (1990), just before its Chapter 11 bankruptcy, while PeoplExpress was just about to reach the same mark ($928 million in 1985) when it was acquired in 1987 by Continental.

Profit levels were non-spectacular with only two carriers showing a tendency to rise above the crowd, New York Air in 1986 (net profit $36 million) and America West in 1989 (net profit $20 million). New York Air can therefore be considered to be the only start-up new-entrant carrier being acquired (1987) in good financial condition if the immediate year prior to acquisition is used as an indicator.

Summary

Most new-entrants have failed or been acquired, leading to pressing questions as to the causes. All jet-operating regional based new-entrants have been acquired by other airlines. Regional based new-entrants operated usually a mixed fleet of turboprop and jet aircraft, with operations centred around feeding agreements with a major carrier on short-haul routes out of a hub.

Charter-based new-entrants operated on long-haul domestic and international routes. They operated mixed charter and scheduled operations. There are four charter-based new-entrants operating and two of those have had some success for a considerable time by entering and exiting scheduled passenger operations repeatedly. Charter carriers have not found a successful niche in long-haul scheduled operations with the exception of Tower Air.

The former intrastate carriers still operating have had considerable success with Southwest Airlines being United States' most profitable carrier since deregulation.

The number of start-up new-entrant carriers has been high, but the failure rate has been just as high with only two first wave start-up carriers remaining, Midwest Express and America West, with the latter emerging from bankruptcy reorganisation in 1994.

---

1 Smaller new-entrants may not even go to court with a perfectly good cause due to the legal costs involved.

2 $t+2 = 3$ complete years of operations.

3 In fact from 1959 to 1963, 128 cities were abandoned by the carriers

4 The FAA Loan Guarantee Program existed before the 1978 Deregulation Act but was expanded with the Act's passage to include eligible commuters, intrastate and charter carriers. Each carrier could gain guarantee of up to $100 million for up to 15 years. The program was based on the FAA guaranteeing a loan amounting to 90 percent of the purchase price of aircraft, if the petitioning carrier was unable to secure uninsured loan elsewhere on reasonable terms, given certain provisions the carrier had to fulfil. The results of the program was to make it easier for new-entrants to secure loans at favourable terms.

5 Charters were called supplementals in the United States, but the term 'charter' will be used in this study.

2 The operating environment

Introduction

An important characteristic of the airline industry is that economies of scale are not considered to be present. This apparent fact, discussed in Chapter 2, makes the airline industry theoretically easy to enter. However, as will be discussed in this chapter, incumbent airlines have erected other barriers to entry that have been quite effective. In addition, infrastructure barriers have limited the availability of valuable scarce resources to new-entrants making competition less viable or simply impossible in many markets. When new-entrants emerge in the form of new or expanding small carriers the staying power of the large incumbents is certainly a barrier to entry unless there are enforced rules to play by. In fact the ground-rules for the treatment of new-entrants were paved before deregulation. The Chicago Midway 'Low Fare Route Proceeding' before the CAB, dealt with two new-entrants that had made an argument for a lead-time or a protected corridor, against competition by the incumbents. In this case the CAB ruled that (CAB order 78-7-40, p. 5)

> It is one thing to grant a new entrant the opportunity to compete; one need have no concern in these circumstances about its ability to meet the public need, since others are present to provide service if it fails to do so. It is a very different thing to make an award to a non-operating firm and then erect regulatory shields that were not there before to protect it in the hope that it will survive.

A dissenting member of the Board, O'Melia, found on the contrary, a reason to exclude incumbents from Chicago's Midway airport and, what is more, from matching the new-entrant's fares for one year in order to protect them.[6]

The Board stated on O'Melia's dissenting view that (CAB order, 32-32)

> New entrants if they succeed must do so in an environment that assures all carriers a fair opportunity to compete - not in one that requires ever increasing regulatory restraints of so flagrantly discriminatory a kind, even for limited

period of time... Moreover, if we impose restrictions to protect Midway Airlines today, we create a precedent for imposing a restriction on that carrier tomorrow to protect another new entrant. Leaving aside for the moment the possibility of preemption or predation by existing carriers, the success new entrants have in carving out their share of the market must depend primarily on their superior innovation or efficiency - not on such extreme restrictions on competition as the ones we are now excusing.[7]

This view was the general attitude to new-entrants in the marketplace, which is not strange in view of the notion at the time that barriers to entry were limited. If frequent flyer programs, CRS bias and yield management systems had existed under regulation, new-entrants might have done better than they actually did in gaining protection.

The Deregulation Act (Section 102a:10) did, however, mention new entry, by calling for

...the encouragement of entry into air transportation markets by new air carriers, the encouragement of entry into additional air transportation markets by existing air carriers, and the continued strengthening of small air carriers...[8]

In order to manifest the above Congress issued in a Statement of Policy, an objective of maintaining a system of convenient and continuous scheduled service for small communities.[9] However, a direct provision for the enhancement of new entry by new carriers was not considered necessary beside the provisions in the act where entry and exit was open to any carrier. Congress did, however, retain the provision to permit the Board to act on 'predatory' fares.[10] Nevertheless, the Senate Committee concerned itself with the possibility of the CAB limiting low-fare competition on the basis of this provision in the Act. As a result the Senate issued in a report (Senate Report 107, p. 11),[11] a limitation on the application of this provision

Thus the Committee would not expect the Board to strike down a low-fare level which represents genuine competition simply because it would tend to decrease the revenues of less efficient carriers in the market or perhaps force from a given market carriers who were not able to provide the price and service mix which the passenger in that market desired.

The argument for the protection of new-entrants is perhaps stronger than ever in view of the fact that they have not been able to mount an effective long-term competition with the incumbents, as almost all new jet-operating airlines have gone bankrupt or been acquired by other carriers. Thus, when the Board talks about 'an encouragement that assures all carriers a fair opportunity to compete' it is perhaps important to recognise that a 'laissez faire' attitude towards the whole industry may not yield what deregulation is supposed to accomplish, namely to maximise the consumer benefit. For, if the incumbents can create effective barriers to entry without long-term reduction of fares, such as a new carrier could,[12] the consumer will be worse off. As a result a 'consumer driven' legislature will approach the maximum consumer benefit only by protecting new-entrants through the 'elimination' of predatory behaviour and unequal access to information markets. The result of such a move by the legislature will of course instate resistance since the large incumbents may loose market-share. Such a resistance can be said to be an indication that the incumbent enters what can be termed as the *conflict contour*. In fact, there is a trade-off between consumer and airline benefit. As one increases it will be at a cost to the other, thus, the larger the pressure and gain on the consumer side the greater the resistance and inefficiencies caused on the airline side.[13] The long-term benefit for both will be more efficiency but better adapted operation to consumer demands in the wider sense of the word. Meaning that not only will the airline industry approach its customers but also other stake-holders, such as environmental protection groups.

The Clinton Government took a favourable stand on new-entrants as the upsurge of new-entrants and tougher stand on anti-competitive behaviour showed. The Clinton nominated Commission to 'Ensure a Strong Competitive Airline Industry'(1993) concluded that new-entry was important in 'sustaining future competition'. Furthermore, it concluded (p.18) that entry of 'new competitors creates downward pressure on ticket prices, reduces expenses for business and individual travellers, and stimulates total traffic.' This favourable attitude was one of the foundations for the 'second wave' of new entry that started in the early nineties following a rather dormant period of several years.

General theory of barriers to entry

General barriers

One of the pertinent issues of deregulation was the freedom to enter the industry. This was rooted in the assumption that the entry of new low-cost airlines would cause fares to come down and the incumbents to lower their costs in order to become competitive. The new-entrants have, however, faced effective barriers to entry not anticipated prior to deregulation.

There are eleven general barriers to entry possible, these are named by Porter in his landmark book on competitive strategy, seven are relevant to this analysis (Porter, 1980, pp.7-13)

(i) The first barrier is economies of scale, which forces the entrant to enter at a large scale, risking forceful retaliation from the incumbents or to come in at a small scale, usually in a niche market but at a cost disadvantage. It has been argued that economies of scale are limited in the airline industry (Levine,

1987, p.401). Moreover, the new-entrants are usually at a cost-advantage, making this barrier rather weak.

(ii) The second barrier is product differentiation, which forces the entrant to spend heavily to overcome existing customer loyalties.

(iii) The third barrier is high capital requirements to compete. This is a particularly hard barrier to overcome if capital is required for unrecoverable cost areas such as advertising or customised information systems. Also the necessity of substantial capital outlays to create presence in a market is definitely a barrier to entry for new-entrant airlines. While aircraft have been available during recessions under favourable leasing terms they are less of a barrier than one may presume.

(iv) The fourth barrier is switching costs, which are the particular costs to the buyer of switching the supplier of the product or service he consumes. In the airline industry, this switching cost is particularly low, thus, lowering this barrier to entry. However, the airlines have sought to increase this switching costs on the individual level through the frequent flyer programs.

(v) The fifth barrier to entry is access to distribution channels. This is a barrier for new-entrants, as airline's distribution outlets are extremely dispersed making it hard to influence individual travel agents. Thus, a small airline may have considerable difficulty in making its presence felt in the market. This is due to the tendency of travel agents to book those carriers that provide them with volume commission overrides[14] or are reputable and well known carriers. On the other hand CRS provide new airlines with an instant access to a large-scale distribution network.

(vi) The sixth barrier is cost disadvantages independent of scale. These can be advantages of the incumbents due to location, contacts, experience and information.

(vii) The seventh barrier is government policy. The government can in spite of liberal law, limit or even hinder entry completely by making seemingly secondary regulation such as licensing or access to necessary resources too strict for most or all potential entrants to overcome. For example, the Australian government maintained its two-airline policy by placing import embargoes on aircraft.[15]

Porter (1980, pp.7-17) mentions, moreover, relative additivity of entry barriers as the foundation of a firm's decision to enter or not. Therefore, if the prevailing prices which balance the potential rewards of entry with the expected costs of overcoming structural entry barriers and risks of retaliation, are higher than the forecast profits, entry will be unlikely.

Levine's air transport barriers

Levine has identified three main barriers to entry in air transport. These are economies of scope, density and information (Levine, 1987, p.419).

(i) Economies of scope are present when advantages result from the number of destinations or market segments served. In air transport, economies of scope can manifest itself in information efficiencies and efficiencies due to exploitation of principal-agent effects,[16] an advantage not available to a smaller airline to the same degree.

(ii) Economies of density is it called when greater utilisation of capacity is achieved by concentrating city-pair markets into a hub and spoke system that allows the gathering of few passengers from each origin into one common destination flight. This boosts the load-factor for a flight that would be otherwise practically empty if it was a return flight between one of the origin points and the destination.

(iii) Economies of information have to do with the advantages of name recognition and brand loyalty. It leads to a preference for an airline that has been present in a market for a period of time rather than for a newcomer, because the consumer has not established a recognition and knowledge of the new product (Fawcett and Farris, 1989, p.19). In such cases it is more comfortable to select a 'known' name although the newcomer may be offering superior product, because the information thereof may not have reached the travel agent or the customer, or the carrier has not 'proved' itself in the market.[17]

Industry background

Financial condition of the airline industry

The financial health of the US airline industry deteriorated rapidly from 1979. Table 2.1 shows the net results of all scheduled US airlines from 1979. There are three periods of losses 1981 to 1983, 1986 and 1990 to 1992. The reasons for the losses in 1981 to 1983 are usually stated as being the recession and the effects of the air traffic controllers strike (PATCO) which limited access to many airports.

Table 2.1 Scheduled airlines' net profit 1979 - 1992

	Profit ($000)	Profit ($000)	
1979	346.845	593.398	1987
1980	17.414	1.685.599	1988
*1981**	(300.826)	127.902	1989
*1982**	(915.814)	(3.921.002)	*1990**
*1983**	(188.051)	(1.869.974)	*1991**
1984	824.668	(2.419.743)	*1992**
1985	862.715	2.350.173	1993
*1986**	(234.909)	1.391.181	1994

* Years of industry losses

Source: Financial Condition of the Airline Industry (1993).

Another reason is that low-fare, low-cost new-entrant airlines and the intrastate carriers emerged in the interstate market in 1981, creating disruption in the market equilibrium, especially in 1986. The loss period of 1986 can be attributed to frequent fare wars and to the debt burden many carriers took on as a result of the many acquisitions and mergers that occurred during that year. The last period of industry losses has been attributed to: (i) the recession; (ii) the Gulf Crisis; (iii) over capacity; and (iv) Chapter 11 carriers. The recession affected demand for air travel, causing less passenger growth than anticipated. The Gulf Crisis reduced demand for international air travel affecting the domestic demand as well.

Traffic growth was high in the mid-eighties causing the majors to place optimistic orders for new aircraft. When these entered the fleet between 1988 and 1992 the growth had levelled off. Thus, the industry's largest carriers suddenly found themselves with about 300 additional aircraft in need of passengers.

Table 2.2 Financial indicators of major US carriers

	Operating expense per ASK				Operating Revenue per ASK			
Airline*	1978	1984	1992	1994	1978	1984	1992	1994
American	0.085	0.081	0.068	0.067	0.088	0.087	0.068	0.069
United	0.065	0.075	0.071	0.060	0.070	0.081	0.068	0.062
USAir	-	0.105	0.088	0.084	-	0.119	0.082	0.078
Delta	0.072	0.091	0.073	0.066	0.079	0.097	0.068	0.065
Northwest	0.108	0.073	0.069	0.068	0.117	0.076	0.066	0.074
TWA	0.110	0.079	0.068	0.067	0.113	0.080	0.060	0.062
Pan Am	0.079	0.079	-	-	0.084	0.076	-	-
Continental	0.068	0.062	0.060	0.062	0.072	0.069	0.058	0.062

* All figures are in 1994 dollars.

Source: Compiled from Air Transport World 1979 - 1995.

In addition, the Chapter 11 carriers allegedly forced yields down due to their protection from creditors and the resulting reduction in debt payments. This association is, however, disputed as the non-bankrupt carriers may emphasise strategic attacks on the bankrupt carriers in order to undermine their financial wellbeing and prevent them emerging from bankruptcy. In either case the result is going to be poorer overall profit performance.

As the deregulation years have gone by the operating expenses per ASK declined, because of cost saving measures at the airlines, especially in the trimming of labour cost, along with other cost saving measures such as fuel efficient aircraft, two pilot aircraft and increased homogeneity of the fleet.

Economic environment

In 1980 to 1982 (*see* Table 2.3) jet fuel prices increased by 65 percent at the same time when the Consumer Price Index (CPI) rose 16.3 percent. The effect of this is the hindering of growth and increased costs. In 1986 the economic indicators show favourable environment and high traffic growth, but losses occurred nevertheless, due to heavy merger activity and the resulting debt burden and inefficiencies. In 1989 jet fuel prices rose again by 46.5 percent in 1989 and 1990. At the same time the CPI started to rise while interest rates offset the cost increase by going down from 1991 to 1992 by 60.5 percent.

Table 2.3 Economic trends since deregulation

Year	Consumer Price Index All Items[1]	%	Consumer Price Index Public Transportation[2]	%	Jet Fuel Index of Cost Per Gallon[2]	%	US Discount Rate Index Middle Rate[4]	%
1980	100.0		100		100	53.0*	100.0	
1981	110.2	10.2	124.1	24.1	106.5	6.5	92.3	-7.7
1982	116.9	6.1	137.6	10.9	112.3	5.4	66.3	-29.2
1983	120.6	3.2	144.2	4.8	99.2	-11.6	66.3	0.0
1984	126.1	4.6	153.1	6.2	88.9	-10.4	62.4	-5.9
1985	130.6	3.6	160.0	4.5	92.8	4.4	58.5	-6.3
1986	133.0	1.8	169.5	5.9	64.4	-31.6	42.8	-26.7
1987	137.9	3.7	175.4	3.5	64.7	0.4	46.7	9.0
1988	143.6	4.1	178.6	1.8	61.9	-4.3	50.5	8.3
1989	150.5	4.8	187.5	5.0	70.4	13.7	54.4	7.7
1990	158.6	5.4	206.4	10.1	90.6	28.8	50.6	-7.1
1991	165.3	4.2	215.5	4.4	78.8	-13.1	27.2	-46.2
1992	170.3	3.0	219.2	1.7	76.1	-3.4	22.8	-14.3

* Unusually high increase over previous year. Prices are annual domestic average except 1983, which is December price.

Source: [1,2] Bureau of Labour Statistics, US Dept. of Labour. [3] ATW 1979 - 1993. [4] Federal Reserve Board.

Traffic growth

The air transport industry is recognisable cyclical because both leisure passengers and to lesser extent business passengers tend to cut travel expenses during a recession. A survey of North American business travellers (Barker, 1990) reveals that although air fares for business passengers are up, annual costs incurred by corporations per staff traveller have decreased by 7.1 percent from 1988 until 1990. Thus, for a large segment of the leisure market, travel is basically a luxury and for many businesses during recession, travel is one of the cost areas affected by a cost cutting program.

As fuel prices came down from 1983 to 1986 with only slight increase in 1987 the average growth was 8.2 percent during the period. In 1989 fuel prices rise again along with the Consumer Price Index that rose from 1.8 in 1986 to 3.7 in 1987, to 5.4 percent in 1990, with slight reduction in 1991 to 4.2. These effects caused reduced traffic growth, with the Gulf Crisis in 1991 causing further reduction. After 1991 the traffic picks up fast with 14.1 percent growth in passenger haulage (*see* Table 2.4). These increases are attributed, as mentioned before, to fare wars caused by too much capacity in the industry.

Table 2.4 Growth in US airline traffic 1982 - 1994

Year	*Revenue pass (000)*	*% Change*
1982	294.102	2.8
1983	318.638	8.3
1984	344.683	8.2
1985	382.022	10.8
1986	418.946	9.7
1987	447.678	6.9
1988	454.614	1.6
1989	453.692	-0.2
1990	465.557	2.6
1991	452.210	-2.9
1992	516.038	14.1
1993	531.390	2.9
1994	576.439	8.5

Source: Compiled from Air Transport World 1982-1995.

Capacity

Over-capacity is one of the factors cited as the reason for losses in the early nineties. The following figure (*see* Figure 2.1) shows the average capacity offered and the resulting average load-factors. It is worth pointing out that average load factors have not declined, but increased during the period. This implies that if over-capacity was present, capacity was well utilised by the travelling public, probably due to lower fares on offer.

To test whether lower fares contributed to the increase in load-factors, one can refer to Figure 2.2 that shows operating profits per available seat kilometre. It is clear that as capacity increased at the incumbent carriers they tried to increase loads by lowering fares. This led to poor operating profit for all the incumbent carriers in 1992. In 1994 American, United and Northwest had reached profitability again, while USAir, Delta and TWA had not. The implication of this situation for new-entrants is that market entry is difficult unless the incumbents can be avoided, but at the same time aircraft are readily available lowering the equipment barrier to entry.

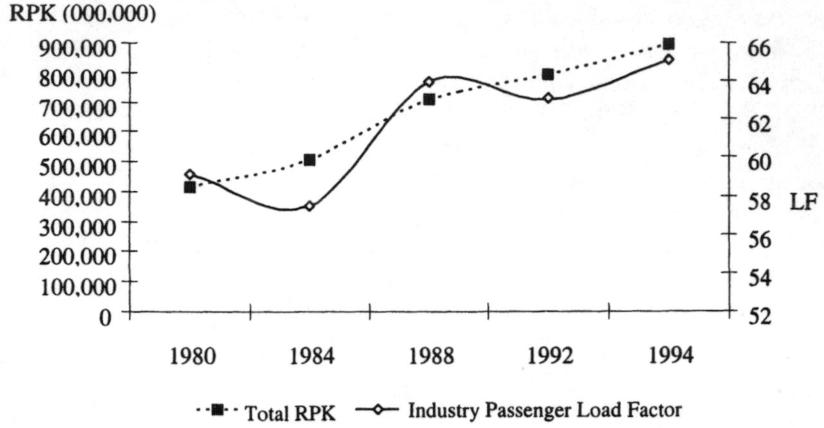

Figure 2.1 US airline capacity 1980 - 1994

Source: Compiled from Air Transport World 1979 - 1995.

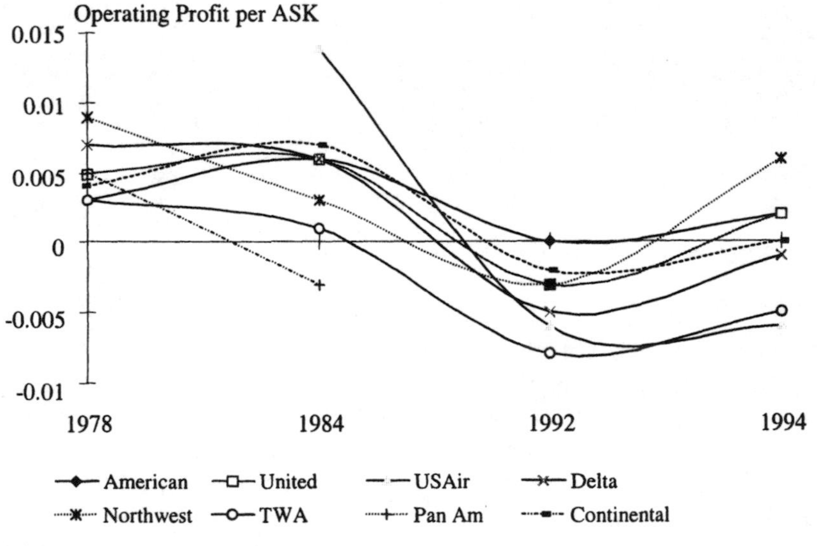

In 1994 dollars.

Figure 2.2 US incumbent airlines' operating profit per ASK 1978-1994

Source: Compiled from Air Transport World 1979 - 1995.

The three largest majors added capacity out of line with passenger growth trends. In the period from 1988 to 1992 the number of revenue passengers grew by 4.4 percent, compared to 30 percent in the four preceding years. The reason may have been the tendency for optimism during the growth period in the mid-nineties and long lead-times in aircraft deliveries from manufacturers at the time. At any rate the large majors were more optimistic than the smaller carriers, as the latter group reduced their capacity, while American, Delta and United added 35 percent. Much addition of capacity during low growth periods increases rivalry in the market, reducing the viability of entry for new carriers.

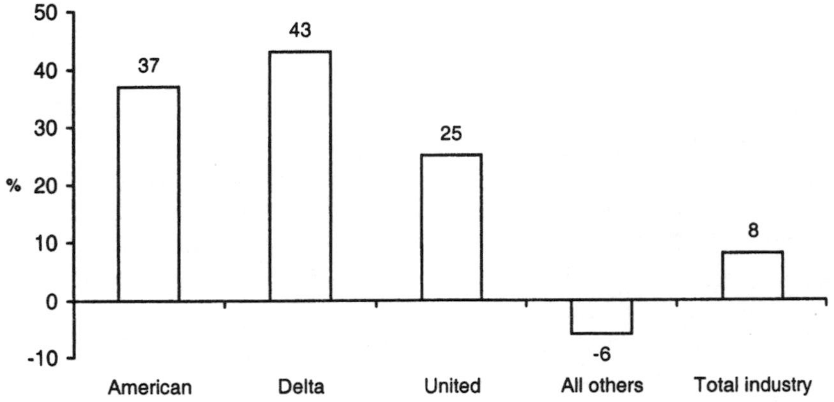

Figure 2.3 Increase in capacity by carrier 1988 – 1992

Source: Based on Financial Condition of the Airline Industry (1993).

Industry fare structure

From 1981 until 1983, 22 new jet-operating carriers emerged causing the incumbents to react with lower fares although they had not shed the extra weight of the regulatory era. Meyer and Oster (1987) reported that as early as 1981 competition had already reached high levels, both in terms of percentage of markets with discount fares offered and reduction of fares measured in terms of discount fare as a percentage of couch fare. The percentage of top 50 markets with discount fares increased from 69 percent in 1976 to 96 percent in 1984. The increase was larger for small markets, for example markets ranking between 151 and 200 increased discount offerings from 39 percent in 1976 to 80 percent in 1984. Meyer and Oster report little change in average discount fares as percentage of couch fare from 1981 until 1984 with the exception of the top 100 markets, where there was a slight reduction. In other smaller markets there was rather a tendency for dissipating difference between the average discount fare and the couch fare.

Hub and spoke route networks

Hub and spoke route networks have had a major impact on the air transport industry following deregulation, creating perhaps the greatest barrier to entry for new entrants. To begin with it is important to define what constitutes a hub, a hub is defined as (Jenks, 1986, p.30)

> ...a pattern of simultaneous arrivals followed by simultaneous departures at any airport, such that a passenger from any arriving flight can connect to any departing flight within a reasonable period.

The FAA definition of a hub differs considerably from the one above '...air traffic hubs are geographic areas, and are based on the percentage of total passengers enplaned in the area.' Hub airports are classified into four types by the FAA, large, medium, small and non-hub airports. The FAA definition does not take into account the hub and spoke concept of the traffic arriving and leaving in banks. Therefore, one can not use the 'hub' concept as defined by the FAA in the same context as that used by the airlines in their strategic planning. In this section we will use the hub concept meaning that traffic is scheduled in banks.

One of the advantages of a hub network is the reduction of the number of linkages necessary to tie the destination nodes in the network. It requires n(n-1) linkages to provide direct flights between the destinations served (n). If, however, a hub is used the linkages are reduced for the destinations served by the hub to (n-1). Furthermore, the hub allows for the operation of larger aircraft with lower seat-mile cost as the geographical catchment area for passengers is much larger for a hub operation than direct service. This boosts load factors allowing more frequency on thinner routes and larger aircraft on high density routes as mentioned before. Another important feature of a hub location is the size of the local market that will be captured by the dominant hub carrier. What is more the hub carrier if in a dominant position can charge relatively higher fares for passengers originating or terminating their journey at the hub airport.[18]

The hub strategy of the major carriers after deregulation was primarily geographic and market-share driven. A carrier well located in the Eastern United States, wishing to gain market-share in the Western part would develop a hub in that region in order to build a market-share. Another way would be to gain instant market-share by acquiring a carrier already operating a hub in the area, just as PeoplExpress did with the acquisition of Frontier, gaining a hub location in Denver.

Hub and spoke strategies can be divided into three phases since deregulation: (i) one or two hub strategy prior to 1986; (ii) multi-hub strategy from 1986 to 1992; and (iii) hub consolidation from 1992. The main problem with the one or two hub strategy was the inability of the hub airport to accommodate constant growth in air traffic and the provision of adequate number of peak hour flights. As a result, the hub airports became overly crowded causing inconvenience to the passenger. This reason and the carrier's wish for geographic expansion led to the construction of secondary hubs. By that action the carrier relieved some of the pressure on the main hub and reduced the inconvenient transfers and lengthy routes for part of their passengers, increasing the passenger's incentive to use the carrier.

As the major carriers concentrated on building large hubs during the early deregulation years they withdrew from direct services, causing their market-share to decline in secondary markets, allowing new-entrants and commuters to gain by filling in the gaps. As deregulation progressed the majors started to establish medium to small size hubs, drastically reducing the leeway for new-carriers.

The inefficiencies of hub operations are substantial in terms of less hourly fleet utilisation due to the aircraft arriving and departing in blocks. Consequently, when the hub airport becomes large the time period it takes each block to arrive and leave becomes larger, thus, creating inefficiencies and greater average passenger waiting time. This may explain the economies experienced by Southwest's direct flights, where fleet utilisation is high compared to the hub airlines.

Concentration

Mergers and bankruptcies, many of which occurred in 1986, marked the change in industry structure and the prevailing concentration in US air transport. This has led to controversy as to the benefit of deregulation for the consumer and the airlines. In general the view appears to be that the industry has become more concentrated as a result of deregulation, although, competition has increased in terms of number of carriers serving each of the high-density routes. Table 2.5 shows the increase in concentration since deregulation both in terms of airlines achieving more than 1 percent total market-share measured in terms of enplanements at the 50 largest airports and the Herfindahl Index that measures concentration at airports. Both of these indicators show that concentration has increased substantially since deregulation. Although this trend may be reversing for the reasons stated in the section on hubs and spokes.

Airlines with more than 1 percent market-share were 25 in 1979 but only 15 in 1991, at the same time total enplanements increased from 310.8 million to 346.5 million with the largest peak in 1986, 389.7 million. The Herfindahl-Hirschman Index (HHI) shows increased concentration, as weighed average for the 50 largest airports increased from 2.224 in 1979 to 3.904 in 1991.[19]

The purpose of merger in deregulated air transport markets is to: (i) gain instant access to markets that would otherwise take considerable time to grow into organically: (ii) eliminate a competitor; (iii) increase debt in order to buffer against a hostile take-over; (iv) to gain a competitive tool such as access to a computer reservation system; (v) gain economies of scope, information and density, to create a barrier to entry or enhance the ability to fight off a competitive threat; and (vi) build critical mass to enhance the staying power of the airline in a fierce competition.

Table 2.5 Number of airlines that achieved 1 percent market-share

	1979	1980	1981	1982	1983	1984	1985	1986	1987	1988	1989	1990	1991
Airlines = *n*	25	22	22	22	21	21	21	21	20	19	18	16	15
HHI	2224	2243	2198	2248	2462	2455	2562	2757	3187	3352	3443	3605	3904
Total enplane-ments (m)	311	287	270	277	301	320	357	390	348	352	350	355	347

Source: Compiled from Maldutis (1993).

It is important to contrast mergers that are the result of an attempt to salvage the leftovers of a bankrupt airline against those that have the sole purpose of gaining the advantage of a system that will improve competitive status considerable. In fact there is little reason for courts to block a merger of a bankrupt carrier, as such an act can cause 'social harm' to those employees that would otherwise keep their jobs. It is rather the period prior to bankruptcy of a carrier that needs to be analysed in order to filter out predatory actions driving a competitor into bankruptcy for the purpose of acquisition or elimination.

Table 2.6 Large mergers of US airlines in 1986

PeoplExpress*	With	Frontier
Texas Air	with	Eastern and PeoplExpress*
American	with	Air California*
Delta	with	Western
Northwest	with	Republic
TWA	with	Ozark
USAir	with	Pacific Southwest Airlines*

* A new-entrant carrier

Source: Adapted from Sawers (1987).

The application of post deregulation competition tools as mentioned before (yield management systems, CRS's, hub and spoke systems, etc.) by the incumbents influenced the many mergers and acquisitions that occurred in 1986. The year was characterised by over capacity and fare wars that had serious effect on profitability, especially in regard to the new-entrants that had less critical mass and therefore less staying power.

Table 2.6 shows large mergers that occurred in 1986, but four of these involved new-entrants. All were taken over by the incumbents with the exception of PeoplExpress' brief take-over of Frontier. The new-entrants taken-over were PeoplExpress and the former intrastate carriers AirCal, PSA and Republic airlines.

Sawers (1987, pp.32-33) argues that as profitability fell in 1985 companies 'with high costs, large debts or non-competitive services were encouraged to seek safety in the arms of stronger firms,' explaining the failure of Eastern, Western, PeoplExpress and Frontier. It must be noted that PeoplExpress is an exception to some of the points stated by Sawers as it had the lowest cost per available seat mile of any carrier in 1985.

Marketing

Advertising

Under deregulation advertising has become an issue as some airlines have tended to emphasise the short-term benefit from capturing the customer's attention through deceptive advertising knowing that a certain percentage of those that make contact will accept the 'true' value of the product even though it was described differently in the advertisement.

The regulator has recognised this barrier to entry and provided some measures to reduce it. The DoT in judging airline's adherence to Section 411[20] of the Federal Aviation Act follows a 'Statement of General Policy' Part 399.80, that lists the following as a breach of the code of conduct in airline advertising: (i) misrepresentation of the quality of service type or size of aircraft, departure times, points served, number of slots, and total trip time; (ii) misrepresentation of fares and charges; and (iii) misrepresentation of discounts stating that they are available when they are not.

Furthermore, Part 399.84 declares advertisements which contain a lower fare than is actually charged to the customer, an unfair deceptive practice, but this practice was often used by the incumbent's when new-entrant entered a market offering lower fare than prevailed. In addition non-inclusion in advertising of code-sharing when present is considered a deceptive or unfair practice as the passenger may not realise unless notified that there may be a carrier or equipment switch enroute. This discriminates effectively against a direct service new-entrant.

To address these and other issues the DoT administered airline advertising standards that constitute allowed practices: (i) taxes can be listed separately as long as they are included in the advertisement; (ii) fares can be advertised as one-way even though round-trip ticket is required to receive the advertised fare; (iii) restrictions on fares must be listed in the advertisement; and (iv) if a low fare is advertised a 'reasonable' number of seats must be made available at that fare. Practice (ii) and (iv) are the most controversial ones. It can be alleged that an advertisement citing fare for one way but requiring round-trip to receive the fare, to be purely misleading. Furthermore, 'reasonable' number of seats is not defined any further for practice (iv) leading to carrier's breach of it.

The DoT has found two main complaints on behalf of airline customers regarding advertising (Airline Advertising Reform Act, 1991, pp.IX-X): (a) lack of availability that deals with reasonable number of seats at an advertised low fare (*see*, practice iv); and (b) lack of adequacy of disclosure about restrictions on fares, that deals with fare restrictions (*see*, practice iii).

Frequent flyer programs

Frequent Flyer Programs (FFP) can make a new-entrant's strategy to gather for business travellers less viable. This is due to the tendency of FFP's members to stick to their carrier in order to accumulate all the miles possible. Thus, the largest carrier that has the most extensive route network (economies of scope) becomes the best choice for the mileage maximising FFP member. As soon as the itineraries of the business passenger are restricted to few routes, other smaller carrier's FFP's may become attractive. However, a major decision in the selection of FFP's by a passenger, are the rewards. As the rewards are used for personal travel, vacation for example, the airline has to offer some exotic vacation destinations such as Hawaii, Bahamas, Bermuda and similar vacation destinations. For some smaller carriers this is not a viable addition to their route system. As a result, their FFP becomes less attractive to the FFP member unless it is joined up with a program that covers such destinations. So one way to break this specific barrier is to make a marketing agreement with some international carrier or another US carrier having non-overlapping route system that includes such destinations.

Just to show how effective frequent flyer programs are in shifting traffic, one can name Midway Airlines that in 1988 suffered in terms of the incumbents' triple-mileage offerings diverting traffic away from the new-entrant. The result was to establish a first-class product primarily to offer it as an incentive in their FFP. Furthermore, in order to bolster foreign destinations a marketing agreement was entered with Canadian Airlines International and Air New Zealand.

A landmark decision regarding the reduction of FFP as a barrier to entry was the Swedish Government's decision to require SAS to open up its FFP to Swedish new-entrants, as part of the carriers' approval to take over Linjeflyg. The Swedish approach to the FFP would, however, render the programs useless as distinguishing marketing factor for an airline in a domestic market, but it would still be effective internationally. It should, nevertheless, be acknowledged that the FFP is not abandoned as result of such a move, due to their popularity and built-in incentive for the business passenger to travel perhaps more than necessary. Thus, the FFP might turn into 'commodity' that everyone expects to be there, but will not consider in the decision on carrier selection, given the unlikely scenario that the Swedish approach will become generally accepted.

Code-sharing

Code-sharing acts as a barrier to entry as it can exclude carriers from entering a hub with dominant carriers, if marketing agreement with the hub carrier(s) can not be secured. This is vested in the fact that the CRS system will show flights as direct on one carrier through the hub, even though there is an equipment or carrier change. Another factor is that the incumbent may charge proportionally higher fares for flights terminating at the hub in order to reduce the incentive to use other than its own or the code sharing partner's flights out of the hub. Furthermore, the code-sharing partner usually gets prime location of gates to minimise walking between connecting flights, but the independent new-entrant may have to settle for poorly located facilities.

Computer reservation systems

The CRS were biased in favour of the owners (hosts), especially on the actual display itself. In 1984 the CAB issued rules that corrected this display biases to a certain extent. Nevertheless, the system's hosts still benefited from their ownership in terms of proportionally more bookings than non-host airlines. This has been dubbed as 'incremental revenues.'[21] Incremental revenues are generated by a combination of 'architectural bias'[22] and travel agents' (TA) identification with the CRS host airline, called 'halo effect'.

The 1994 regulation addressed four main issues (Airline Competition Enhancement Act, 1992, p.2)

(i) Prohibited 'bias' in the listing of airline schedules on CRS screens. This prohibition prevented CRS from continuing the practice of displaying the schedules of the airline owning the CRS above the schedules of other airlines.

(ii) Required CRS owners to charge all airlines the same 'booking fee' for listing their schedules and issuing tickets through the CRS. Prior to this prohibition, CRS owners were charging airlines different fees, sometimes related to the extent to which an airline competed with the CRS owner.

(iii) Prohibited CRS owners from leasing CRSs to travel agents for terms of more than five years. The intent of this rule was to furnish more opportunities for competition in marketing CRS systems to travel agents.

(iv) Prohibited CRS owners from requiring that a travel agent use a particular CRS system exclusively. This provision was also intended to promote CRS competition.

The alleged biases left in the CRS after the passing of the 1984 regulation and directly affect new-entrants, are shown in the listing below (Avmark, 1987c, p.19)

(i) Individual carrier identity: Displaying flights/fares for carrier YY ahead of those for carrier XX by means of over-ride of other display priority parameters. Displaying fares for carrier YY in addition to those for carrier XX whenever fares for carrier XX are requested.
(ii) Carrier's status of participation in the system: Because carrier XX is not a co-host, not enabling any enhancements for carrier XX through the system. Similarly, because XX is a participating carrier: a) excluding from the display flights by carrier XX that compete with those of carrier YY, connecting flights by carrier XX.
(iii) Priority given to on-line transfer: Displaying carrier YY/YY connection ahead of carrier XX/ZZ or XX/YY connection despite other inferior connection parameters for the former. Where the connection is domestic/international , a wholly domestic carrier or a foreign international carrier loses display priority.
(iv) Code-sharing: Carrier XX and carrier ZZ making agreement for designation of carrier XX/ZZ connection as carrier XX/XX to retain priority under above parameters.
(v) Dual-listing: If code-sharing then using also separate, additional listing (using different flight parameters if necessary to avoid detection) of carrier XX flight for local traffic purposes.
(vi) Restriction on display of fares: Limiting the number of classes of service types of fare which may be listed (in some instances fewer classes have been available for participating carriers than for a vendor carrier).
(vii) Change of gauge without change of flight number: Retention of single flight number where a change of aircraft is required en-route in order to achieve display priority. This practice can also lead to dual or multiple listing where there are several feeder services for a long-haul service with the same flight number.
(viii) Departure time, arrival time, length of flight time: Falsification of flight schedules by carriers, individually or jointly, to achieve display priority.

Therefore, some of the more important sources of bias left in the CRS after the regulation were 'functional differences.' The two most commonly named being last-seat availability and 'autovalidation'. Last-seat availability has been cited as one of the causes for TA's to prefer the host carrier, as last-seat availability has not been available through the primary display of some CRS, requiring the TA to spend time to enter a 'direct-link' with the non-host carrier. This has even failed due to 'connection interference' causing the booking to fail although the TA is in a good faith that it actually went through to the non-host's system. Therefore, TA's often feel less secure to use this cumbersome facility in view of the consequences for the passenger. The second source of bias is autovalidation that has to do with the host carrier receiving initially the whole ticket amount when multi-segment ticket is issued on two or more carriers. The usual rule is that the validated carrier should be the first segment or longest segment carrier. On some CRS the system will autovalidate on the CRS's host carrier if it is carrying the passenger on any segment of the trip, unless the TA validates the ticket on a specific carrier.

The following listing shows the most common complaints over CRS manipulation (Avmark, 1987c, p. 20)

(i) Control of participation: Outright refusal to accept a (foreign) carrier as a participant, or acceptance only under unduly burdensome or discriminatory conditions.
(ii) Control of sales information: a) Manipulation of a participating carrier's fare and flight information to that carrier's disadvantage; b) Evaluation of and response to a competing carrier's revised schedules and fares before they are officially announced.
(iii) Control of marketing information: Information generated through a CRS exclusively available to vendor or sold only at excessive fees (including, for example, data to identify travel agents who might be induced to direct their business away from competing carriers or analyses of reservation patterns with a view to amending tariffs).
(iv) Control of reservations policy: Reservation for flights on routes where vendor is a dominant or monopoly carrier conditioned upon use of the same carrier wherever available for any other segments of the journey.
(v) Control of ticket validation: Designation of vendor as validating carrier on all tickets or on any ticket containing a coupon for that carrier (whether first coupon or not) in order to achieve improved cash flow.
(vi) Control of system enhancements: 'Last-seat' availability or advance issue of boarding passes available only for vendor carrier.
(vii) Inequitable access fees: a) Through inequitable allocation of costs amongst vendor, participating carriers and travel agents; b) through fee structures that vary amongst participating carriers; c) through excessive fees for enhancement facilities.

Even though nearly all bias could be eliminated from the computer reservation systems, it is likely that *incremental revenue* will be present, unless the system is fully de-hosted. The options left to the host airlines are still numerous. The host airlines feel that since the CAB eliminated the bias that created much of the incremental revenues for the host, compensatory rates for booking on host flights had to be introduced. Furthermore, they feel that architectural bias is not the reason why TA's choose to book some carriers more than others, but rather the commission overrides offered by the host airlines (McNamara, 1992, p.265). If that is the case there is a much less interest by the regulator to regulate such practices as they are generally considered to be a part of the normal business relationship between the TA and the airline.

Certain CRS owners included in their CRS agreements with TA, clauses that 'tie' the owner's commission levels to the CRS usage. These clauses are actually purposefully created to prevent the TA to install more than one CRS system in the agency, even though the agent wished to provide its customers with extra service by installing software that biased the display by showing more airlines, or lowest fares across or shortest possibly itinerary. They were not able to do so as the CRS agreements usually contained a clause prohibiting the use of third party software on the basis of technological incompatibility. This further reduced the new-entrants' chances of being listed advantageously on the basis of low fares or direct flights.

Airlines and travel agents felt increasingly uneasy towards the CRS hosts ability to control competition, leading to a lawsuit brought against American and United. The plaintiffs alleged that the CRS hosts were taking advantage of their dominant position. The Court of Appeals ruling brought about under the Sherman Anti-trust Act, stated that (McNamara, 1992, p. 277)[23]

> Airlines generally subscribe to every CRS because the CRS's charge the airline *per booking*. The $1.75 fee to secure a booking is of little consequence because a $300 or $400 fare may otherwise be lost. This is not to say that a CRS can charge its airline subscribers any fee that it desires, no matter how high. Basic economic theory tells us that an airline will withdraw from the CRS if the cost of using it causes the marginal cost of providing a flight booked on the CRS to exceed the marginal revenue gained by the booking.

This ruling rejected completely the notion that hosts misused their position, on the grounds of how low their booking fee was as a portion of the total ticket price.

Congressional Subcommittees, on the other hand, felt the need to take a close look at the CRS dominance and in 1992 a bill on 'Airline Competition Enhancement' was presented to the US Congress to amend the Federal Aviation Act of 1958. The bills' purpose was (Airline Competition Enhancement Act, 1992, p.5)

> ...to enhance competition among air carriers by prohibiting an air carrier who operates a computer reservation system from discriminating against other air carriers participating in the system and among travel agents which subscribe to the system, and for other purposes.

The reason for the bill was still the alleged hosts' advantage even though the display bias had been eliminated. The bill was not passed but initiated regulation by the US Department of Transportation regarding CRS.

The United States' Department of Transportation (DoT., 1988) analysed the substance of incremental revenues and found that (*qtd. in* Anderson, 1992, p.147) [24]

> ...airline revenues in 1986 were about 14 percent higher for United and 15 percent higher for American because of incremental revenues. These were only moderately lower than the estimates of incremental revenues for the pre-rule period.

Another important aspect of the CRS issue is the importance of the systems revenues and profits which the CRS owners can attribute back into the airline's operation to buy aircraft, international routes, slots and not the least withstand fare wars.[25] The US Department of Transportation estimated that in 1988, based on older data, adjusted annual rate of return for Apollo (now COVIA) was approximately 50 to 55 percent and 75 to 90 percent for SABRE.[26]

Table 2.7 CRS profit estimation 1988 to 1991

Year	SABRE	COVIA (Apollo)
	Net operating margin %	Before tax profits $(mill)
1988	16.9	na
1989	16.2	90
1990	14.1	32
1991	13.9 (110 million profit)	15

Other financial information for these two large systems was not publicly available.

Source: Compiled from Airline Competition Enhancement Act (1992).

Table 2.7 indicates roughly the profit of the largest systems. If profits and incremental revenues[27] are added together it is clear that the CRS contribution to American and United has been of major importance in their growth and competitive position in the market.

Following numerous congressional hearings on CRS bias, the hosts have started to remove most of the alleged sources of bias. SABRE has for example stated that it has removed all differences in order to make the system 'absolutely identical' in every aspect to each participant (Airline Competition Enhancement Act, 1992). This identical treatment will, however, in many instances come at a cost as in some systems there are a number of service levels at different fee levels. Thus, the higher the service the higher the fee.

The whole question of CRS bias revolves first and foremost around the possible effects on the competitiveness of new-entrants. Beauvais (1993, p.54), then Chairman of America West, stated on the issue of non-host carriers in a CRS

> Our pricing is being regulated by American. We are being regulated in our pricing levels and structure, and if you deviate you are punished. In our opinion, being regulated by an airline is not good for anything, particularly the consumer and the industry.

Contrary to the above view held by non-host airlines the COVIA CRS partnership states that (Conley, 1993, p.171)

> CRS is the reason new airline entrants can immediately get their products in front of the people who sell them, without any up-front costs. Deregulation, with the entry of so many new carriers, could never have taken off so quickly without CRS.

The two quotations above show a very different views to the CRS, one says that they seriously distort competition for non-host airlines and especially vulnerable new-entrants and the other says that they are an important tool for new-entrants to make instant market presence at minimum cost. Both views are right in their own way, but the bias allegation can only be eliminated if CRS's will be de-hosted by law.

Although it seems to be logical that the CRS vendors can use market pricing for their services, it is nevertheless, questionable if one group of carriers is treated unfavourable in comparison to others in this respect. The DoT (1992, p.XL) stated back in 1988 that

> The carriers charged the highest fees tended to be new-entrants such as Midway that also suffered the most from display bias. These fees raised the costs of such carriers and reduced their ability to offer lower fares than the incumbent carriers. In addition, the fear of loosing access to a major system caused some carriers to promise a vendor that they would not compete aggressively against it as a condition to maintaining their participation in the system.

Anderson (1992, p.LVI) on behalf of United States General Accounting Office stated during a Congressional hearing in 1988 that the [28]

> ...market power of CRS vendors does inhibit new entry and threatens the ability of new-entrants to survive...

The counter argument has been that the CRS's hosts should be in full right to charge for their services based on traffic feed into the system and the importance to the travel agent to be able to book on a particular airline. Both of these arguments are highly unfavourable to new-entrants as they provide little traffic initially and are of little importance to TA's, being less known and generally less trusted due to poor track record in the past.

A clause limiting the ability of a travel agency to install other CRS's, along with a clause that ties the lease-price charged to the agent for the CRS to the number of tickets the agent sells on the CRS's host airline, has in the past limited the new-entrant's chance of having equal opportunity of selling its seats in the system, based solely on price and quality. However, although CRS's host advantage may have been to the disadvantage of new-entrants in the past this will be negligible in the future as such systems will become increasingly a neutral commodity. Thus, CRS ownership will not be to the airlines advantage in any other form but as an investment.[29,30]

To conclude, one must point out that the 1984 ruling on CRS's bias was not beneficial to all new-entrants. The reason being that many smaller carriers relied on connecting traffic (interlining) from the majors. What happened was that connecting flights fell into the third category of screen priority. This caused serious drop in bookings as TA's have a tendency to book high proportion of flights from the first screen instead of scrolling through all the screens before making a selection. Air Wisconsin ran into difficulty after the ruling, as 80 percent of their flights were made by TA's at the time and 40 percent of total traffic was connection with United's flights. The change in ruling led to a loss of estimated 20.000 passengers in the first half of 1985 (ATW, 1985c). As a result of the ruling on CRS bias the connecting carriers were effectively thrown into the arms of the incumbents, as for many the only way to survive was to get 'associated' in order to get code-sharing agreement and maintain previous traffic levels.

Travel agents

New-entrants face a particular barrier from volume incentives to travel agents. Such incentives can be in the form of VIP club memberships, overbooking privileges, override commissions and free tickets. These incentives provide the agents with competition tools to favour good clients and build loyalty to their agency. Thus, volume incentives and especially commission overrides can have major impact on agencies' profitability. In view of the fact that many customers leave the choice of airline up to their travel agents (TA), volume incentives can be an important distribution strategy by airlines. In 1987, 41 percent of business travellers and 55 percent of leisure travellers left airline choice to the TA's (Travel Agency Market Survey, 1987). The same survey showed also that 51 percent of TA's selected the carrier they had commission override agreement with, some of the time.[31,32]

A new-entrant is usually much smaller than a competing incumbent carrier, so the potential benefit from a new-entrant's commission override scheme is much smaller than that of the incumbent's, because the volume breaks are higher but booking volume larger due to larger route network. As a result it is logical that the TA will select the incumbent if selection is possible. Pricing is of course a factor in the selection but price matching is the usual practice of the incumbents if a lower fare new-entrant enters their market, thus, nullifying the TA incentive to book the new-entrant anyway.

Yield management systems

Sophisticated yield management systems (YMS) can act as barrier to entry for new-entrants, as these allow the high-volume incumbent carrier to under-cut any fares offered on joint routes at a minimum yield reduction. A state of the art YMS was not available on the open market to begin with, creating an adavantage for the original developers such as American Airlines. It is also clear that taylorfitted YMS such as the one in operation at British Airways was until the nineties not within the reach of smaller airlines. In that sense there will be an ongoing development gap between the large financially strong carriers and small new-entrants in terms of YMS.

Quality of service

Table 2.8 (new-entrant airlines) and Table 2.9 (incumbent airlines) show trends in complaint rates. Most complaints filed are on flight related problems, baggage mishandling and customer service, in that order. In 1983 just to take an example, flight problems were 26.5 percent, baggage complaints 16.3 percent and refund problems 14.9 percent.

Looking at the changes in complaint rates, the high increase in 1979 can be explained by an industry wide decline in on time performance and the CAB's efforts to make it easier to file complaints.[33] As on-time performance improved the complaints declined. The high increase in complaints in 1987 through 1988 can be attributed to airport congestion at hub airports causing delays and missed connections. The congestion at the hub airports during these years can be explained by the havoc in scheduling caused by the high merger activity during 1986. In addition, unrealistic scheduling was an important factor, escalated by carriers' attempts to tamper with scheduling in order to gain better CRS display position.

If one examines the complaint rates of individual airlines one can see that the airlines at the bottom of the list were all having labour disputes due to cost cutting or mergers if not both. Eastern had serious union fights, Northwest suffered from merger problems affecting labour and organisation, and Continental had serious customer service disputes as indicated by their complaint record. The reason for the high rise in Hawaiian's customer complaint rates were problems with a new international service. A biasing factor resulting in higher complaint rates during 1987 could be the extensive publicity of service problems in the period. After 1988 the complaint rate drops considerable indicating smoother operations at most airlines filing.

The importance of examining complaint's rates is related to the hypothesis that good service breeds success and bad service failure. The problem is, however, the relationship, namely whether the problems of the carrier lead to poor service or whether the poor service leads to the carrier's problems. Examining failed vs. non-failed carriers shows a marked difference in complaint rates. The overall average for non-failed carriers was 2.14 complaints per 100.000 passengers, compared to 5.28 for failed carriers.

Table 2.8 New-entrant airlines' consumer complaints 1981 - 1991

Complaints per 100.000 passengers

	1981	1982	1983	1984	1985	1986	1987	1988	1989	1990	1991	Avg.
Regional												
Air Wisconsin										0.22	0.00	0.11
Horizon									0.63	0.11	0.44	0.39
Intrastate												
Air Florida	12.5	8.5	5.21									8.74
AirCal	2.12	1.17	0.94	0.46	0.55							1.05
MarkAir										1.84	1.31	1.58
PSA	1.92	0.83	0.81	0.51	0.83	1.03	2.09					1.15
Southwest	0.82	0.74	0.37	0.33	0.36	0.46	1.59	1.24	0.81	0.56	0.46	0.70
Start-up												
America West				0.67	na	0.94	3.42	2.24	1.41	1.65	1.76	1.73
Braniff (II)				1.22	2.20	1.44	4.77	4.14				2.75
Jet America				2.04	na	3.19						2.62
Midway				1.45	3.37	1.29	5.83	2.67	1.64	1.42	2.06	2.47
Midwest Exp.											0.00	0.00
Muse				0.55								0.55
New York A				1.40	2.30	4.36						2.69
People Expr.				2.90	4.54	7.90						5.11
Charter												
Am. Trans Air							4.81	na	1.28	3.05	1.63	2.70
Capitol	30.8	26.8	28.6									28.73
Tower Air									5.29	3.09	4.19	4.19
Transamerica	5.6	5.86	4.34	5.24	2.58							4.72
World	22.3	10.5	3.39	6.11	11.2	18.3						11.97
NE Average	10.9	7.77	6.24	1.91	3.10	4.32	3.75	2.57	1.84	1.49	1.32	4.20
Incu. Average	3.07	2.24	1.66	1.57	1.73	2.05	8.55	5.01	2.44	1.89	1.56	4.17

Empty squares denote non-availability of data or non-operating year

Source: Compiled from Air Transport World 1981 - 1992.

However, comparing incumbent carriers' average complaint rates for each year with new-entrant carriers shows that complaints have declined considerably. This decline is particularly great after the charter-based new-entrants, Capitol and World, terminated their scheduled operations.

Service quality does seem to have two important parts to it in the eyes of the passenger. The first is deliverance on service features, especially in terms of staff's interaction with the customer. Carriers with less service features such as Southwest Airlines in the eighties and early nineties can earn high quality reputation given that attention is given to each feature. The second part is service features because some passengers will associate quality with the sophistication of the service. So some target groups associate quality with the number of service features as well as deliverance.

Table 2.9 Incumbent airlines' consumer complaints 1978 - 1991

Airline	1978	1979	1980	1981	1982	1983	1984	1985	1986	1987	1988	1989	1990	1991	Avg.
						Complaints per 100.000 passengers									
Aloha	1.88	2.12	1.08	0.84	0.82	0.41	0.26	0.12	0.25	0.46	0.93	0.30	0.32	0.43	0.73
Alaska				2.34	0	0.61	0.55	0.51	0.72	1.49	1.25	0.88	0.59	0.48	0.94
Delta	1.87	2.21	1.41	0.90	0.79	0.70	0.65	0.66	0.56	2.19	1.38	0.72	0.55	0.47	1.08
Piedmont	4.84	5.42	2.91	1.33	1.23	0.68	0.64	0.68	1.04	2.97	1.80				2.14
Hawaiian	2.21	1.61	1.55	1.35	1.04	0.67	1.44	1.55	2.93	8.44	7.34	4.19	2.34	1.68	2.74
Republic		6.40	5.28	2.63	2.02	1.34	0.73	1.33	2.18						2.74
Frontier	6.76	5.14	3.44	1.84	1.35	1.00	1.59	1.14							2.78
USAir/All	5.68	8.94	5.03	3.46	1.97	1.09	1.22	1.50	1.38	3.51	2.12	2.16	1.26	0.63	2.85
American	5.90	10.0	5.68	2.89	2.29	1.31	1.09	1.33	1.39	3.84	2.07	1.22	1.04	1.42	2.96
Ozark	5.73	9.27	4.95	1.99	1.12	0.90	0.93	0.73	1.06						2.96
United	3.67	7.95	3.62	2.28	2.10	1.42	1.70	2.48	2.56	6.60	2.82	1.98	1.37	1.47	3.00
Western	4.29	9.14	4.96	2.08	1.95	1.60	1.65	1.48	1.27						3.16
Eastern	5.58	6.77	4.51	2.47	1.56	1.35	1.11	1.60	2.42	13.1	10.1	6.48	2.23		4.56
Northwest	11.1	8.75	4.90	2.81	2.34	2.27	1.68	1.69	2.67	18.6	6.21	1.95	1.33	0.98	4.81
Continental	5.63	8.69	5.27	2.69	1.55	5.93	3.89	4.21	3.56	24.6	11.9	3.29	2.09	1.21	6.04
TWA	9.84	12.3	11.8	6.60	5.15	3.33	3.69	3.35	4.13	12.4	7.80	5.31	5.63	4.46	6.84
Pan Am	12.8	16.2	13.0	8.91	4.61	3.60	3.95	5.04	4.64	13.0	9.50	0.81	3.91	3.89	7.42
Braniff (I)	6.17	14.4	9.45	4.42	6.18										8.12
Texas Int'l	6.40	10.6	13.0	6.55											9.14
Average	5.90	8.11	5.66	3.07	2.24	1.66	1.57	1.73	2.05	8.55	5.01	2.44	1.89	1.56	4.17

Source: Compiled from Air Transport World 1979 - 1992.

After 1986 the new-entrants have maintained lower complaint rates than the incumbent carriers, probably due to the incumbents' problems with integrating their route systems after the frequent mergers of 1985-1987 and the resulting shake-out in the industry.

Infrastructure

Congested airports

Airport congestion is one of the barriers to entry even though congestion did not generally exist at US airports in terms of total slots offered. Congestion did however exist in terms of slots offered at peak demand periods. This means that at such an airport a new-entrant will be at a disadvantage by not being able to offer its passengers the most competitive schedule.

At a congested airport the incumbent has a number of alternatives to hinder the success of the new-entrant. Firstly, it can monopolise the peak hour slots, pushing the new-entrant into accepting a less convenient flight schedule, thus, limiting load factors at the outset. This is especially effective if the new-entrant is aiming for business passengers. Secondly, it can leave the less desirable facilities to the new-entrant, for example, the gates furthest from the passenger lounges, older run down less appealing facilities, and release gates for connecting flights that are as far away from each other as possible within the terminal area. Such moves can seriously harm the new-entrant's image. Thirdly, the incumbent can charge the new-entrant excessively high prices for ground services monopolised by an agreement between the incumbent and the airport authority. In such cases, the new-entrant has to have its passengers come in contact with the incumbent's service personnel that can provide poor service on purpose.

Slots

The FAA's High Density Rule is a limiting factor, as it restricts access to slots at four airports: Washington National, Chicago's O'Hare and New York's Kennedy and La Guardia. The airlines can buy and sell slots at these and other airports but refrain from doing so unless under a major financial pressure, because of an airline's tendency to protect its market position even though it does not need some of the slots it possesses.

When slots are scarce and bought and sold as in the United States, they become an asset that involves cost of acquisition upon entry in a congested market. The incumbents on the other hand may have acquired the slots free of charge if operating at the airport before the regulation allowed slot trading. This can exclude the new-entrant competing on the basis of low cost and fares unless the carrier is on marketing terms with the incumbent. This rests on the fact that the incumbent can rely on a number of tools to fight a small competitor at an airport: sandwiching, fare dumping, frequency increase and so on. This argument turns the proverb of 'it being better to be a large fish in a small pond rather than small fish in a large pond', into a fact. This can be seen clearly when the section on market-share is examined, as new-entrant carriers operating from dominant position at airports such as Midway at Midway Airport, Southwest at Love Field, America West at Phoenix and PeoplExpress at Newark, were in a better position to protect their turf. The prerequisite being that such carriers can consume the capacity of the airport in peace during the early stages of the operation. Presidential Airways attempted to fill a gap at Washington Dulles Airport. Immediately after the initiation of operations, United Airlines as well as New York Air entered the airport on large scale, thus, destroying Presidential's niche. The lessons from these experiences are that, if possible, the new-entrant should strive for a high frequency service out of a secondary airport in the vicinity of a large or congested airport in a highly populated area. Exactly what America West, Southwest, PeoplExpress and Midway did.

Under the High Density Rule slots were distributed by committees' representing airlines and airport authorities. As new-entrants demanded access to the slot controlled airports the system crumbled as almost all slots became controlled by the incumbents. Due to this problem and the resulting dead-locks in allocating slots, the DoT amended the High Density Rule in December 1985 by allowing slot trading (GAO, 1990).[34] Under the new system existing slots were allocated according to slot holdings in December 1985. However, in April 1986 the airlines could trade them subject to prior approval from the FAA.

In order to facilitate allocations to 'other' airlines the DoT provided for a 'use or loose' rule that required an airline to use the slot 65 percent of the time or be subject to reallocation through a lottery process. The new-entrants seemed to have a decent chance of obtaining slots under the new system. Yet, it was not so in reality as the incumbents leased their unused slots making it virtually impossible to reallocate slots according to the use or loose clause, as the incumbent was considered to be using the slot although it was actually leasing it to another carrier. What is more the incumbents actively acquired slots through airline acquisitions concentrating the majority of slots to few major carriers. This has led to a very effective barrier to entry for the new-entrants and a lucrative source of income for the majors. In fact if a new-entrant wishes to buy a slot it would have to invest large sums of money for a single slot at the four major airports. To lease is, therefore, the obvious alternative. However, it increases the cost of the new-entrant diluting its competitiveness somewhat with the incumbent. What is more, the incumbent can actually select to lease its slots only to airlines that are not competing directly or are code-sharing partners. Furthermore, leasing is usually short-term, making it hard for a new-entrant to sink capital into building a route that can be lost suddenly. In fact only 9 percent of leases in 1988 were for more than 180 days with most lasting only 60 days (GAO, 1990, p.28).

In order to facilitate new entry, the FAA in 1986 held a special lottery of 152 slots withheld at the High Density airports. Only new-entrants were eligible to participate. Regardless of this provision these slots eventually ended up with the incumbents and only 13 of the 152 slots were utilised by new-entrants in 1990 (pp.22-24). This shows clearly the problems associated with designing effective strategies to lower the slot barrier. In this case it would have been possible to attach a restriction on these slots, requiring them to be utilised by new-entrants only. That, on the other hand, would have lessened their value for the new-entrant holder, making them disadvantaged compared to the incumbent in case of market exit or due to other reason necessitating the liquidation of the slot holding.

Restricted access to gates

Even though the new-entrant can acquire or lease slots, lack of airport facilities can still deter entry. In the United States the airlines lease airport gates and all other facilities on long-term exclusive leases. This gives the airline full control and the ability to exclude other airlines and new-entrants, in particular, from using these facilities at congested airports. The federal government has, however, encouraged the use of 'preferential-use leases'[35] to provide access to facilities that would otherwise be idle. The fact is, however, that gate leases made on the basis of exclusive use gives the lessee full control of the facility while preferential lease allows the airport to allocate the use of it to other airlines if the lessee has not scheduled the use of the facility. If the lessee then decides to use the facility the newcomer has to give it up. In the case of a new-entrant it may have to negotiate the use of facilities under exclusive-use with the incumbent, its competitor. In such case it may be too easy for the incumbent to refuse such lease and, therefore, actively close the airport to competitors although there are unused airport facilities available.

GAO (1990) reported that 88 percent of 3,129 gates at 66 medium to large airports were leased. Of the airports surveyed 26 percent had no unleased gates and 85 percent of the gate leases were for exclusive use. The total number of subleases was 131 in 1990 of which other carriers than majors had 53 percent. In addition to this, 60 percent of all gate leases in 1990 had 11 or more years left to expire (GAO, pp.35-38). While the majors had 2,468 gates leased in 1990, the national airlines had only 240 and regionals 30 (GAO, p.74). This is 8.8 and 1.1 percent of the total gates respectively. At the same time the nationals have 4.9 percent of the total U.S. revenue passenger kilometres and the regionals 0.3 percent. In that sense the allocation of gates seems fair, if it was not for the reason that gate allocations will actually hinder growth and preserve the major's size regardless of efficiency. That is the real problem, since if there is a carrier that can serve the public at a lower fare than the incumbent, that airline should be allowed to serve those that are willing to use it. Under present system the barriers to entry are too extensive to allow such a simple policy to work in reality.

What made the picture even bleaker for new-entrants was that only 16 percent of all leased gates contained a 'use or loose' clause. In the cases where such provision exists it will usually require the lease holder to keep the gate idle for up to 3 months before the gate will be reallocated (GAO, p.35). The outlook for small airports is somewhat better as 37 percent reported that they did not lease any gates and half of the leased gates are 'preferential-use' leases (GAO, p.38). One of the reasons for this difference is that many small airports do not have loading bridges to aircraft so they do not register as having gates.

Restricted access to airport facilities

An incumbent can stockpile airport facilities in order to block possible entry of other carriers. This can sometimes be circumvented by the new-entrant by establishing facilities on its own, but such endeavour raises the entry costs dramatically. At some airports this is not even possible as the incumbent may have in its lease a clause giving it ability to block any further construction at the airport. In view of the risk for the airport to have one dominant large carrier that may exit, leaving the airport suddenly with much less traffic, many airports started to attract carriers by including a 'preferential use' clause in their leases. Such clause gives the airport authority ability to lease to other airlines airport facilities not used by the leaseholder.

In addition to gates, other facilities are being leased on exclusive terms. These include ticket counters, passenger waiting rooms and baggage claim facilities. What this points to is that limited access to airport facilities is a barrier to entry, especially at concentrated airports but to lesser extent at small airports. The major carriers can effectively control access to facilities through their exclusive facility leases, a situation that puts the new-entrant in the position of having to negotiate with its competitor. The most effective way of solving this stalemate is if the airport is effectively building facilities and giving new-entrants priority. The problem with that is severing of relations with large customers namely the incumbents and reverting as well to a short-term solution as the new-entrant is more likely than not to disappear and its leases ending up with the incumbent carrier anyway. Thus, exposing the new-entrant as a weak political bet.

Restriction of airport expansion

If we examine the expansion of airports to see if developments actually open up space for new-entrants, we see that the prospect is rather gloomy. Environmental issues have increased community resistance to airport expansion and 'majority in interest' (MII) agreements between the airlines and airports have also created a strategic element to expansions. MII agreements give airlines, having majority of operations at the airport a saying in matters that could affect their interest, namely expansion plans among other major issues (GAO, 1990, p.45). The logic behind MII is straightforward. The airports needed backing from the users in order to fund expansion projects often initiated by major airlines. The airport fees are then used to pay off the bonds. If bond payments become exceedingly high the only way to make ends meet is to raise the airport fees. As a result it is in no way strange that the airlines would in some way protect their interest, namely with MII. The problem is, however, when the MII are used strategically to block off airport expansion that would benefit new-entrants or other competitors. GAO (p.48) reported that 75 percent of airports with MII find that such agreements limit or delay expansion of airports and 89 percent of all medium to large airports report that one or more factors hinder expansion to some extent.

Environmental impact restrictions

Environmental issues such as pollution are causing ever more constraints at airports. The one affecting the airlines the most is noise. Noise control has raised the barriers to entry for new-entrants in number of ways. First, by curtailing the ability to use older cheaper aircraft not meeting noise regulation standards. Second, by placing a limit on the maximum number of operations at some noise sensitive airports, effectively closing it down for new-entrants due to 'grand-fathering' of slots. Sometimes creating 'fortress' airports for incumbents. Some early new-entrants operating Stage 2 aircraft were limited to airports allowing such aircraft, thus, effectively barred from other airports.

In order to show how environmental issues can affect new-entrants we can look at AirCal's problems at John Wayne Airport (JWA) California, which was AirCal's main airport. As of March 1982 the Airport Board adopted an access plan designated to reduce the noise impact in the area. The plan limited authorised average daily departures (ADD) at the airport to a maximum of 41, to be divided among the five airlines then serving JWA. AirCal was cut from 27 to 23.5 departures. The plan had also subsections subjecting each airline to a possible 10 percent reduction each quarter, dependent on how well it performs with regard to noise limitation. In December 31, 1982 AirCal was down to 19.92 ADD and on November 30th, 1984 it had only 14.6 ADD. The airline blamed estimated losses of $2.5 million in 1982, $15 million in 1983 and $17.5 million in 1984, on the ADD plan (ATW, 1984).

Equipment and financial barriers

Equipment barriers

New entry increases dramatically when aircraft are readily available in the market, due to recession or other causes leading to equipment availability. There are three main sources of aircraft for new-entrants; (i) used aircraft market buying/leasing; (ii) new aircraft from leasing companies; and (iii) new aircraft bought from the manufacturer. The two former ways are the two most commonly used by new-entrants with the first one being the general option taken by most early new entrants. Since the mid-1980's the noise abatement regulation have had serious impact on airlines' aircraft renewal and selection. As a result, there have been cheap older aircraft available to new-entrants that have not been operable to all airports due to noise restrictions, as mentioned before. The regulator, in order to facilitate new-entry provided exemption from some of the noise regulation for a period of time (DoT, 1993). In fact, new-entrants that began operations after the interim Stage 3 phase-in deadlines were not subject to any Stage 3 requirements until the next interim deadline.[36]

Rick Pranke, a banker (Airfinance, 1994, p.18) made it clear, following the 1990's upsurge of new-entrants, that

> ...traditional bank sources will remain sceptical about the new-entrants, except banks and lessors looking to offload aircraft.[37]

These words indicate why the equipment barrier is lowered as well as the financial barriers during periods of excess availability of aircraft. The conclusion is then that the equipment barrier is lower during periods of recession in air transport than during growth periods, unless airlines are retiring older aircraft due to noise abatement laws or an period of over optimistic aircraft acquisitions.

Financial barriers

The availability of capital to new-entrant airlines is a much noted barrier to entry causing a large number of start-up attempts to fail. At the dawn of deregulation a number of airlines were successful in raising share capital through financial markets. These were carriers such as Midway, PeoplExpress, Muse, New York Air and Jet America. Airlines appearing after that were received with less enthusiasm by venture capitalists. In fact the whole airline industry has been poorly rated in financial markets since deregulation and especially new-entrants in view of their poor overall performance.[38] More recent carriers have used self-financing during the early period and then raised public money as the airline has proved itself. Such self-financing can be in the form of employees capital injection in addition to funding from private investors.[39] This method of initial capital formation appears to be the norm for past 1990 new-entrants. However, the availability of capital for new-entrants will reflect the availability of risk capital for high risk endeavours, causing fluctuation in this barrier to entry.

Legal and regulatory barriers

Legal barriers

Legal and regulatory barriers can be built around government policy taking protectionism attitude towards existing carriers. This is, however, not prevailing in the US deregulated market although there have been changes in the pro-activity of governments towards new-entrants. There are, nevertheless, a number of fundamental problems related to the laws and regulation that can be considered to raise barriers for new-entrants. These are the anti-trust law, noise regulation, slot allocation regulation, carrier licensing, CRS regulations and TA regulations. The general conclusion is that these are barriers that are being reduced by the lawmaker and the regulator, especially in terms of anti-trust law, CRS regulation and by ensuring TA's independence from the CRS owners.

The licensing of air carriers can also work as a barrier to entry, by adopting so stringent requirements for new carriers, that only very few will ever get airborne. The fact of the matter is that very few carriers applying for licence fulfil the requirements for licensing. One of the FAA requirements is the production of operations manuals on all aspects of the operation from uniforms to emergency evacuations, proving flights (50 hours) and emergency evacuation tests (Airline Business, 1990b). These requirements are usually deemed as necessary for the safe operation of the carrier and are, consequently, not questioned. Other relevant source of legislation is social legislation, involving labour, drug and alcohol testing and so forth. As social legislation and technical requirements are costly to meet, these raise the financial entry barrier for new-carriers.

Merger regulation

It became an issue in the deregulation process that the industry might become concentrated. In order to keep the checks and balances in mergers and acquisitions the CAB was given control over mergers and agreements according to a standard set forth by the Bank Merger Act.[40] Under section 408(b) of the Deregulation Act the Board (Lowenfeld, 1981, section 4.27, p.4-70): (i) shall approve a merger, unless it finds it not consistent with the public interest; but (ii) shall not approve a merger if (following section 7 of the Clayton Act) the effect of the merger may be substantially to lessen competition or to tend to create a monopoly; unless (iii) the anti-competitive effects of the merger are outweighed in the public interest by its probable effect in meeting significant transportation conveniences and needs of the public, and less anti-competitive alternatives are not available.

Section 414 dealt with the exceptions from the antitrust laws and states that the Board

> ...may excempt any person affected by its order from the operations of the antitrust laws...

Furthermore the CAB

> ...may not excempt such person unless it determines that such excemption is required in the public interest.[41]

When the Act's Sunset Clause was effected the supervision of mergers and agreements, as well as antitrust immunity was transferred to the Department of Justice (DoJ) under supervision from the Department of Transportation. On January 1, 1989 the Department of Justice took full charge of domestic-airline-antitrust issues. The Department of Justice has been considered to take a tougher stand on airline mergers and CRS issues than the DoT. The DoJ blocked the proposed deal between USAir and Eastern on the latter carrier's Philadelphia gates and the Toronto route, in view of USAir's dominant position at the airport and it being Eastern's main competitor on the route. Furthermore, it opposed the Sabre-Datas II joint venture, leading to its cancellation, that resulted in Datas II merger with Pars. In February 1991 the DoJ blocked United's bid for Eastern's slots and gates at Washington National on the basis of Sherman Section 1, as the proposed sale had a less anti competitive alternative, namely Northwest becoming the eventual buyer of the package.

Bankruptcy law

Chapter 11 of the US bankruptcy law has played a role in the structure of the US airline industry, reason being the protection against creditors it provides. In fact, such protection has major influence on the cost structure of the carrier involved, allowing it to compete by offering lower fares. In reality Chapter 11 is a way for a bankrupt carrier to remain in possession of its assets under court supervision, while it attempts to reorganise. If the carrier can gain approval for its reorganisation plan, the carrier can emerge from bankruptcy, if not it will enter Chapter 7 bankruptcy that means full liquidation under the control of a trustee.

A loophole in the bankruptcy law enabled airlines to declare bankruptcy in order to lower cost structure, but it was closed in 1984 following the heavily criticised bankruptcy of Continental Airlines.

The Chapter 11 carriers' effect on the industry

Chapter 11 bankrupt carriers can operate for extended periods depending on the time it takes to negotiate a reorganisation plan, sometimes for years. Such carriers face pressure to maintain cash flow to cover day to day operating costs. Therefore, they may lean on fare discounting in order to maintain adequate demand levels, as many passengers might otherwise avoid flying with a bankrupt carrier.

A way to raise working capital through other means than stimulating demand through low fares, is the so-called 'debtor in possession' (DIP) protection of lender to a Chapter 11 company. Under the scheme the injection of loans is encouraged through special protection scheme because priority of payment ahead of other creditors is guaranteed by law. America West secured loans from Northwest and Guinness Peat Aviation through DIP. In fact the scheme has in some cases induced a financially troubled carrier to declare bankruptcy in order to secure needed loans only available under DIP. This is what is alleged to have happened in the case of Pan Am and Midway. A further development in bankruptcy as a management tool was the so called 'pre-packaged' bankruptcy, where the airline arranges for DIP financing and reorganisation plan before declaring bankruptcy, in order to reduce the bankruptcy period and increase the carrier's chances of emerging.

Taking Pan Am (I) as an example of the impact of DIP financing, it was alleged that the carrier needed cash and was negotiating a short-term loan, but the financial institution involved would not provide the loan unless the carrier declared Chapter 11 bankruptcy, to secure the loan under the DIP scheme. Similar situation occurred with Midway that could only secure a $25 million loan upon declaring bankruptcy. The problem with this development for the airline and the financier is that the airline's image is diminished causing sudden drop in income, due to many passengers and travel agents avoiding the bankrupt carrier. Therefore, one can assume that this inducement to file for bankruptcy to be fatalistic to the carrier but a secure short-term option for the creditor, as he will recover his investment as far as there are assets to cover the secured loan.

Chapter 11 bankruptcy as a management tool originated with Continental's bankruptcy in September 1983. The purpose of the bankruptcy that was allegedly unnecessary due to $60 million cash reserves and non-default on loans, was primarily to resolve a labour dispute (Bernstein, 1991). The bankruptcy was utilised as an instrument to re-negotiate all labour contracts allowing the carrier to lower its cost structure instantly.

An important question of the whole bankruptcy issue is whether bankrupt carriers seriously bias the competition structure by fare cutting fuelled by their protection against creditors and therefore lower cost structure. The large Chapter 11 carriers, America West, Continental and Trans World had among them 18 percent of the industry traffic in 1992. The former president of America West, Conway (1993), remarked that the effect of the Chapter 11 carriers was overstated as the bankrupt carriers do not gain any advantage of the bankruptcy as the effect will not be positive on operating costs. Furthermore, the carriers will have to pay for large portion of their costs up-front in cash. In addition, he stated (Conway, p.643) that the stigma of bankruptcy would bleed off traffic.

It may be precisely this traffic bleeding that has made it so difficult for bankrupt carriers to emerge from Chapter 11. The reason being that the passenger takes a perceived risk by travelling with a bankrupt carrier.[42] So in order to facilitate the customer's willingness to undertake such risk the fare must be attractive, inducing the Chapter 11 carriers to offer attractive fares and maintain the necessary cash flow.

Predatory behaviour

If the new-entrant's expectations as to the force of the incumbents reaction to entry is high, it can deter entry and, therefore, form a barrier. Many countries do enforce 'fair' competition laws that can be a powerful buffer against unjust competitor's actions. For example, the alleged predatory actions of British Airways against Virgin Atlantic, the European new-entrant, weakened British Airways as a competitor with respect to this potential barrier. This is due to the scrutiny BA may experience from competition authorities and the media if new cases of alleged predation occur.

Another important issue is predatory actions or intentions as actions by the incumbents along such lines can easily crush a small airline, unless the new-entrant has something unique and unmatchable to offer in the market. In view of this, anti-trust enforcement is an important issue for small airlines. Although, the meaning of the term 'predatory' is subject to controversy.[43] There have been two basic views of what constitutes predation: (i) that of offering 'any price below cost'; and (ii) the 'motive' of driving a competitor out of business or out of a market.[44] An important example in this regard was Northwest's reactions to the new-entrant Reno Air in 1993. Northwest had terminated its service out of Reno in 1991, thus, leaving a market space for Reno Air, which commenced three daily flights to Northwest's Minneapolis hub. The incumbent attempted to 'discipline' the new-entrant by starting a service to Reno again and issue plans to operate flights from Reno to three destinations in competition with the new-entrant. However, after objections and government pressure Northwest withdrew its plans in Reno. The question is, nevertheless, if these actions by Northwest should be termed as predatory or simply aggressive competition?

A similar case involved United and Pacific Express, where the new-entrant alleged predatory actions after United Airlines started to operate flights on Pacific Express's San Francisco route. However, United defended its case successfully on the grounds that its move was a logical extension of its network growth. Contrariwise, Northwest entered the Reno market again after it left it on the basis of inefficiency of operations. Thus, it seems that by entering the market again just after Reno Air came about, that the sole intention may have been to discipline the new-entrant or to force it out of the market. However, the case never went before the courts making the true intentions unclear and predatory behaviour unproved.

Human capital barriers

Employee barriers

A possible barrier to entry is experience accumulated with time, making entry costs high, as the incumbents have accumulated cost saving experience not readily available to the new-entrant. The classic experience curve involves the increase in workers efficiency, layout improvement and increase in specialisation that occurs with time. For the experience curve to be a barrier to entry it needs to involve experience that is not readily available to new-entrants. Porter (1980) assumes that the new-entrant will have inherently higher costs than the incumbent at the outset. In air transport this does not hold as most new-entrants have lower costs.[45] Thus, the general assumption must be that experience is not a major barrier to entry in air transportation compared to many other industries. New-entrants can usually benefit from ex-airline employees becoming redundant during recession or frequent cost reduction exercises by large carriers, gaining employee experience instantly and often at minimum cost. In fact, most new-entrants in the 90's have been established by employees of bankrupt carriers or laid-off staff from the majors.

Summary

The intense rivalry that has characterised the industry since deregulation, is because of excess capacity, market-share orientation, Chapter 11 carriers, 'spiteful' behaviour or deterrent strategy to prevent new-entrance.

Barriers to entry are primarily in terms of market power, shortage of capital and congestion rather than incumbents' cost economies of scale. The first start-up new-entrant, Midway Airlines, was the first to face numerous barriers to entry, it tried to gain protection at Midway airport but was denied such protection because it was deemed to be neither in the carrier's nor the consumers' interest. That effectively laid the basis of new-entrants' treatment in the deregulated environment.

Frequent flyers programs are one of the most effective tools of the incumbents after deregulation. New-entrants found it difficult to compete with large carrier's frequent flyer programs, but have made their programs more attractive to passengers through marketing agreements with such carriers. Code-sharing was a necessary feature of the hub operating new-entrant in order to gain priority on CRS screens after a change in regulation that demoted interlining flights in screen priority, causing a drop in bookings. The code-sharing alliance agreements have, however, caused loss of independence and in some cases eventual acquisition by the incumbent due to the vulnerability of the smaller carrier in such a marketing pact. The problem can be compared with the 'one customer' dependency problem that is often related to bankruptcies.

Computer reservation systems (CRS) have created market power for the hosts that have been the largest major carriers: United, American, Eastern and Delta. The systems have provided the carriers with extra revenue and profits. Which is generated from the tendency of agents to book the flights of the system owner rather than the competitors and termed as 'incremental revenue.' CRS bias caused a substantial incremental revenue due to the hosts display priority of own flights. Such biases along with a number of other advantages of CRS ownership are being neutralised creating a more level playing ground and reducing the distribution barrier to entry.

Volume incentives have been used by the airlines in order to create travel agents' loyalty and preference. Such programs are important for the TA's as the normal commission level is seldom enough to run an agency. The downside of this practice is that new-entrants, usually with little volume, will find it hard to break the loyalty formed in this way.

Yield management systems have been found to be an important competition tool for incumbents as they allow complex fare differentiation and reduce yield erosion of very low fares. Such capability raises a serious barrier to entry for a comparably low frequency, low-cost, no-frills and low-fare carrier.

Airport congestion raises barriers in the densest markets, especially at the High Density Rule Airports that have slot restrictions. Slot trading was allowed in 1986 creating much wealth for the largest carriers that had most of the slots at the congested airports. After that the new-entrants had to buy or lease slots in order to gain access to the largest airports. In order to do so the new-entrant had to be code-sharing with the slot owner in order to be reasonably secure, as most of the slots are leased on very short leases, usually for only two or three months at a time. Gates are not readily available to new-entrants rather than slots at airports, as the incumbent can acquire more of these facilities than necessary in order to be in control. Such ability depends, on the form of leasing for these facilities at the airport. Majority-in-interest (MII) clauses can give predominant incumbent carriers the ability to veto expansion plans at airports, that could benefit new-entrants. Therefore, raising infrastructure barriers further.

Environmental protection and health regulation, especially, noise abatement has caused massive changes to airlines in terms of costs and access to some airports. The availability of the largest single capital and cost outlay for an airline, the aircraft, has had effect on the ability of new airlines to start operations. During recessions and industry consolidation aircraft become more readily available reducing this barrier to entry. Legal and regulatory barriers can be hard for new airlines to overcome as much cost is involved with fulfilling some of the requirements for carrier licensing. Such requirements are usually safety related and therefore not questioned. There has, however, been some opposition to recent costly regulation on drug and alcohol testing.

Anti-trust enforcement is important for the new-entrants as such regulation can hinder too much concentration in the industry and anti-competitive behaviour of the larger competitor. The enforcement of such regulation has, however, been very problematic due to the difficulty of defining and proving predatory behaviour.

The human capital barrier is mentioned and it is concluded that this barrier is not a large factor for new-entrants after 1986, due to layoffs and bankruptcies that have created a large pool of experienced people looking for work with the airlines. Many of the past 1990 new-entrants have been formed and staffed by these people.

The industry has had three main loss periods since deregulation, 1981 - 1983, 1986, and 1990 to 1993. The alleged reasons for industry losses were increases in fuel prices, merger activity and over-capacity. Concentration has increased since deregulation as in 1979, 25 carriers had 1 percent market share or more at 50 of the largest airports, but in 1991 there were only 15 carriers. Hub and spoke networks were considered one of the most important strategic tools of the industry following deregulation. Market-share analysis of airlines shows that those airlines having dominant position on one or more airports were more likely to survive at least for longer periods than those not having such a position. In the last few years there has been increased attention on direct service carriers such as Southwest as its constant profit performance is better than that of many larger carriers. Southwest Airlines' efficiency is first and foremost, because of: high fleet utilisation, quick turn-around at gates, direct short-haul services, high quality but no-frills type of service and gradual growth.

Carriers have in the past decided on bankruptcy in-order to secure loans from loan institutions that want DIP protection. This has lead to untimely bankruptcy that could have been avoided. Chapter 11 carriers operating under protection from the creditors during reorganisation have to offer attractive fares to maintain demand as passengers and travel agents may circumvent the bankrupt carrier. At the same time incumbents can initiate fare wars in order to undermine the financial condition of the bankrupt carrier eliminating a competitor.

Quality of service measured in terms of complaint's rates has increased from 1988, while in 1979 the average rate reached its highest or 8.11 complaints per 100.000 passengers. The period 1987 to 1988 was also poor due to problems in route system integration following the high merger activity in 1985-1987, as well as unrealistic scheduling in order to gain better CRS display listing.

---

6 It played a role in this case that Chicago's Midway airport was on the verge of failure due to lack of services at the time.

7 Midway majority opinion, at 31-32.

8 See Section 102(a) (10) of the Federal Aviation Act of 1958 as amended in 1979.

9 See Section 102 (a) (8) of the Federal Aviation Act of 1958 as amended in 1979.

10 See Section 1002 (d) (4) (B) of the Federal Aviation Act of 1958 as amended in 1979.

11 Senate Report 107.

12 Most new carriers have lower cost structure and can, therefore, reduce fares for all passengers. Furthermore, the sustainability of their fare structure is long term but for the large incumbents low fares are usually short-term or capacity controlled.

13 This is along the lines of the cost of safety. The cost of a perfectly safe car would be immense and not viable because it would cost the customer more than he is willing to pay. Thus, there will be an equilibrium between safety costs and price in the market. The same goes for airlines as the maximum benefit to the consumer is a fare approaching zero and constant departures to each destination. Such a system is inconceivable but can be approached given that the priorities are decided. That is, should the system strive for primarily low fares and high frequency; low fares, high frequency and high service standard? The ultimate balance has to be a segmented equilibrium between the service demanded and the price the customer is willing to pay.

14 A new-entrant can certainly offer such overrides. The travel agent will, however, rather book a larger carrier that generates more booking volume. This is due to the fact that volume breaks are higher thus pressing the agency to book more on the large carrier in order to maximise the agency's income.

15 A good introduction to Australian deregulation can be found in Button (1991), pp. 48-82.

16 The principal agent effect refers to the principals' attempt to create incentives for the agent in order to shape his behaviour due to lack of direct control and imperfect information on his behaviour, or conversely create incentives or strategies to prevent negative results from an agent's behaviour (Levine, 1987, p. 419).

17 Being a new-entrant in a market where failures of such carriers have been frequent or entry and exit have occurred frequently, can raise entry barriers as potential customers and travel agents avoid the newcomer.

18 An antitrust suite was brought against American, Continental, Delta, Midway, Northwest, Pan Am, TWA, United and USAir over conspiracy to fix prices through

to and from hub cities, through a CRS. The airlines lost the case and a $364 million antitrust fund was created from which passengers can claim vouchers in order to get discount off selected flights with the above carriers, provided the passenger made a trip with one of the carriers through one of the 34 named hub cities.

19 HHI above 1800 indicates high concentration, while HHI below 1000 indicates low concentration.

20 Section 411 of the Federal Aviation Act states that the FAA has the duty to: '...investigate and determine whether any air carrier, foreign air carrier, or ticket agent has been or is engaged in unfair or deceptive practices or unfair methods of competition in air transportation or the sale thereof.'

21 Incremental revenues are defined as 'added revenues resulting when agents using CRS book more travel on the airline owning the CRS than the agents would normally make on that airline.

22 Architectural bias is it called when every function of the CRS is not open to all participants in the system. 'Functional Equality' is the term used to describe a system where all functions of the system are equally open to all participants.

23 This was a 1989 trial in the Federal District Court in California involving among others Northwest and Alaska against SABRE and Apollo's host airlines American and United. The court found no antitrust violations and the plaintive appealed the judgement. *See* (91 Daily Journal D.A.R. 13279) and U.S. Supreme Court of denied certiorari (112 S. Ct. 1603, 1992).

24 Pre-rule, meaning before the CRS regulation was introduced in 1984.

25 This has been possible by the hosts as the CRS's have been run as departments within the host airlines, rather than as separate companies. Some of the small CRS were de-hosted, but the large ones COVIA and SABRE remained hosted.

26 Note that this estimate is not reliable as an estimator for current profitability.

27 In a study (DoT, 1988) it was estimated that in 1986 the halo effect from the two largest CRS SABRE and Apollo increased revenues by 40 and 36 percent respectively and incremental revenues increased revenues likewise by 15 and 14 percent.

28 This GAO report was quoted in a Hearing Before the Subcommittee on Public Works and Transportation House of Representatives on The Airline Competition Enhancement Act of 1992.

29 The CRS owners indicated in a Congressional Hearing on the Airline Competition Enhancement Act of 1992, that the profitability of the CRS had been drastically reduced due to intense competition between the systems and low booking fees that have not followed increases in the Consumer Price Index. As most of the CRS do not release their accounts it is not possible to evaluate this statement at this time. However, it indicates that CRS are perhaps not as good an investment as in the past. Nevertheless, it must be recognised that the construction of such a system involves very high sunk costs as the creators of Galileo and Amadeus found out and resulted in partnership with the U.S. CRS.

30 SAS decision to withdraw from Amadeus ownership reflects this shift in strategy, but SAS considered that ownership of superfluous benefit based on the EC's equal functionality requirement. As the European flag carriers will be under increased pressure to be profitable in a competitive deregulated environment they will place increased importance on disassociating themselves with the CRS unless they will become a major source of income instead of a drain. In such an environment the CRS will not play a major role as a barrier to entry for new-entrants. With the neutrality of

CRS the airlines will, however, find other ways of creating favourable bias towards their product. These are in the form of sales-incentives or 'commission overrides' and 'limited availability fares' to selected 'favourable' agents.

31 The 1987 Travel Agency Market, pp. 28-45.

32 Due to the sensitivity of the question it is likely that the actual practice of selecting the incentive carrier is much more widespread than the numbers indicate.

33 Complaint rates are calculated from filings from the airlines and from DoT data. This way of counting the complaints could incorporate inaccuracy that is hard to estimate. The complaint rates are nevertheless a indicator of airline service quality and is the only publicly available source.

34 Slot sales have decreased since trading was activated but leasing increased, which indicates that the incumbents will retain control in order maintain this barrier to entry, as reported in the report from GAO (1990).

35 A preferential-use lease grants the lessor the right to provide the facilities to other airlines if the facilities would otherwise be idle.

36 Note that the Committee (*see* DoT, 1993) recommended that new-entrants should be required to meet the same requirements as other airlines in all aspects.

37 Quoted words by Rick Pranke of Chase Manhattan Bank.

38 America West regardless of initial success was never rated higher than B+, United as BB+ and Alaska although profitable for decades as BB+. According to S&P's rating system of the financial condition of firms for investment purposes the average grade for U.S. airlines in 1993 was B+, which is a middle speculative grade.

39 Reno Air took this route and raised an initial $2 million and took out a IPO later. Kiwi raised $10 million from its employees, later the carrier took out private equity placements raising the initial capital base. ValuJet started out with $3.4 million provided from the founders, later when the airline had established itself it took out a private placement of $12 million.

40 See 12 U.S.C. Section 1828 (c) 5, and (5) and Section 1842(a).

41 See Section 414 of the Airline Deregulation Act of 1978.

42 Using a credit card reduces this risk as credit card companies will not honour payments to bankrupt carriers for unused tickets. Travel agents can also validate the tickets on another carrier in order to delay the payment to the bankrupt carrier and therefore reduce the risk of the passenger in case the carrier goes under within three or four weeks, which is the processing time of the payment through the validated carrier.

43 See Section 101 of the Act. ' Predatory means any practice which would constitute a violation of the antitrust laws as set forth in the first section of the Clayton Act (15 U.S.C. 12).

44 See Section 2 of the Sherman Act.

45 In fact if the classic experience curve traits are analysed we find that costs actually increase as an airline ages, workers' efficiency increases in the beginning but then levels off and may decline as occurred at PeoplExpress when the employees were literally burning out due to the high work load and the stresses associated with providing high quality service and up-beat attitude all the time.

3 The anatomy of a new-entrant

Introduction

When researching the new-entrants it soon became evident that information is scarce on the smaller airlines in comparison to carriers such as Southwest, America West and PeoplExpress. As a result, these airlines are mentioned to a greater extent than other airlines in the book. This should not skew the historical overview as the general underlying principles of their initial success and later failure is coinciding with other new-entrants in most respects.

Management

Education/experience

Little information is available on the education of new-entrant airlines' managers. In a survey conducted on new-entrant airlines' managers, a part of this research project, it was found that managers (n = 45) of new-entrant airlines have completed an average of 16.1 years formal education. That means that they have on the average an undergraduate degree. Of those that responded in the survey, 12 had master degree, 23 undergraduate degree, 2 had some college education, and 4 high school or flight school. Contacts and experience rather than education seem to be most valuable for founders of new-entrant airlines. The question of whether education makes the establishment of important contacts easier to accomplish is beyond the scope of this book, but worth having in mind. It is a fact that Harvard Business School (HBS) graduates have started some successful carriers, such as Donald Burr of PeoplExpress, Fred Smith of Federal Express (small package service and cargo) and Rollin King, a HBS graduate that suggested the formation of Southwest to Herbert Kelleher.

If one examines the track record of new-entrant airlines' founders one can easily establish that experience in the airline industry is a prerequisite to getting the airline flying. Managers and front-line staff at new-entrant airlines are usually professional people coming from either large incumbent carriers with the motivation of doing things differently or coming from bankrupt carriers wishing to stay in the industry. The former motive was the reason for PeoplExpress formation while the latter goes for Reno that was created by former Pan Am and Eastern employees as well as America West that was formed by ex-Continental staff. In fact jet-operating airlines have to have management staff with airline experience in order to function adequately from the beginning. It must be noted that PeoplExpress required no airline experience when recruiting customer-managers (front-line staff). Apparently to facilitate job flexibility and team spirit, but they expected resistance to their concepts by veteran airline employees.

The importance of good connections and relevant experience is apparent if Donald Burr of PeoplExpress is examined. He had gained important experience as president of National Aviation, a Wall Street company specialising in airline investments, then climbing from the executive vice presidency to presidency at Texas International. This experience gave him extremely good credentials and connections to raise capital and start an airline, facilitated by his Harvard MBA degree (HBS, 1983). Mike Hollis of Air Atlanta had similar background but he earned a law degree after graduation from Dartmouth College and started his carrier with the investment firm Oppenheimer & Co, as VP-Public Financing. Then he ran his own law practice in Atlanta and served as an assistant to the DoT's Urban Mass Transportation Administrator, followed by various other public sector posts (ATW, 1985b). What Hollis lacked compared to Burr was aviation experience, a factor that may have influenced Hollis optimism of the success of a premium service strategy in the face of known difficulties with such a strategy.

Paul Quackenbush of Empire Airlines graduated from Yale University and entered the Navy. After earning his commercial licence and air transport pilots licence he managed a fixed base operation, aircraft sales outlet in Hawaii, worked in marketing at Aloha Airlines, then at Air America as training and operations pilot, and finally once again as a Fixed Base Operation manager at Oneida County Airport from where he founded Empire Airlines (ATW, 1982b). Mark Morris of Air 1 had considerable experience as a pilot, manager of small specialised airline and then of DHL Airways a small passenger cargo carrier. In the mean time he had been general manager of St Lucia Airlines for few months until it was nationalised. His period as a consultant got him interested in forming Air 1 after his proposal for such an operation was turned down by a client (ATW, 1984a). Although William Lyon and George Argyros that took over AirCal in 1982 had no airline experience, their senior staff was highly experienced with a total of over 90 years experience in 1984. William Slattery the original president and CEO of

Braniff (II) came from TWA were he was vice president of sales and services. Harold J. Pareti the founder of Presidential co-founded PeoplExpress and was previously employed by Texas International as assistant secretary and staff vice president of governmental affairs (HBS, 1983). Most of the carrier's employees were actually ex-PeoplExpress employees. Thus, lending Presidential considerable experience from another new-entrant, which was unusual as most new-entrants have been staffed by ex-employees of the incumbents.

Personality

Starting a new-entrant is first and foremost an entrepreneurial exercise making the founder's personality an important element. Ari Ginsberg and Ann Bucholtz (1989) undertook meta-analysis to establish if research on entrepreneurs actually proved any difference in leadership traits of entrepreneurs compared to business leaders of established companies. The study found that the definition of what constitutes an entrepreneur varied greatly making their comparison troublesome. A general definition covering an airline founder could be adopted from a study by Smith & Miner (*see* Ginsberg and Bucholtz, pp. 32-40) that defined entrepreneurs as being simply persons involved in the founding of a business. Their study was limited to businesses experiencing fast 'growth rates,' defined as an increase of more than 1.5 employees per year, a far to little growth to cover new-entrant airlines. According to the study entrepreneurs scored higher than ordinary managers in the sample on self-achievement, feedback of results, personal innovation and for the total score of all examined factors. The amazing fact about the new-entrants is the unusually large scale of the initial operations, the complexity of the start-up and the fast growth of the operation. All requiring a truly special entrepreneurial qualities that need to be researched specifically in view of the unique case of new-entrant airlines.

Domineering and charismatic personalities are common among new-entrant airline CEO's. One can name Acker at Air Florida,[46] Burr, Muse and Kelleher on the charismatic side. The true benefit of the charismatic leader to a new-entrant is media coverage and employees' willingness to follow the leader (sometimes blindly) based on his vision. The airline's strategy has, however, to take into account this ability of the founder and integrate it into the airline's image. Herbert Kelleher of Southwest is well known for his stunts where his image is portrayed as a 'fun loving eccentric' in a positive way. This image may be originally his own, or cleverly managed and escalated by his closest staff, but the talent has to be there and Mr. Kelleher certainly possesses it richly. Lamar Muse used similar tactics at Muse Air, having been well seasoned at Southwest where he was president until 1977. Donald Burr, although highly charismatic did not use the 'fun' factor but became a 'saviour' from high-fares. His charismatic features were, however, greater internally through his management philosophy that was highly motivating for the staff during the early years of operations.

Locus of control

Table 3.1 shows the composition of the board of directors for few new-entrants. It does not make a distinction between directors that have financial interest in the company as mentioned above in the People's Express case, but such directors are sometimes regarded as insiders rather than outsiders. Of the carriers shown in the table MGM Grand Air (1987-1995) had the largest and most monumental board with famous names such as Lee Iacocca the former chairman of Chrysler Corporation. Regardless of that the carrier was financially unsuccessful during its operational period and eventually sold the operating certificate to Champion Air in 1995.[47]

Duchesneau and Gartner (1990) found a link between very high *locus of control* and unsuccessful or failed firms. Therefore, it is of interest whether the top executive is performing more than one role at once as representation of centralisation. Such as being the airline's chairman, CEO and president or some other combination of the sort. Under this form he is less likely to be challenged, although decision making will be quicker. Such form of management suits start-up companies often particularly well, but the structure becomes a liability as the company grows and gets more complicated (Flamholtz, 1990).

Table 3.1 Examples of new-entrant airlines' composition of board of directors

Airline	Insiders[b]	Outsiders	Total	Notes
America West[a]	3	5	8	Emerged from Chapter 11 in 1994
MGM Grand Air	4	10	14	Folded
Southwest	1	6	7	
PeoplExpress	1	4	5	Acquired

[a] This is the board of directors until Sept. 1992, after receiving a financial package the board was changed. [b] Insider in this context is someone with an executive function within the company.

Source: Financial statements for 1992, except for PeoplExpress where HBS Case (490-012) was used.

A criticism of having a combined CEO and chairman is that the idiosyncrasy of one person can influence decision-making to a greater extent than if the person was working closely with a separate chairman. Argenti

(1973) has suggested that the combination of top roles is associated with failure due to the resulting lack of checks and balances. The tendency to autocracy and lack of balance is further escalated if the combined chairman/CEO nominates his delegates to the board of directors. For example, PeoplExpress board of directors was composed of stakeholders, investment bankers that were involved in the airline's financing, one of which was a large shareholder. This was the combination of the board until 1985 when a Harvard professor[48] joined the board (Prospectus, 1983). Employees had no representative although they were the majority shareholders in the company. It may have been to the company's benefit to have an employee nominee at the board level in order to represent employee issues, that had become a major problem as early as 1982, due to the airline's fast growth (Business Week, 1985, p.65).

The difficulty with unbalanced boards, for example high representation of venture capitalists, such as characterised PeoplExpress is a swing towards their interest of financing expansion and acquisition. If marketing, operations and finance are equally represented into inside and outside directors it is more likely that the board will effectively perform its duties.[49]

Decision-making

Decision-making is the function that ultimately makes or breaks a company. A skill affected by factors such as information quality and quantity, experience, environment and management aspirations. If we make an example of PeoplExpress, decision-making at the carrier was until 1985, made up of management teams that were assisted by advisory staff committees. The decision-making flow was from nineteen management teams reporting to the chairman through weekly staff meetings or to the co-ordinating councils that would make recommendations to the chairman. The management teams usually bypassed staff committees that never had substantial role. One must recognise that no other management officer (top manager) had much flair, as the chairman was the only person associated with daily operations, that sat on the airline's board of directors, as mentioned before. In view of the working load that People's Express organisational structure placed on the employees, it is highly likely that the increased pressures of changed competitive environment led to threat-rigidity[50] in PeoplExpress decision making. Burr as an individual had the greatest influence on the company's destiny due to his central role in all decision making.

Research on stress and anxiety provides some insight into behavioural tendencies in such situations. Withey (1962, p.118) reported that individual's anxiety in a crisis situation leads to 'a narrowing of the perceptual field and a limitation of the information that can or will be received', leading to a rigid response. Putting this into context with PeoplExpress, we find that the chairman was criticised for deciding on the Frontier acquisition too quickly.

Previous major decisions by Burr seemed to be 'thought-out' but the Frontier acquisition should have been seen clearly as incompatible with the situation at PeoplExpress. Thus, it is highly likely that mounting pressures from the competitive environment had increased stress levels at the airline to such an extent that threat-rigidity in decision-making occurred.

Another supporting factor was the decision to step-up employee pressures knowing of employees' frequent complaints of excessive job pressures, long-working hours and burnout (Business Week, 1985). The evidence seems to point out that new original solutions to the airline's problems were not adopted, as the situation craved.

The issue of threat-rigidity must be considered a highly important focus point for managers of new-entrant airlines due to the pressures that are associated with the territory. It is perhaps more important to build in check points for this phenomena at new-entrant airlines than most other firms due to the fast growth and speed of changes that affect such airlines. As discussed before the check points should be established through the composition of the board of directors and the management structure, where no one person can hold ultimate power.

Organisation

Organisation structure

New-entrant airlines have selected to establish organisation structures that have allowed the necessary cross-utilisation of employees in order to attain maximum employee efficiency and lower costs. Employee staff-committees and advisory councils have been used in order for employees to have a saying in the running of new-entrant airlines founded on theories of participatory management.[51] Such policy had an added importance due to the new-entrant airlines' wish to stay non-unionised. Thus, if employees are owners and participate in decision-making or at least have a say, there would be less reason for employees to get organised within union.[52]

No airline went farther into employee programs than PeoplExpress, which organisation structure was apparently highly decentralised. In 1982 it was composed of nineteen management teams, four staff committees and advisory councils. The advisory councils were composed of service managers, flight managers and maintenance managers. Then each advisory council nominated two of its members to the co-ordinating council that met with Burr (HBS, 1990, p.7). Employee cross-utilisation was an important idea in order to increase efficiency, but seemed to have been made into a ritual at PeoplExpress, to such an extent that employees complained of being moved too much around learning no one function fully and being constantly wasting time re-learning tasks over and over again. Some employees got away with ignoring the concept and stayed in one line or staff function in order to address the growing problems of the airline's fast growth (HBS, p.12).

The fast growth at PeoplExpress caused the airline, apparently, to outgrow its organisational structure. Hence, in August 1982 PeoplExpress introduced team managers, as the management teams' span of control was too large. The team manager's role was to ensure that their team members had all the resources and support they needed. In 1984 there was still a major change to the organisational structure as the heavy emphasis on cross-utilisation lead managers to conclude that employees identified too much with their staff functions rather than operations. As the number of employees was totalling over 3000 in 1984 the team spirit of the early days was disappearing.

In order to revitalise the 'old' spirit PeoplExpress introduced operations groups of about 300 people each. The groups were formed around aircraft types, so there were to begin with six 727, three 737 and one 747 group. Each group of 300 employees was then broken down into teams of 20 people, each led by a team manager. The groups then controlled a section of the company such as an airline within the airline, in charge of specific gates, routes and planes. This structure was never fully implemented but showed early signs of success (HBS, p.15). PeoplExpress was out of the ordinary in terms of organisation structure. Other new-entrants adopted a more traditional organisation structures, usually segmented into the marketing, operations and finance functions.

Southwest's organisation structure is departmentalised but decentralised with relatively little concentration on the top. In 1972 to 1973 the main departments were operations, marketing, ground operations and the comptroller. Lamar Muse was at that time the president and treasurer with Herbert Kelleher as secretary and general counsel reporting directly to the president (HBS, 1974). What is worth special attention in Southwest's Organisation Chart is that ground operations are separated from flight operations giving it more independence. This configuration is probably the heart of Southwest's emphasis on fast aircraft turnaround that has maintained the company's high efficiency to the present day.

It can not be concluded that the type of organisation structure has played much role in new-entrants' failures. However, an organisation structure unable to grow as fast as many of the new-entrants did, certainly did have an impact on their fortunes.

Employee issues

New-entrants usually adopted low cost approach to operations, effectively paying less for more work. Therefore, employee issues, were a matter of priority due to its correlation with quality service and motivation. A 'we care attitude' or 'you are working for yourself' became the buzzwords. America West, for example, ran day-care centres and employee assistance programs.

The assistance programs dealt with problems ranging from substance abuse to personal financial difficulties (Airline Executive, 1990a), ratifying clearly to employees a care attitude resulting in increased employee loyalty and motivation to work towards organisational goals.

Cross utilisation or flexible job descriptions were widely accepted in order to increase efficiency. The concept was put to use very efficiently by PeoplExpress that called all its employees 'managers,' front line people were 'customer managers,' the crew was, 'flight managers' and maintenance workers, 'maintenance managers'. In fact the employees were trained to take on assignments as diverse as baggage loading to being a flight attendant, with pilots taking on flexibility tasks as well. These programs worked to begin with but the airline's fast growth soon created intense pressures on employees causing many to find a policy of such cross-utilisation[53] hindering efficiency. This system of extreme cross-utilisation disintegrated slowly due to employees not having time to take it too seriously during the latter half of PeoplExpress life-cycle (HBS, 1990, p.12). America West, on the other hand, did not confer the 'manager' title on all its staff such as PeoplExpress, but defined itself as a people oriented airline, not only in terms of service to passengers but also internally (Airline Executive, 1990a, p.19)

> In a service business where you expect to do a good job with customers, your first priority is to do a good job with your employees...It's a matter of survival.

America West has used 'peer review hiring' where hiring committees are made up of workers. The committees apparently seem to have better insight into who will perform and fit into the environment present (Airline Executive, p.20). To emphasise its employee policy even further, America West maintained an open door policy throughout its growth, giving top managers the ability to feel the pulse and be in direct contact with what was happening in the airline (Airline Executive, p.21). America West cross-utilises gate personnel so that any gate personnel can go on board as flight attendant if necessary. Many non-unionised new-entrants utilise such flexibility in order to increase efficiency without going to the extreme and make cross-utilisation into a philosophy such as PeoplExpress did.

Stock-participation programs became common among the new-entrants and both PeoplExpress and America West had such programs. At People the employees were initially required to buy shares at one fourth of their market value and optional shares at one half of market value (ATW, 1993b, p.19). During the first years of operations many of the early employees had shareholding of substantial worth. At America West employees spent 20 percent of their first year salary to buy stocks at 15 percent below market value and optional stocks of up to 20 percent of salary after that (Airline Executive, 1990a, p.18). Furthermore, profit sharing-programs were considered important for the new-entrants in order to avoid labour trouble during 'good times'. Both PeoplExpress and America West offered their employees profit-sharing plans. At America West employees were given 15 percent of pre-tax profits and at PeoplExpress employees could earn as much as 30 percent of their base salaries under the profit sharing program. As the airlines fortunes disintegrated the problems with profit sharing and stock-participation programs appeared. One was the dilution motivation when stock prices decline, creating more problems from the programs than if they did not exist. The reason for the escalation of the associated problem was that the new-entrant airlines used these programs to justify low pay scales compared to the incumbents. Consequently, the stock-participation programs took on added value and importance to the employees. As soon as the stocks go down it is harder for the employee to accept the lower pay scale, so if the economic climate is right he or she will start to look for work elsewhere. PeoplExpress, for example, had problems retaining pilots after 1985 due to their ability to get positions with carriers paying higher wages, demanding no involvement in tasks unrelated to flying, such as People did.

Southwest, contrary to most new-entrants, has not kept costs down by paying low salaries, as its salary level is comparable with the industry average even though the company is unionised. This actually prevents the problems PeoplExpress had when things turned bitter, as losses will not affect employees' financial resources the way it did at PeoplExpress.

Union relations

The notion after deregulation was that cost-savings had to be accomplished by reducing labour costs below the industry average. The new-entrants, unlike the incumbents, were in a good position to attain much lower labour costs by hiring non-unionised labour at a much lower salary levels in exchange for profit sharing or stock participation, as already discussed. Low salaries and prolonged losses at America West, for example, started to cause disillusion among the staff leading enough customer representatives to sign union election cards in 1987 to call for a union voting.[54] In order to raise support for non-unionisation the management raised base pay by 16 percent, leading to a meagre 14 percent in favour of union representation (Feger, 1987, p.54).

Due to the lack of unionisation, strikes were almost unheard of at the new-entrant airlines. Moreover, strikes have not been frequent since deregulation if the years 1979 and 1980 are excluded. Those strikes that have occurred have been related to extraordinary situations at the incumbent airlines and usually benefited new-entrants by opening access to new-markets or increased demand on established routes.

A further factor resulting in fewer strikes is that the unions were under increased pressure after the demise of Eastern, having been accused of overplaying their role resulting in severe job-losses. At any rate the unions have been under much pressure by airlines in the deregulated environment due to the incumbent airlines' need to lower costs through wage concessions. As well as the new-entrant airlines' ability to maintain low wage scales and stay non-unionised. However, the co-operation between the management of the unionised airlines and unions, has lead to improved communication programs benefiting both parties (ATW, 1986b, p.25). Thus, the three facets of airline labour policy that led to less tendency for disputes, are: (i) increased union co-operation with management; (ii) increased communication with employees; and (iii) employee-friendly atmosphere, that works against union representation.

Organisation evolution

The evolution of early new-entrants organisations was characterised by fast growth and displacement as training and the necessary infrastructure such as information systems lacked the necessary sophistication. Internal communication that was characterised by informality of the entrepreneur organisation broke down as formal communication channels and organisation charts become ineffective and are often resisted by the early staff that 'miss' the informal close atmosphere of the 'early days.'

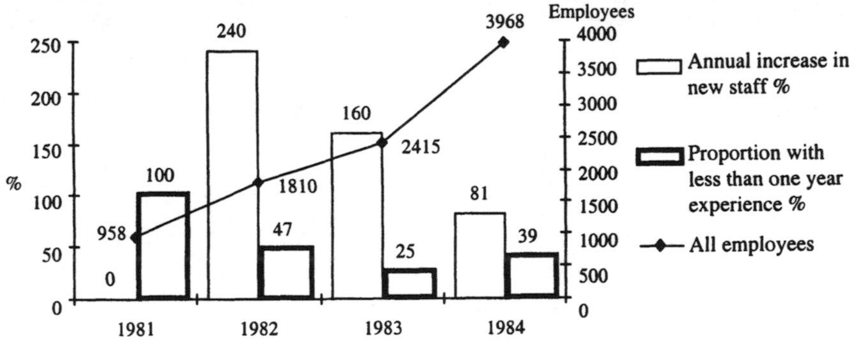

Figure 3.1 PeoplExpress employment growth rate and proportion with less than one year on the job experience

Source: Compiled from DoT Form 41.

The hiring gap (*see* Figure 3.1) is created due to the fast growing organisation's inability to absorb employees with adequate experience fast enough to actively solve impending problems associated with growth. The reality is that hiring enough people may not be the main problem, but rather making the newly hired employees productive fast enough to keep up with the organisation's need. The fact being that the faster the company grows the larger the proportion of newly hired employees not functioning properly.

There were two factors that hindered PeoplExpress in functioning properly in terms of employee training. First, the intense growth caused the company to reduce the requirements it set initially for new employees' personality to fit the organisation. Second, the religious emphasis on cross-utilisation increased the training requirements. This reduced the efficiency of the labour force rather than increased it as employees spent considerable time re-learning their functions as they shifted around, rather than concentrating on becoming specialists in one function. With a quarter to one-half of the labour force being new employees, each year, there was a great extra burden on the existing employees to integrate them into their tasks, as existing employees had their hands full. In fact, most were putting in more than 60 hours per week (HBS, 1990).

PeoplExpress is a typical example of an organisation that was very effective for a while but fell behind due to changes in the environment it could not adjust to with its available resources. As a result PeoplExpress attempted a 'discontinuous' change[55] in cost structure, product design and organisation structure, in order to shift itself to profitability. Such sudden shift is riskier for a company having been caught by new environmental developments such as People did, than if the organisation is adjusted incrementally. PeoplExpress could have developed a more sophisticated internal booking system making yield management possible. It could have entered the business passenger segment earlier. It could have developed another organically grown hub in the Midwest earlier and it could have grown slower in order to reduce the adverse effects of the Newark facilities on its service.

Marketing

Fare structure and yields

Yield is useful indicator of revenue trends within an airline but less so for comparison between airlines. The reason being that a low-yield carrier can have high load-factors and therefore be profitable, while the opposite can also apply. As a result it is important to examine yield in the context of other profitability factors such as load-factors and specifically profit margin. Furthermore, sector distances affect yield in such a way that yield declines usually with increased sector distances, reflecting the same trend in costs.

From Table 3.2 it is clearly apparent that regional based new-entrants have the highest yield per revenue passenger kilometre (.269) while charter based new-entrants have the lowest (.068). The former group operates commonly on short-haul routes linking with larger carriers. Such operations incur higher costs due to higher landing, terminal and fuel charges per each kilometre flown due to the short sector distances. As a result, it is not surprising to see high yield figures for regional based new-entrants, as the costs have to be matched. The reverse is true for charter based new-entrants as their sector distances have been relatively long compared to all other new-entrant carriers.

The high yield of premium service new-entrants (.196) is of course in direct relation to their high cost service in addition to relatively long sector lengths. The former intrastate carriers show their spectacularly low yield compared to stage lengths just such as the start-up new-entrants. This reflects the low cost of these carriers as can be seen in Table 3.9.

Table 3.2 Revenue of new-entrant airlines - US cents per RPK

Airline	1980	1981	1982	1983	1984	1985	1986	1987	1988	1989	1990	1991	1992	Mean
Regionals														***.269***
Air Wiscons.				.374	.352	.336	.280	.317	.274	.236				.310
Horizon Air						.322	.273	.260	.275	.279	.289	.275	.253	.278
Aspen						.236			.254	.213	.249			.238
Empire			.240	.258	.257	.242								.249
Premium														***.196***
MGM Grand								.306	.237	.268	.232	.186	.170	.233
Air Atlanta					.289	.186	.119							.198
Midwest Exp.						.175	.157	.236	.164	.152	.135	.122	.115	.157
Intrastate														***.111***
Air Califor.	.143	.144	.134	.136	.149	.136	.120							.137
Southwest	.107	.108	.095	.097	.093	.089	.084	.077	.079	.074	.076	.072	.089	.088
PSA	.140	.141	.122	.120	.130	.126	.122	.121						.128
Air Florida	.106	.099	.095	.071										.092
Start-up														***.101***
New York A.		.133	.152	.171	.155	.129	.114							.142
Sunworld					.108	.109	.102	.126						.111
Florida Exp.					.097	.104	.095	.091						.097
Midway	.300	.186	.156	.137	.188	.133	.102	.078	.090	.089	.080			.140
Presidential							.088	.099	.135	.132				.114
Muse Air		.139	.108	.093	.088	.087								.103
Jet America			.117	.083	.095	.100	.072							.093
America W.				.080	.081	.085	.079	.074	.077	.083	.074	.065		.078
Braniff (II)					.076	.070	.061	.056	.068	.067				.066
People Expr.		.088	.087	.062	.061	.064	.058							.070
Charters														***.068***
Arrow Airw.				.052	.059	.072	.067							.062
Tower					.062	.052	.056	.054	.046	.041	.045	.048	.054	.051
Capitol Air	.102	.060	.057	.062	.039									.064
World	.073	.060	.055	.056	.051	.047	.042							.055
Tower					.118	.129		.116			.088	.082	.106	.106
Mean	.139	.116	.118	.124	.127	.138	.110	.144	.155	.148	.141	.121	.131	.068

* The carrier was delinquent in filing with the DoT, the data may be inaccurate as a result. All values are 1992 dollars.

Source: Compiled from DoT Form 41.

In Table 3.2 one can observe that Southwest Airlines is decreasing its yield over the years but at the same time its cost per available seat kilometre stays relatively fixed. This reflects that Southwest's unique low cost advantage is decreasing in terms of cost margins.

Supply/capacity

The capacity offered by the new-entrant is one part of the equation leading to success or failure. If the capacity is too much compared to demand the carrier has two alternatives either to cut extra capacity down or reduce fares in order to stimulate demand. Southwest shows a reduction in yield and load-factor fluctuations indicating increased stability, as Figure 3.2 shows.

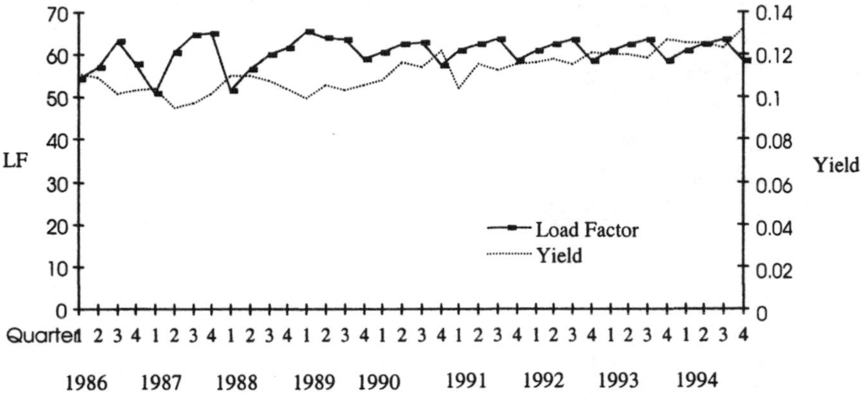

Figure 3.2 Yield and load-factor at Southwest Airlines: quarterly data 1986 - 1994

Source: Compiled from Thomson Financial Networks - CD, 1993.

If the new-entrant has homogenous segment strategy such as PeoplExpress had from 1981 until 1985, emphasising the low-fare market only, rather than mixing both business leisure passengers, there are going to be weekday and seasonal fluctuations in demand.

Figure 3.3 shows seasonal fluctuations at PeoplExpress became larger as the company grew larger. The main fluctuations follow the main summer holiday months of July and August. If the revenue passenger miles (RPM) for September each year are examined one can spot a trend where the reduction in RPM is increasing from 1983 until a large drop occurs in 1986. Conversely, an increase in demand occurs in March and December every year, becoming increasingly larger every year.

In Table 3.3 new-entrant's ASK and its yearly growth is tabulated. The average growth for all new-entrants listed in the table is quite high or 39.6 percent from 1980 - 1991. The airlines showing average growth over 100 percent are Muse Air and PeoplExpress, but both had high growth in the year following initiation, the reason being that they started operations around mid year; Muse initiated operations in June 1981 and PeoplExpress in April 1981. As a result the growth numbers become inflated for the following year. If the average excludes the first year the growth becomes 49.3 percent for Muse and 76.3 for PeoplExpress. It is nevertheless apparent that the growth of Muse in the first one and a half years was quite high but one has to take into account that the initial capacity it offered was low compared to PeoplExpress and New York Air.

Carriers growing in the 80 to 100 percent band were Air Atlanta and America West.[56] However, Air Atlanta started operations in February 1, 1984 so the first year counted eleven months, while America West started operations on August 1, 1983. The level of growth at America West during the first two years was projected by dividing the capacity of the first five months of the first year of operations by five and then multiplying by 12 giving the projected full year capacity. Upon using this simple method the total projected capacity for the first year becomes 1869.4 and the growth rate for the second year becomes 204.4 percent. Hence it is apparent that the growth was high even though operations began in August 1983.

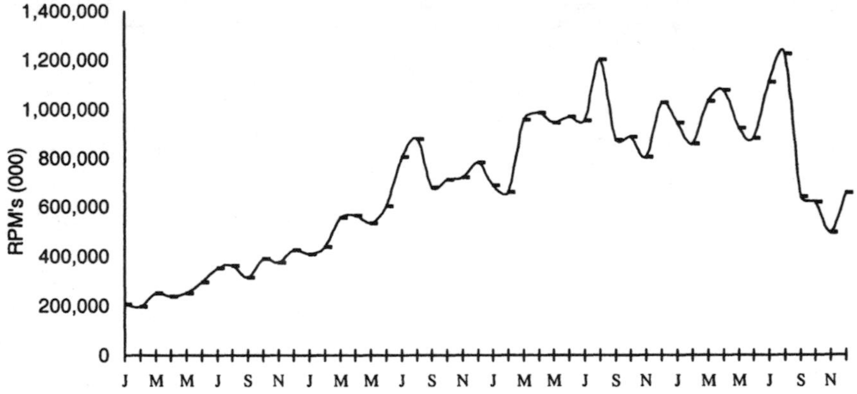

Figure 3.3 PeoplExpress RPM by month from 1983 - 1986

Source: Compiled from DoT, Form 41.

Airlines growing in the 40 to 80 percent band were Empire with 70.1 percent, Florida Express with 58 percent, World with 50.2 percent, Midway with 46.6 percent and New York Air with 41.6 percent. Although most of the airlines in the table have failed, except Midwest Express, Southwest and Tower, it is impossible to generalise on whether high growth as such is the main contributing factor to the new-entrant's demise. It is, however, apparent that many of the carriers increased capacity intensively just before their demise: Empire by 189.9 percent in the last three years of operations, Air California increased capacity by 144.7 percent in its last two years of operations, Midway by 35.1 percent, Muse Air by 70.4, PSA by 53.5, PeoplExpress by 63.3 percent, Sunworld by 52.2 percent (cut down capacity by 22.1 percent in the year of its demise), and World by 50 percent in years four and three before closure (cut down capacity by 28.4 percent the following two years). It is quite common that following high growth period there is sudden drop or cutback of capacity. This shows a marked contrast with Southwest that grows at a rather constant rate. The reason for new-entrant's tendency to grow fast may be an urge to achieve critical mass in order to be more competitive in the market and the tendency to look at fast growth as synonymous with success.

Table 3.3 Yearly growth of new-entrants' ASK

ASK Growth %	1980	1981	1982	1983	1984	1985	1986	1987	1988	1989	1990	1991	Mean growth
Light-speed													
Muse Air			508.3	7.5	53.5	16.9							164,1
People Expr.			239.8	159.6	80.5	63.3	1.7						109,0
Hyper													
America W.					390.5	-1.7	127.0	94.8	16.2	12.8	34.1	11.9	85,7
Air Atlanta						123.0	47.9						85,5
Empire		149.1	11.5	105.3	71.0	13.6							70,1
Florida Exp.						98.9	59.2	16.0					58,0
World		279.8	-0.7	0.4	50.0	-1.0	-27.4						50,2
Very rapid													
Midway		109.8	51.0	5.9	-24.8	127.1	94.8	32.9	19.4	15.0	35.1		46,6
New York			51.0	-4.8	33.4	76.8	51.7						41,6
Midwest Exp							34.3	4.9	69.8	77.2	43.6	9.4	39,9
Republic	132.3	69.4	10.3	7.3	4.2	7.4	14.9						35,1
Capitol Air		116.9	60.6	-37.9	-2.5								34,3
Arrow Airw.					117.0	-27.0	5.1						31,7
Air California		43.7	10.6	-58.1	33.4	76.8	67.9						29,1
Aspen						67.6	4.7	19.8	9.9				25,5
Jet America					59.9	13.6	3.0						25,5
Rapid													
Sunworld						45.0	52.2	-22.1					25,0
Tower						6.4	-5.5	65.5	41.5	3.3	-5.9	39.2	20,6
Air Wiscons.					42.7	28.3	29.1	9.1	15.3	10.9	10.0	16.9	20,3
Southwest		36.0	21.5	28.9	26.2	9.2	15.1	14.2	16.7	10.6	11.3	22.1	19,3
Air Florida		77.1	-5.8	-19.3									17,3
Normal													
Horizon Air							14.3	6.8	17.5	-22.2	61.9	9.2	14,6
Braniff (II)						-19.6	52.4	8.4	26.0	-6.9			12,1
PSA		7.0	18.6	16.2	2.6	-10.2	49.5	4.0					12,5
Negative													
Mid Pacific						0.3	0.7	-12.2					-11,2
Presidential								-43.2	-21.5				-32,4

Source: Compiled from DOT Form 41. Note that empty cells in the table are for years during which the carrier was not operating, or due to non-availability of data.

Demand

The airline's passenger load-factor is the most widely used indicator of airline performance. However, the load-factor has its limitation as there is no use in maintaining a high load-factor if the demand is stimulated by too low fares or aircraft utilisation.

Table 3.4 New-entrant airlines' load factors

Airline	1980	1981	1982	1983	1984	1985	1986	1987	1988	1989	1990	1991	1992	Avg.
Charter														
Tower				86.5	82.9	88.9	81.7	89.3	85.5	88.7	85.7	78.4	76.0	84.4
Capitol Air	77.4	80.4	77.9	77.0	72.5									77.0
American Tr.							60.6	73.5	67.0	88.9	74.1	78.2	70.4	73.2
Arrow Airw.				67.7	71.2	74.2	67.8							70.2
World	62.2	77.3	66.5	64.8	65.3	70.8	66.4							67.6
Carnival											65.4	69.1	63.2	65.9
Start-up														
Pacific East				72.3	79.7									76.0
Florida Exp.					68.0	69.4	66.7	63.9	63.1	55.9				64.5
Braniff (II)						68.0	57.7	65.5	64.7	62.8				63.7
People Expr.		58.3	61.2	74.6	69.8	61.1	57.2							63.7
Jet America			64.6	71.3	59.3	66.4	60.2	56.3						63.0
Air Florida	59.0	64.3	59.5	62.4	66.2									62.3
Braniff (II)I												56.4	66.4	61.4
MGM Grand								69.2	63.1	73.7	56.2	53.7	50.2	61.0
America W.				51.7	52.5	62.4	61.0	56.1	57.9	57.7	61.0	63.6	61.4	58.5
Pacific Expr.				57.1										57.1
Sunworld				52.6	51.9	59.3	51.7	56.5	69.1					56.9
New York A.	51.0	62.7	54.9	57.3	56.0	56.4	54.1							56.1
Republic	50.2			54.4	50.1	58.8	60.1							55.9
Mid Pacific							58.1	53.5						55.8
Midway	49.2	59.7	55.4	48.4	50.9	58.1	59.0	57.4	56.0	56.8	58.5	58.8		55.7
Midwest Exp					23.7	38.8	55.7	65.1	65.4	60.0	56.2	54.7	55.7	52.8
Kiwi													52.6	52.6
Air One				47.4	50.8									49.1
Golden West		46.9	51.3											49.1
Cascade		48.5	47.7											48.1
Presidential							46.1	47.3	46.0	49.4				47.2
Muse Air		35.8	41.8	50.9	47.1	47.0								44.5
Regional														
Aspen	55.9	49.9	55.3	na	na	49.8	48.9	46.6	49.5	53.2	55.0	61.8		52.6
Horizon Air						50.4	51.4	50.4	49.9	52.3	49.6	51.5	53.6	51.1
Air Wiscons.	55.8	51.8	46.3	42.7	40.5	51.6	48.8	46.9	na	na	45.5	45.2		47.5
Imperial		44.2	50.8											47.5
Empire	51.2	56.1	47.8	47.3	43.4	40.7	40.6							46.7
Markair						42.4	44.5	47.2	49.6	50.0	47.5	38.6	38.4	44.8
Air Midwest				40.9	41.9									41.4
Intrastate														
Southwest	68.2	63.6	61.6	61.6	58.5	61.2	58.3	58.9	57.7	62.7	60.6	61.1	64.5	61.4
Air California	67.8	58.2	51.4	58.2	55.1	56.6	53.2	54.5						56.9
PSA	55.4	53.0	54.9	55.2	53.4	56.5	56.0	55.7	51.4					54.6

Source: Compiled from DoT Form 41.

Table 3.4 shows that the two new-entrants with highest load factors are both charter-originated operating primarily on long-distance routes. Tower Air has done rather well through the years due to its very narrow niche, flying between the US and Israel. Capitol, on the other hand, had extensive problems during its period of scheduled operations, which indicates that the high load factor was not enough to fend off losses. American Trans Air, Arrow Airways, World and Carnival are also charter based, all having fairly high average load.

To further the point of non-relationship of load-factors with financial wellbeing of airlines, one can examine Braniff (II), having high load-factors in spite of all its financial problems and undulating strategy. The reason was the competition at its Dallas-Forth Worth hub, where two stronger competitors retaliated fiercely against this largest airline start-up in history, leading to a scaling down soon after operations started both in terms of applied aircraft and cities served. In fact, the cities served were cut down by half six months after start-up (Avmark, 1987a, p.19). In this way the airline maintained its load-factor although it had cost drastic fare cuts in the face of the high unit costs of its full service strategy.

There are two main reasons for low load-factors, one is over-capacity on routes either due to too high frequency or high fares. Thus, it is not uncommon for carriers offering premium service geared towards business travellers to have lower load factors than low-fare or mixed carriers. Air Atlanta, Muse Air and Air One fit this profile well. Air Atlanta, for example, was well capitalised but could not sustain the low load-factors it had in the beginning. Although, the load-factors improved, the airline was not able to sustain operations, the main problem being the drop in traffic during the weekend unlike PeoplExpress that had problems during mid-week.

Regional based new-entrants show medium to low load-factors, because of operating a mixed fleet of prop and jet equipment on very short-haul routes. Such operations are usually linked with an incumbent's operation making it less able to compete for load as departures are under the influence of the incumbent. On the plus side is that regional based new-entrants' loads are usually composed heavily of business passengers, leading to higher yields.

Some new-entrants experienced sudden reduction in load factors immediately preceding failure. The explanation is the tendency of travel agents to 'sell away' due to 'rumours' of imminent failure. Another explanation has to do with increased competition intensity from the rivals as soon as the word of financial problems spreads around.

Finance

Access to capital

Initial capitalisation is important for the future performance of any new venture. Airlines are especially capital intensive compared to other new-ventures, not only in terms of aircraft acquisition, but also in terms of financing of fast growth. Start-up financing can be divided into several sources: (i) term loans; (ii) private placements; (iii) public financing (bonds and stock); and (iv) revolving credit. Table 3.5 shows few examples of new-entrants start-up financing. However, note that FAA loan guarantees were higher than total initial capitalisation for PeoplExpress and Midway. Furthermore, on can see that high capitalisation is no guarantee of success as Braniff (II) and Muse Air both folded despite being well capitalised initially.

Term loans are usually for more than one year but less than 15 years and amortised regularly during the term. Private placements, on the other hand, are direct business loans just such as term loans but with maturity of more than 15 years. Such loans are usually secured on assets, stocks, bonds or equipment. The advantages of term loans and private placements are the avoidance of costly Security and Exchange Commission filings, flexibility of changing the loan indenture as there is only one lender and less time to arrange the loan than it is for bonds or public financing. The disadvantages are high drain on cash as the loan is amortised regularly and places commitment on the borrower due to the long-term relationship with the lender (the lender may want to be represented on the board of directors). The private placement market declined substantially in the early nineties due to less participation of life-insurance companies and the increase in the availability of public financing to lower quality issuers.

Public financing is usually in two basic forms, bonds and stock. These are usually called fixed income securities. Public financing requires the service of investment bankers. With a bond offering, the investment banker carries some risk as 'underwriter' that is the function of issuing bonds for distribution, during which the distributor bears the risk of fluctuation in bond prices. When the investment banker decides to become an underwriter for a bond issue, he will pay the company the face value of the bonds less the commission and then distribute the bonds to buyers, a function that can take a considerable time in some instances. This risk bearing of the investment banker leads to a necessity of good relationship between the company and the banker often requiring a considerable investigation into the company's affairs before the banker will accept being an underwriter. In the case of start-up companies the founders will have to sell the idea and prove to the bankers that it is worthwhile in terms of return on investment before they will consider it.

Table 3.5 Start-up financing obtained by new-entrants

Airline	Capitalisation	Type of capitalisation	FAA loan guarantees
Southwest	$ 8 m (Pre-dereg.)	Stock $7m [a]; debt $1.2 m [b]	
People Expr. '80	$ 25 m	Stock $24 m [c];private contr. $1 m [d]	$58.0m
America West	$33 m	Equity	
Braniff (II)	$71 m	Loan $38 m; equity $ 20 (Hyatt); cash $13 m [e]	
Midway	$13.7 m	Equity 11.7 m; bank credit 2 m	$24.1m
Jet America '81	$23.4	Equity 12m ('81); principals equity 1.2m; convertible subordinated debentures 10 m ('82)	
New York Air	$33.2 m		
Muse Air	$110 m		
Pacific Expr.	$30 m		
Reno Air	$8.0m	Private investors $2m; stock and stock warrants $6.0m (IPO).	
ValuJet (Former charter)	$17.4m	$3.4 from founders; $14m private placement(IPO).	
Kiwi Intern.	$14.2m	Employees, mostly pilots $10m; Rombac $1m. Credit line $1.7m; $1.5m loan guarantee.	

[a] Common stock, $1 par value, 2.000.000 shares authorised, 1,1058,758 issued at December 31, 1971 at $1 par value. Capital in excess of par value $6,012,105. [b] 7% convertible promissory notes. [c] 3 million shares at $8.5 per share (No airline had raised start-up money with stock-offering before). [d] Burr put up $355,000; Gitner $175,000 and other managing officers $20,000 to $50,000 each. FNC Capital Corp., a subsidiary of Citicorp put up $200,000. [e] From Braniff (I), bankruptcy estate. Dalfort Corporation an affiliate to Hyatt Corporation was the original stockholder of Braniff holding 93 percent of the voting power.

Source: Compiled from Air Transport World (1980-1995) and PeoplExpress 1984 Prospectus.

Many start-up airlines never get past this hurdle and can not gain enough capital to start. If a company can secure the consent of an investment banker to become an underwriter it is called a flotation. Both preferred, common stock and bonds fall under this term. Flotation can be costly for the company, proportionally more expensive as the flotation is smaller. Bond flotation is considered to be less costly than stock flotation and common stock flotation to be more expensive than preferred stock offering. The cost as a percentage of the total flotation can range from as low as 0.10 percent for large offering of 100 to 500 million dollars up to 10 percent for offering of less than 500 thousand dollars.

Common stock carries voting rights at annual meetings and entitlement to a share of the company's net profit in the form of dividends. The company can, however, withhold profits if it is felt to be in its best interest to reinvest to secure future profitability or to avoid bankruptcy. The advantages of common stock is that the company doesn't necessarily have to pay dividends, it does not have any maturity but is bought and sold, after issuance, on the market.

Stock issuance is sometimes more receptive on financial markets than debt issuance due to its higher expected gains than bonds or preferred stock and because of capital gains being taxed at a lower personal income tax brackets than interest on debt. The disadvantages are the possibility that the founder looses control as voting right is extended to new stockholders. That is one of the main reasons why many companies avoid the issuance of common stock. The cost of underwriting and distributing is considerably higher than for other issuances and the dividends are not deductible as an expense for the company as interest payments on bonds are. Preferred stock has claims and rights ahead of common stock but behind bonds. Preferred stock does usually not carry voting rights. They usually carry a preferred dividend, meaning that the company will service preferred stock ahead of common stock in terms of dividend payments, but the company does not have to pay dividends to preferred stockholders if the operating environment does not allow such a payment.

Revolving credit is a financial package that can be drawn for any purpose but is often used to resolve short-term capital needs until other financing has been arranged. America West just as PeoplExpress gained the use of a revolving credit facility. In April 1990 America West secured a $50 million revolving credit arranged by five banks that played a role in the carrier's secured financing. The money was used immediately to finance the airline's expansion applying $40 million to finance the acquisition of a Boeing 747 (Airline Executive, 1990a, p.20).

There were five airlines that entered a positive market for equity financing at the dawn of deregulation. These were Midway,[57] New York Air, PeoplExpress, Muse and Jet America. Subsequent new-entrants had a harder time finding start-up capital because of the poor track record of the early new-entrant airlines (Meyer *et. al.*, 1984, p.119). According to Ronald Schmid (1992) new-entrants will not have much probability of success unless they are well capitalised and have access to lease finance packages. In his view, the reluctance of banks and leasing companies to finance aircraft for new-airlines can seriously inhibit the access of new-entrants and undermine the regulatory efforts to enhance competition.

New-entrant airlines are rated lower by aircraft financing companies than incumbent carriers. Thus, new-entrants are at a disadvantage from the beginning. In view of how large a portion the aircraft acquisition is in the total cost structure of an airline this must be viewed as a major handicap for a new-entrant. One important aspect of the early deregulation in the United States, favourable to the new-entrants, was an option in the law to lower the financial barriers of entry for a period of time. This option was the Deregulation Act's revival and expansion of the FAA's Aircraft Loan Guarantee Program.[58] Under this scheme the FAA could guarantee a loan up to $100 million for a period of up to 15 years, given that the carrier could not obtain uninsured financing on reasonable terms elsewhere (Meyer *et al.*, p.112).

The Loan Guarantee Program insured the lender against default, thus, allowing the carriers to achieve substantially lower rates on capital than was prevailing at the time, given the risk involved. According to Meyer *et al.*(1984, p.113) there were 149 aircraft bought under the scheme, by 20 carriers during an initial three year period from the beginning of deregulation. New-entrants received 85 per cent of the total figure guaranteed and thereof New York Air, PeoplExpress, Midway Airlines and Muse Air, 23 per cent. The benefit of the Loan Guarantee Program for the new-entrants, was (Meyer *et al.*, p.112)

> ...loan guarantees reduced the debt service drain on cash flow by lowering interest rates, extending the loan terms available, and, most important, making financing possible where it had previously not been available.

The Loan Guarantee Program was criticised by the existing carriers as unfair. As a result, important changes were made to the program; first, an imposed $100 million ceiling in 1982; second, a limit to the size of aircraft purchased under the scheme (aircraft of less than 60 seat and 18.000 pound tow). This wiped out the availability of this program to new jet-operating airlines as most were considering aircraft larger than 60 seat.

To conclude one can say that access to capital is the single largest obstacle to starting-up an airline. The early new-entrants can not be said to have suffered from under capitalisation but the new-comers had less funding, leading to increased dependence on debt capital.

Aircraft acquisition

Aircraft acquisition is the single largest cost item in running an airline and the largest in terms of capital intensity. Most new-entrants have had to decide whether to own or lease. Leasing is the most common way to acquire aircraft for new-entrants due to its greater flexibility and lower start-up capital requirements.[59] Furthermore, leasing was treated as cost rather than debt, therefore, not affecting the carrier debt structure. As a result, there was greater flexibility to acquire capital and add debt.[60]

Examining Table 3.6 one can see that most new-entrants started by leasing aircraft rather than buying. PeoplExpress, however, started out by buying large number of aircraft in one lot or 22 in all. No other new-entrant has had such a bold initial equipment acquisition, until Braniff (II) leased 30 idle ex-Braniff (I) 727's. It must be noted, however, that PeoplExpress bought its aircraft and had much lower initial capitalisation than Braniff (II).

Table 3.6 New-entrants' aircraft acquisition

Airline	Type of initial aircraft and financing	Financing
Air Atlanta	Bought five 727-100s and arranged for sale/leaseback with General Electric Credit Co.	Leased
Air California	In 1984 signed up for 12 737-300s to be delivered in 1985, leased from International Lease Finance.	Leased
Air Florida	Various schemes due to aircraft trading. Utilised the Loan Guarantee Program to finance a $85m transaction, financed five 727-200, under 'cross-border tax leasing' (double dip) were lenders in the US and UK get tax breaks which they share with the airline in lower lease rates.	Leased and bought
Air 1	Seven 727-100s bought from Pan Am and Piedmont for $2.5m each.	
America W.	18 used 737-200s on lease, lease-purchase or purchased. Leased 737-200s from International Lease Finance. (two purchased for $5m and some from GPA) Three aircraft delivered in 84 purchased for $39.1m) In 1989 AW owned only 17 of its 86 airplanes the rest was leased.	Leased and bought
Braniff (II)	30 Boeing 727-200s in 1984 leased from Braniff's (I) Bankruptcy Trust (initially at $2.7 million per month).	Leased
Empire Airl.	Two bought directly from Fokker in 1980, Four F-28's bought through bidding, two purchased from Altair Jets. Aircraft were financed through public offering.	Bought
Florida Exp.	20 F28-200s, 400s(6) one half is leased from IMM under long-term non-cancelable leases and the other half is was purchased by the carrier.	Leased and bought
Horizon Air	Two F-28s bought	Bought
Jet America	Leased two MD-80s from McDonnell Douglas Finance Corp. and GATX.	Leased
MGM Grand A.	Three Regent Air's 727's bought in 1987 for $16.5m and three Air Italia's DC-8-62s for $16m.	Bought
Midway Airl.	Three leased DC-9-10s from McDonnell Douglas. In 1989 the carrier sold and leased back 16 DC-9-30 to cover the acquisition of Eastern' assets in Philadelphia of which the 16 aircraft belonged.	Leased
Midwest Exp.	Two DC-9s bought for $2.7m and $3.3m and a DC-9-14 bought in 1983 for $3.5m. K-C Aviation a subsidiary of Kimberly Clark bought the aircraft for Midwest Express that is also a subsidiary of K-C.	Bought
PSA	Bought 30 MD-80, 20 BAe 146s, 4 DC-9-30s from 1978 to 1986. With the 146s starting service in 1984.	Bought
PeoplExpr.	Bought 22 737-100s for $90m in 1981. Bought 4 737-200s in 1982. Bought 20 727-200 for $4.2m each and leased 1 747 from bankrupt Braniff, bought 10 used 727s from McDonnell Douglas at $4.2m each and 15 727-200 adv. from Delta for $91m. The latter two purchases were not delivered all at once but spread to 1984. In 1984 the carrier leased two more 747-200 and 100.	Bought and leased(only 747s)
Southwest	Bought initially four 737s for $16.2m(1971). In January 1982 it operated 25 owned 737-200 adv., by 1986 it owned 17 B737-300s and 46 B737-200s. In 1991 it leased three ex-AirCal 737s and bought 11 new 737s bringing the fleet to 120 737s. Southwest unlike other carriers tends to add used aircraft to the fleet during recessions due to better prices, a strategy enabled by strong financial status.	Bought (few leased)

Sources: Compiled from Air Transport World 1982 - 1991, Airfinance (1993), Lloyd's Aviation Economist (1984).

Large initial fleet seems to have caused Braniff (II) much trouble, while PeoplExpress seemed to be able to absorb the capacity of its 22 Boeing 727 aircraft very quickly. One explanation is that Braniff (II) started operating in a different environment, than PeoplExpress in 1981.

In a growth market airlines tend to expand by acquiring aircraft at premium lease rates. However, the leasing companies pursue to minimise their risk and new-entrants are dependent on favourable lease terms in order to be cost competitive, making the availability of suitable leasing agreements fairly limited. When the market situation is reversed as occurred in the early 1990's, lessors are faced with rentals that may not cover the loan payments and even a fleet of idle aircraft. In such a situation the leasing company will offer terms that cover some of the loan payments rather than maintaining idle aircraft in the lease portfolio and face financial ruin or bankruptcy as a result. In this market situation the conditions for starting an airline become favourable from this perspective.

Many new-entrants have tried to minimise the effect of aircraft acquisition on cash flow and the debt structure by acquiring older aircraft during stagnation or declining values, usually during economic recession, leading to entry during periods of economic recession, when market rivalry is more intense. Nevertheless, most of the new-entrants have enjoyed high growth rates (*see* Table 3.3). This has placed intense pressure on financial resources making leasing the most viable option to acquire aircraft at a faster pace without harming the balance sheet. Such an alternative does, however, place extra burden on the airline's cash flow.

Profitability

Airlines are highly sensitive to customer and travel agents' trust, as the customer usually buys a ticket in advance in good faith of it being honoured on the day of travelling. The ticket is, therefore, as such a short-term investment to the customer. In the meantime, from when the ticket is bought until it is used, the passenger wants to be assured that the airline will still be around when he or she undertakes the trip. As a result, any rumours of bankruptcy will reduce the number of potential travellers willing to use an airline subject to such adversities. What is worse, the travel agents will avoid booking the airline. If they use it they might mark another airline as the designated airline meaning that the revenue will go to that airline first and then to the troubled carrier, delaying the troubled carrier's use of the cash for some weeks. This will increase the passenger's ability to recover the fare in case of a failure. Thus, a rumour of imminent failure of a carrier will result in sudden drop in cash flow and in conjunction to other factors this drop in demand can result in a quicker demise of the carrier. Airlines that have been affected in this respect are America West that showed dramatic drop in profitability in 1991 with operating losses mounting to 104.7 million.

Table 3.7 New-entrants' operating- and net profit 1979 - 1992

Op. profit Net profit	1980	1981	1982	1983	1984	1985	1986	1987	1988	1989	1990	1991	1992	Cumu lative
Regional														
Air Wiscons.				8.1	10.1	5.7	6.2	14.1	22.7	1.6	0.7	-26.8		42.4
				4.0	4.4	1.9	3.1	6.1	17.8	0.4	1.3	-37.3		1.7
Horizon Air						-3.3	-0.9	2.9	2.8	-2.5	0.6	8.0	7.3	14.9
						-9.1	-3.7	-5.1	2.6	1.9	1.1	3.6	3.3	-5.4
Empire		1.0	-0.7	4.6	6.1	-1.5								9.5
		0.5	0.5	20.1	2.3	-4.2								19.2
Aspen						1.4	-0.7	-1.1	-0.6	-5.4	-2.0			-8.4
						0.4	-0.2	-1.3	-0.1	-5.5	1.4			-5.3
Intrastate														
Southwest	48.8	48.5	39.2	68.6	68.6	70.3	81.3	41.3	86.1	97.6	81.6	62.0	182	913.9
PSA	2.6	-16.0	-17.4	-10.0	31.0	31.9	23.0	20.6						65.7
	4.2	22.7	18.6	-12.6	-4.8	-0.6	-3.1	-24.7						-0.3
Air California	12.2	0.3	-20.7	17.3	24.5	12.8	3.7							50.1
	9.9	4.4	-24.0	3.4	11.2	9.3	-1.6							12.6
Air Florida	9.5	-12.1	-33.5	-5.8										-41.9
Start-up														
Mid Pacific		-0.9	2.4	2.4										3.9
		-1.1	0.5	2.7										2.1
Midwest Exp						-3.5	-1.6	5.3	5.7	7.5	5.1	0.6	4.1	23.2
						-1.8	-0.3	3.2	3.8	4.8	3.0	0.1	2.0	14.8
Muse Air		-5.5	-4.7	4.6	-3.3	8.3								-0.6
		-4.0	11.5	-2.0	-17.0	-8.7								-20.2
MGM Grand								0	-0.5	na	-4.1	-3.5	0.1	-8.0
								-2.4	-5.4	-2.6	-15.0	-8.9	-14.7	-49.0
Jet America				-8.3	-1.4	3.0	2.0	-1.6						-6.3
				-8.8	-3.1	-3.7	-8.5	-15.8						-39.9
Florida Exp.					-1.6	5.2	3.8	-13.8						-6.4
					-3.1	4.1	1.9	-12.1						-9.2
Sunworld					-0.6	2.5	-4.6	-18.6						-21.3
					-5.3	2.5	-5.3	-15.2						-23.3
New York A.		-9.5	-12.4	8.6	-0.6	7.2	-11.1							-17.8
		-11.6	-23.3	4.5	-6.8	-2.4	36.1							-3.5
People Expr.		-7.2	10.5	19.6	20.2	33.4	-124							-47.1
		-9.2	1.0	10.4	1.7	-20.1	-199							-215
Air Atlanta					-19.7	-14.2	-14.4							-48.1
					-23.1	-45.5	-19.4							-88.0
Midway	-4.5	8.8	4.5	-12.3	-12.9	0.9	11.1	25.0	13.5	-13.5	-84.5			-63.9
	-4.9	7.6	0.3	-15.0	-22.0	-3.6	9.0	13.0	6.5	-21.7	-139			-17.0
Presidential							-26.0	-32.2	-13.1	-10.2				-81.5
							-24.0	-28.5	-15.2	-15.6				-83.3
America W.				-6.5	-8.6	18.7	4.0	-35.4	18.1	48.1	-31.6	-105		-98
				-6.3	-15.4	11.4	3.0	-45.7	9.4	20.0	-74.7	-222		-320
Braniff (II)					-91.1	18.6	-12.3	-17.8	-13.1	-57.6				-173
					-75.4	15.2	-9.0	-10.4	-19.8	-147				-246
Charter														
Tower					-1.0	2.0	3.2	9.0	10.8	10.2	11.7	19.0	9.1	74.0
Capitol Air	-3.4	4.5	-13.0	-10.7	-0.6									-23.2
	-5.4	20.5	-21.2	-11.2	-1.6									-18.9
Arrow Airw.					-15.1	-0.1	-3.8							-19.0
					-13.6	0.2	-3.8							-17.2
World	-28.8	9.6	-30.5	-1.3	-13.3	-2.0	-66.4							-133
	-28.2	-20.2	-58.4	-29.4	-18.0	-14.9	-28.0							-197

Source: Compiled from DoT Form 41.

Other examples of a sudden drop in profitability in the last year of operations are Braniff that had escalating losses from 13.1 million in 1988 to 57.6 million in 1989, Midway that had escalation in losses from 13.5 in 1989 to 84.5 in 1990, and PeoplExpress that experienced an operating profit of 33.4 million 1985, but 123.6 million loss in 1986. Although the proportion of these losses attributed to sell away or customer avaidance can not be clearly established it is certain that it is a contributing factor.

Table 3.7 shows that new-entrants have not been profitable in the long-term, with few exceptions such as Southwest and Midwest Express. It is only recently that new airlines and incumbents alike have started to pay attention to Southwest's profitable strategy, the only sustainable long-term new-entrant strategy. Perhaps the slow growth feature of that strategy is what counts more than anything else in securing profitability.

Cost structure

The new-entrants had cost advantage over incumbent carriers operating under the regulation regime where profits were almost guaranteed by the fare control mechanism of the CAB. Therefore, the start-up new-entrants could exploit their cost advantage and the intrastate new-entrants could utilise their experience of operating in a pre-deregulation competitive environment.

The start-ups could operate without unionised staff with lower wage scales and more flexible job descriptions. Table 3.8 shows clearly that new airlines benefit from lower wage scales. In 1985 the average yearly salary per employee of the new-entrant carriers, was 23 thousand dollars, while the incumbents average was 40 thousand dollars. This difference is very large in view of the labour intensity of airlines. Looking at the table closer it becomes apparent that there is considerable difference between the various sub-groups of new-entrants, as intrastate originating new-entrants have similar wage scales as the incumbent carriers, while start-up and charter based new-entrants paid about 50 percent less in wages per employee.

Although low labour cost is extremely important for airlines, non-unionised operation may not be the only way to achieve low cost structure. Southwest airlines, for example, is fully unionised and pays competitive salaries as the table shows, achieved through high aircraft utilisation that cuts down the size of the fleet and utilises staff better. Comparing new-entrants' costs in general terms (*see* Table 3.9) the intrastate carriers were at a cost disadvantage (.072) compared to the start-up carriers (.062) although Southwest Airlines was the exception. The higher costs indicate two things. First, that the Californian intrastate carriers and Air Florida had not had as much incentive to keep costs down as Southwest had under regulation, and secondly that they attempted to imitate the incumbents as they gained interstate route rights instead of developing a defensible niche in the market.

The average costs show some decline from 1980 until 1983, but then increase until 1985. In 1986 fuel costs declined dramatically and costs per available seat kilometre drop as a consequence. In this year, however, many carriers failed or were absorbed by larger incumbents leading to higher debt structure and route inefficiency, that caused an increase in costs again. The general conclusion that can be read from the table is that many new-entrants actually reduced their costs over the years, rather than the other way around.

Table 3.8 Comparison of average pay per employee in 1985

Incumbent airline	Average pay per employee	New-entrant airline	Average pay per employee
	1985		1985
Incumbents		*Regionals*	*Avg. 37,498*
Delta	46,862	Air Wisconsin	31,825[a]
TWA	46,106	*Intrastate*	-
USAir	44,949	PSA	43,968[b]
United	42,792[a]	Southwest	36,615
American	42,777	Air California	31,910
Northwest	42,617	*Start-up*	*Avg. 18,837*
Eastern	41,888	Braniff (II)	26,663
Pan Am	38,885[a]	Midwest Express	22,195
Western	36,316	America West	21,619
Piedmont	34,341[a]	New York Air	19,908
Continental	23,205	Muse Air	18,762
Incumbents' average	*40,067*	Midway	17,015[b]
		PeoplExpress	16,918[a]
		Presidential Airw.	16,184[b]
		Sunworld	10,270
		Charter	*Avg. 18,268*
		Tower Air	21,022
		World Airways	15,514
		NE average	*23,359*

Source: Compiled from DoT Form 41. Incumbent data based on Button (1989b). [a] 1984 data. [b] 1986 data.

Debt structure

Corporations have two basic ways to raise capital, through equity or debt. These two methods differ greatly in terms of the effect on financial performance.

Chow *et al.* (1988) reported that poorly performing airlines in terms of earnings per share (EPS) tended to issue fixed-cost instruments, long-term debt and preferred stock.[61] This financial structure led to less ability of such carriers to adapt to variability in earnings before interest and taxes (EBIT). It is suggested that one of the reasons for utilising such financing schemes was to utilise interest deductions to shield profits.

They argue further that the issuance of equity may indicate to the market that future earnings may not cover increased debt interest. Thus, airlines have to adjust to their environment in ways that may limit their future options or increase leverage causing less flexibility in an adverse environment.

Table 3.9 New-entrants' costs in U.S. Cents per ASK

Airline	1980	1981	1982	1983	1984	1985	1986	1987	1988	1989	1990	1991	Mean
Regionals													
Empire		.133	.118	.107	.105	.106							.114
Aspen						.120	.127	.133	.138	.129	.165		.135
Air Wiscons.				.157	.138	.186	.141	.144	.142	.133	.128	.128	.144
Horizon Air						.129	.128	.165	.142		.146	.142	.142
Premium													***.134***
Air Atlanta					.108	.111	.122						.113
MGM Grand								.292	.189	.206	.199	.142	.206
Midwest Exp						.094	.096	.118	.103	.090	.079	.072	.093
Intrastate													***.137***
Southwest	.058	.053	.054	.052	.049	.050	.042	.044	.043	.044	.045	.040	.048
Air Florida	.102	.080	.080	.069									.083
PSA	.083	.083	.074	.072	.070	.087	.069	.069					.076
Air California	.094	.085	.079	.076	.078	.078	.069						.080
Start-ups													***.072***
People Expr.		.063	.051	.040	.043	.040	.041						.046
Jet America			.058	.052	.053	.051	.045						.052
Muse Air		.096	.052	.047	.045	.040							.056
Braniff (II)					.070	.047	.044	.048	.051	.054			.052
America W.				.056	.074	.050	.049	.046	.047	.050	.049	.048	.052
Sunworld					.058	.061	.061	.068					.062
Florida Exp.					.066	.066	.060	.065					.065
Midway	.104	.099	.086	.076	.090	.083	.060	.054	.052	.054	.056		.074
New York A.		.096	.087	.092	.090	.081	.069						.086
Presidential							.051	.077	.085	.086			.075
Charters													***.062***
World	.102	.080	.068	.055	.045	.046	.056						.065
Capitol Air	.097	.062	.057	.059									.069
Tower					.088	.099		.094			.082	.079	.088
Arrow Airw.					.112	.111							.111
Mean	.092	.085	.072	.072	.077	.083	.074	.101	.099	.094	.105	.093	

*All figures are 1992 dollars.

Source: Compiled from DoT Form 41.

The debt to equity ratio for new-entrants is usually very poor. Although, airlines in general have high debt structure although new-entrants as a segment is higher than the average for all airlines.[62] If the debt structure in the last year of operations is examined in Table 3.10 for each new-entrant, one can see that only three new-entrants Southwest, PSA and Midwest Express have positive equity compared to long-term debt.

Table 3.10 New-entrants' long term debt and equity 1980 - 1992

L.-t. debt Tot. stock. eq	1980	1981	1982	1983	1984	1985	1986	1987	1988	1989	1990	1991	1992
America W.				17	91	129	257	321	390	486	640	801	
				23	33	70	66	77	71	107	43	-145	
Southwest	77.9	58.9	106	158	152	297	259	250	368	353	326	616	699
	107	177	241	314	360	463	508	524	577	649	608	632	854
People Expr.		56	60	247	326	502	502						
		16	49	102	191	211	289						
Republic	650	721	797	805	740	651	413						
	118	72	56	6	37	196	369						
New York A.		41	41	39	73	75	337						
		22	16	42	35	33	96						
PSA	140	267	412	432	354	339	241	227					
	100	197	249	287	282	272	167	345					
Braniff (II)					3	6	9	11	33	188			
					42	57	49	38	12	-132			
World	370	343	287	240	216	199	126						
	89	69	15	-15	23	8	-25						
Air Wiscons.				49	48	75	66	75	60	63	91	125	
				47	51	61	65	72	89	90	91	59	
Midway	14	33	53	50	42	35	30	38	73	143	111		
	9	23	40	46	25	45	56	57	83	116	-26		
Muse Air		0	77	84	121	74							
		32	45	66	49	62							
Jet America			11	11	69	66	54						
			-0.1	0.8	15	6	3						
Tower					0	43	45	45	51	43	45	61	54
					-0.8	-1.7	0	-3	3	5	10	17	18
Air Atlanta					31	45	52						
					-16	-32	-42						
Air California	35	76	88	90	78	43	43						
	22	62	38	42	53	75	79						
Air Florida	175	266	119	33									
	29	53	-32	-54									
Empire		4	27	25	33	30							
		9	9	17	19	15							
Presidential							22	5	9	30			
							25	7	-37	-50			
MGM Grand								15	35	38	60	200	28
								19	13	17	17	76	61
Florida Exp.					0	1	23	23					
					-2	14	25	12					
Arrow Airw.					13	14	16						
					-16	-17	-21						
Capitol Air	9	26	11	10	6								
	-3	-1	-22	-34	-35								
Horizon Air						4	10	6	15	27	14	5	4
						-11	-15	-1	4	5	6	10	13
Sunworld					1	1	0.4	1					
					2	14	8	-6					
Midwest Exp						10	12	10	40	35	26	1	0.3
						6	6	9	13	17	20	20	22

* All figures are rounded to the nearest million.

Source: Compiled from DoT Form 41

If individual years are considered it is apparent that three carriers have fared better than many in this regard, namely Southwest, Braniff (II) and Midway. Southwest stands out having had positive equity throughout the deregulation years.

The otherwise poor debt to equity ratio for new-entrant airlines indicates that new-entrants are highly sensitive to fluctuations of the economy, especially interest rates. Furthermore, it suggests that financing through equity offerings was a problem for new-entrants due to their poor profitability and track record.

PeoplExpress financed most of its debt with public debt securities that were typically 10 year certificates with no principal payments for the first five years. This led to low repayments compared to the amount of debt or $1.5 million in 1986 on $500 million outstanding (Airline Business, 1986). This strategy deferred debt payments to later years in the hope that the restructuring of the airline would better enable it to service that large amount of debt. It is apparent that PeoplExpress had fully extended its financial abilities in terms of public debt securities and seriously severed its relations with the banks after the Frontier acquisition, thus, hindering the tapping of financial resources after the large 1986 loss.

Operations

Route structure

Route structures are different depending on the new-entrant's origin. For example, charter-based new-entrants tend to operate long-haul international routes, while regional based new-entrants operate very short-haul feeder routes and start-up and intrastate new-entrants fall into the short to medium haul category. That category seems to be the one category that works best as into that category fall the new-entrants that are still operating, as well as the *hyper growth* new-entrants. However, stage-length tells only part of the story in terms of the route structure. In fact, there are five basic route structures that new-entrant carriers could adopt under deregulation. The first structure is 'short-haul to and from a hub,' used by a hub carrier such as America West in Phoenix or a feeder carrier such as Air Wisconsin at Chicago's O'Hare. The second structure is 'short-haul point to point,' that characterises the most successful new-entrant Southwest and Morris Air, a relatively successful carrier that was acquired by Southwest in 1994. The third structure is 'medium-haul to and from a hub to small to medium sized cities,' that characterised PeoplExpress, Midwest Express and Midway. The fourth structure is 'long-haul international destinations,' which was mainly the domain of the former supplemental carriers, Capitol, World, Tower and American Trans Air. The fifth structure is 'long-haul domestic,' which was operated by MGM Grand Air that flew between New York and Los Angeles offering premium service. The selected route structure is one of the basic features of the new-entrant's strategy and will be discussed in the following chapter.

Table 3.11 Average stage length in miles

Airline	1979	1980	1981	1982	1983	1984	1985	1986	1987	1988	1989	1990	1991	1992
Short-haul														
Mid Pacific								126	127					
New Y. A.		214	287	333	300	321	379	387						
Air Califor.	249	289	329	341	340	350	371	411	444					
Muse Air			241	296	362	381	389							
PSA	299	319	335	349	351	360	361	362	367	363				
Air Wiscons.					110	105	127	123	128	na	na	158	161	
Aspen	145	147	153	137	na	na	na	156	152	165	189	186	231	
Empire	179	149	150	163	163	169	172	187						
Florida Exp.						381	400	397	392	428	425			
Presidential							na	498	397					
Horizon Air						160	165	156	151	146	145	148	154	160
Southwest	265	276	278	297	303	321	333	354	368	380	375	376	374	378
Medium-h.														
Braniff (II)						734	na	1033	963	806	704			
America W.					544	456	399	402	442	458	480	544	596	629
Midwest Ex.						636	606	531	569	551	570	629	659	699
Midway	310	347	487	442	448	489	501	598	620	614	662	636	673	
Air Atlanta						555	597	526						
People Expr.			396	538	457	531	617	630						
Air Florida	324	286	410	428	435	582	1080							
Sunworld					532	492	458	422	375	821				
Long-haul														
Jet America				1735	1428	1358	1176	887	830					
MGM Grand									2475	2475	2471	2475	2475	2475
Arrow Airw.					1303	1353	1219	1190	1173	1033	1478	1606	1416	
Capitol Air		3173	2262	1959	1384	1611								
Tower					2829	2889	2829	3438	3664	3670	3654	3473	3154	2810
World		1756	1519	1512	1938	1943	1828	1606						

Source: Air Carrier Traffic Statistics, RSPA National Transportation Systems Center, Cambridge, MA.

Table 3.11 indicates that most new-entrants move towards longer-haul markets during their life-cycle as the increase in average stage lengths show. One interpretation of this can be that an original short-haul niche strategy is inadequate in the long term causing the new-entrants to seek longer-haul routes to maintain growth. The consequences of such developments are numerous and may induce major operational and strategic changes such as different equipment, head-on competition with the incumbents and drop in service levels due to poorer facilities at congested larger airports.

Fleet structure

Fuel efficient, small, two pilot aircraft characterise the fleet of most new-entrants with the exception of the regional based new-entrants that have operated a mixed fleet of turboprop and jet aircraft. Another characteristic has been to keep the fleet homogenous by operating only one type of aircraft. Southwest has been able to keep this rule, while PeoplExpress operated both B727's and B737's and added B747's when London was added to its route system.

The Boeing 737 has been the most popular aircraft, characterising the fleets of PeoplExpress, America West, Southwest and Morris Air. As is widely known maintenance costs are usually lower for two engine aircraft compared to three engine aircraft such as Boeing 727. Furthermore, seating configuration in smaller two engine jets allows it to be operated with two flight attendants if seating is below 100. This is what Midwest Express and America West have utilised as a cost cutting measure by operating Fokker F-28 aircraft. Another reason for using two engine aircraft is lower fuel consumption. America West estimated in 1989 that it was actually 22 percent more fuel efficient than the average for other carriers, or 60 ASM per gallon compared with industry average of 47 ASM per gallon.

Information- and communication systems

The internal information and communication system brings together information in the company, including analysis of problems faced and challenges from the outside. The right processing and channelling of this information to the relevant sections of the company provides for effective decision-making, given that the information is relevant, timely and accurate. If information flow is examined it can be divided into different compartments, such as computer based information and processing systems, formal paper based communication systems in the form of reports, letters and internal newsletters and finally formal and informal interpersonal communication.

In the airline industry there are four basic internal computer based information systems. First, the traditional accounting system that has usually an integrated management information module build in. Second, operations system that is centred around the airlines in-house CRS system. This system has current booking status of all flights operated by the airline. The in-house CRS can then funnel this information into management reports citing load-factors divided into classes, production units and yield. The last named function has actually been developed into a sub-function as a management tool to maximise yield, a yield management system (YMS). Third, the external commercial CRS systems ran first as in-house hosted systems and later became de-hosted. Fourth, operation, scheduling and maintenance system dealing with the day to day operation of aircraft.

Some new-entrants such as Southwest and PeoplExpress circumvented commercial CRS, but most new-entrants have been at least participants at the basic level by listing their schedules, but most at higher levels allowing TA bookings. The CRS do generate management reports given that the airline is a full member of the system. The in-house system is, however, usually linked to the commercial CRS meaning that the most accurate up to the minute information are stored in-house, so there is no reason to produce reports from the external system unless the internal system is highly inadequate in that respect. Later the new-entrants could link an internal yield management system to the CRS interface allowing yield maximisation.

Examining PeoplExpress one can see that the carrier had a problem with inadequate in-house CRS system mainly due to the systems inflexibility and simplicity. Indicating that PeoplExpress had not recognised the importance of computerised reservation and yield management systems until too late, probably taking the stand that the cost savings of maintaining a simple basic system would be more important than developing a sophisticated in-house CRS system. The result was inability to respond to changes in strategic environment that was two faceted: i) the increased importance of CRS as a marketing tool; and ii) the development of sophisticated yield management system by American, that set the phase for other airlines. The result was PeoplExpress inability to respond due to financial limitations and time lag to develop such a system.

Summary

Senior managers at new-entrant airlines have usually been highly experienced airline professionals. The airline experience of the founder seems to be important in order for the start-up new-entrant to gain enough funding. There is a tendency for start-up airline's founders to be charismatic and autocratic, traits that seem important to get the airline off the ground but a liability as the airline's size increases. The new-entrants chief executive officers' objectives are various, often stated in the media as: to make profit, to prove that things can be done differently and to enjoy media attention. There is a tendency for roles to be centralised at the top at new-entrant airlines. The new-entrant's founders are often combined chairman, CEO or president, thus enjoying almost unchallenged power. This centralisation may be important for the organisation to begin with but becomes a liability as the airline gets larger and more complicated.

PeoplExpress was famous for its employee programs and was considered highly decentralised, but had combined chairman CEO that can be considered a warning sign of too much centralization at the top. Many of the new-entrants were highly 'people oriented' in order to keep the unions away and pay lower salaries for more employee efficiency than prevailed in the industry. The usual bait for attracting employees on such terms was to offer profit sharing and stock-ownership programs. These programs are two-edged sword for the new-entrants as they become a liability and disheartening for the employees when profitability drops or does not materialise.

Fast growth of the early successful new-entrants imposed a serious strain on organisation structure as large portion of the organisation was composed of 'new' employees that were still gaining experience and training. Information systems that take considerable time to develop and implement lag behind making the organisation inefficient as the infrastructure is not capable of handling the increased complexity of a fast growing airline. New-entrant airlines have grown very fast in most cases and behave differently in that respect from most other industries. To give in to the potential for fast growth may actually be one of new-entrant's greatest liabilities.

New-entrant's capacity to demand ratio, as represented in the passenger load-factor, has been good, with the charter-based new-entrants at the top of the list and regional based new-entrants at the bottom. The load-factor is not a sufficient indicator of efficiency by itself so it is necessary to look at yield, costs and aircraft utilisation as well.

New-entrant's overall profitability has been poor. The losses increase fast as the airline nears bankruptcy because travel agents and passengers alike avoid such airlines. This implies that airlines in a financially poor condition are highly vulnerable to press treatment in their crisis. New-entrants are highly leveraged, making them vulnerable to adverse conditions in the economy, especially increases in interest rates. The reason is their tendency to use fixed cost instruments instead of equity financing, leading to inability to raise equity capital as financial health deteriorates, with the founders attempting to retain power and abstain hostile take-overs.

A new-entrant's cost structure is generally lower than that of the incumbents but they were not able to utilise the advantage fully after the introduction of yield management systems by the incumbents. The main facets of the lower cost structure are lower salaries, higher employee utilisation, greater aircraft utilisation and leaner organisation structures. Aircraft acquired by the new-entrant jet carriers have tended to be second-hand, fuel efficient, small size two engine jets. In order to further the savings the fleets have been kept as homogenous as possible. The most popular aircraft among start-up and intrastate new-entrants has been the Boeing 737.

Although most of the new-entrants have been acquired by other carriers many of the new-entrants participated in the merger 'mania' in 1986. Some of the airlines attempted to over-take other airlines but were not successful. The attempts were costly in terms of management time and capital and affected the profitability of the carrier involved. The mergers that occurred were usually not beneficial for the new-entrants.

The information and communication system of the new-entrant is the central function that allows effective decisions to be taken. Due to the new-entrant's fast growth this function is often lagging behind causing information and communication problems.

---

46 Formerly the president of Braniff.

47 MGM Grand Air's majority shareholder was billionaire Kirk Kerkorian. A fact that is adequate explanation in itself as to why the airline has had so much staying power regardless of constant losses from the outset.

48 The professor was perhaps not that much of an outsider being Burr's friend from the chairman's days at Harvard. This nomination was nevertheless important but too late to have any major impact on company policy.

49 The function of the board of directors is the overall supervision of management and accountability for the conduct and policies of the organisation.

50 For a detailed discussion on threat-rigidity see Staw, et al. (1981).

51 Donald Burr stated that his ideas were based on Douglas M. McGregor's book, *The Human Side of Enterprise*, McGraw-Hill, 1960.

52 Note that non-unionisation is important, not primarily to pay lower wages, but to retain flexibility in the organisation of the workforce.

53 The management had actually declared how much time each Customer Manager should spend in each function.

54 Labour organisation in the US at non-organised companies has to go through a certain process. First of all there has to be employee dissatisfaction with any of the issues which the union can influence. These are usually wages and work conditions. If someone requests the union to come in it will arrange for a voting on union membership. Management at non-union companies will usually have organised their management in such a way that union organisation would be unlikely, by promoting 'people' orientated staff policy and 'we care' attitude. Furthermore, they will in the case of 'low wages' compared to the industry average, offer profit sharing and stock participation programs. If the employee feels satisfied and secure and the company on its way to profitability whereas the employees will gain from the incentive programs he or she is unlikely to will not vote for an union representation.

55 A sharp change in philosophy.

56 In the book *Growing Pains* (Jossey-Bass, 1990), Eric G. Flamholtz proposed some rules of thumb regarding classification of the intensity of companies' growth rates. He considered a growth rate of 15 percent per annum or less to be 'normal' growth, 15 to 25 percent as 'rapid', 25 to 50 percent to be 'very rapid', 50 to 100 percent to be 'hyper' and growth in excess of 100 percent to 'light-speed' growth. Table 3.3 has been segmented according to this proposition in order to show the intensity of new-entrants' growth. The growth rates are based on capacity rather than revenue growth.

57 Midway actually led the way after having spent over three years trying to obtain financing for their up-start, the followers actually benefited from their pioneering work.

58 The program included commuters, intrastate and charter carriers.

59 There are number of different leasing forms in the airline industry; (i) leveraged lease (tax-lease); (ii) Japanese levereged lease; (iii) US ownership - FSC; (iv) German tax-based lease; (v) European export credit; (vi) Commission - FSC; (vii) US Eximbank;

(viii) UK tax lease; (ix) French lease. *See Airfinance Journal*, Handbook 1993/94, May 1993, no. 150.

60 Following deregulation lower fares and increased disposable income in the Developed World, led to a thriving aircraft leasing business due to airlines rapid growth leading to their need to add aircraft without being able or perhaps willing to add debt. This development led to the formation of aircraft leasing companies, that reduced risk for banks as now the banks would lend the lessor that could repossess aircraft much faster than the banks would, in the event of bankruptcy or lease payments default. As a result, the financially poor operators could acquire aircraft faster and easier and in larger numbers than before. This, occurred for new-entrants just as well as other carriers.

61 Preferred stock has claims and rights before common stock but behind bonds. Preferred stock is similar to bonds in some ways but different in the way that the company can decide not to pay dividend in years of negative earnings unlike bonds whose failure to pay interest will foreclose the debenture. Bonds can be of a secured and unsecured nature, meaning that a secured bond will be secured against some specific assets of the company, while the unsecured one is not secured against any specific assets but against assets not already pledged. Thus, unsecured bonds are used by either financially very strong companies or financially weak companies. In the latter case the company wants to preserve their remaining assets, if any, against pledging for future use if necessary. Long-term bond issues call for long-term relationship between the borrower and the lender that is described in the 'indenture' that is a highly detailed document of relevant information. Identure for stock-offerings is however much simpler in nature. Common stock carries with it full voting rights but claims to assets behind, bond holders and preferred stockholders that do not have voting rights.

62 For a good overview of this high debt of the airline industry, see: Financial Condition of the Airline Industry (1993).

BIRMINGHAM COLLEGE OF FOOD

4 Competition strategy

To succeed and survive in an industry,
the firm must match the aggressiveness of its
operating and strategic behaviours to the changeability of
demands and opportunities in the market-place.
Igor Ansoff (1987)

Introduction

Strategy comes across as a relatively wide concept affecting all aspects of the business operation. Strategy is defined in the Collins Dictionary of Business (Pass, *et al.*, 1991, p. 586), as

> ...a unified set of plans and actions designed to secure the achievement of the basic objectives of a business... BUSINESS OBJECTIVES represent the goals of the organization, i.e. the economic (and social) *purposes* for which the business exists; strategy is the *means* used to attain these goals.

Tregoe and Zimmerman (1979, p.10) define strategy as

> a framework that guides those choices that determine the nature and direction of an organisation.

The definitions state, therefore, clearly that the business has to have some 'destination' before it can select the path that leads it there. Strategy as such is the selection of the path. The problem arises when strategy is selected without any clear destination, apparent for some new-entrants and manifested in a change in the airline's basic definition of its own being. In such a case it can be alleged that the carrier has shifted from one 'goal' on which its strategy was based, to another 'goal' that leads to a total change in the selection of 'paths.' Such shift can cause a major havoc among staff and customers resulting in a sudden increase in 'problems' facing the carrier, making it shift once again to the old ways in the hope of 'surviving.'

Porter's competition forces

Porter (1980, p.4) identified five forces that affect industry competitors and cause *rivalry* among firms, whose strength determines the potential profitability in an industry. The forces are made up of the bargaining power of suppliers, threat of new entry, bargaining power of buyers, threat of substitute products or services, and rivalry among existing firms and have differing intensity.

If we examine the airline industry one can assess that the bargaining power of suppliers is low, hence the ability of airlines to switch suppliers easily, because suppliers do not have to provide any specifically designed products for individual airlines: an airline can easily buy a Boeing instead of an Airbus aircraft. The second item, the threat of new entry, is a larger force in air transportation. Although the larger airlines have been successful in fighting off new-entrants in the past, more and more of the competition instruments of incumbents are being neutralised,[63] making new-entrants a greater threat than before. Hence, the threat of entry is enhanced by favourable policy climate, a sort of government strategy to reach a goal of lower fares and more service through enhanced competition. The bargaining power of buyers is low as fares are determined by the rivalry among players rather than by the bargaining power of the buyers, as they are extremely many and not united. Fourth, the threat of substitute products is a reality in short-haul markets where the passenger can select to drive instead of to fly. This is exactly what makes low fares so important in such markets and why there is often so much extra traffic generated when fares go below a certain level.

The focal point of Porter's model is the rivalry among competitors, which is usually rooted in an attempt of one or more competitors to increase market-share. This is especially so in a period of low industry growth, when company growth can only be achieved through snatching customers from the competitors. Porter's strategy framework has been criticised by researchers for its lack of accurate portrayal of strategy performance and questionable generalisability (Miller and Dess, 1993). In fact the strategy - performance relationship appears to be more complicated than indicated in Porter's work. This view is backed by the *PIMS* research program and pointed out in Miller's and Dess work (p. 577). To his credit Porter does use the term 'generic' for the basic strategy alternatives, which indicates clearly that more sophistication is necessary to design a tailor made strategy for specific industry or corporate situations. Therefore, one can view Porter's work as a framework for strategy analysis and selection rather than a detailed strategic tool for all imaginable situations.

The Prisoner's Dilemma

The so called 'prisoner's dilemma' can contribute to the understanding of airline behaviour under oligopolistic competition. The simple matrix shown in Figure 4.1 depicts that if an airline reacts to a competitor's fare reduction by reducing its own fares, both will maintain their market-share but will be worse off. However, one reduces fares without a reaction by the other, an increase in market-share and profit will be the result. The most beneficial action for both would be to hold prices, maintaining the market-share and present profit levels. This is what is called a cartel situation, because the prerequisite to maintain this situation is an agreement not to break the fare equilibrium.[64]

While collusion is illegal in the United States the cartel-state is not inconceivable. The airlines can decide unilaterally on a fare in a market by following a price leader. However, such a situation is inherently unstable as the environment can change, for example, during recession when excess capacity may be in the market. An effective cartel needs policing and that can not be done legally. Yet cartel discipline is possible through threats signalled through CRS among airlines (Avmark, 1993).

In a market with low entry barriers, rent will attract a new-entrant usually with lower cost structure. Thus, it is necessary for the incumbents to raise entry barriers in an industry with inherently low entry barriers. One way of doing so is to adapt a 'deterrent' strategy where the airline will minimise profits whenever there is a likelihood of new-entry. In a situation where both players react to one another and the payoff becomes negative, the only long-term benefit to either one is if one exits the market and previous profit levels can be reinstated. In such a situation the staying power of the players becomes the issue and profits are sacrificed for market-share. The problem is, still, that as the profit levels are reinstated new-entrants will emerge and a price war will reoccur. The only way out of the dilemma for the new-entrant is to develop a niche that is hard for the competitors to enter.

		Airline B	
	Airline A Results / Airline B Results	Lower Price	Hold Price
Airline A	Lower Price	(50) 50 / (50) 50	(75) 200 / (25) 0
	Hold Price	(25) 0 / (75) 200	(50) 100 / (50) 100

(XX) = Market-share

XX = Profit

Figure 4.1 The Prisoner's Dilemma

In air transport the scope for niche marketing is, however, limited due to the commodity nature of the product. Geographical niches are possible but easy for the competitors to enter due to the inherent ease of moving the 'plant' the aircraft from one market to another. Operational niches where the airline operates direct services instead of hub and spokes are more suitable to the time sensitive passengers. Such a strategy has worked well for Southwest Airlines but due to the airline's long-term profitability other airlines are taking up similar strategy and entering direct services.[65]

The Darwinian model of natural selection

In an economic system where behavioural freedom is almost limitless in economic terms, there is going to be what is termed as 'economic natural selection.'[66] The framework is important as a crude way to explain the behaviour of large powerful airlines in a market with weak airlines, as well as giving a simple explanation for the poor overall profitability in the US airline industry in the early nineties.

The theory, derived from evolutionary biology (*see* Hamilton, 1970; Eisenberg and Wilton, 1971), uses the act of *spite* to explain the behaviour of firms that have market power in a competitive market of few. Spite is the behaviour trait of harming both oneself and another, in the belief that such act will only lead to short-term loss but long-term gain as the competitor will be harmed more. Schaffer (1989, p.30) states

> When firms have market power[67], the potential for 'spiteful' behaviour exists. A firm which forgoes the opportunity to maximise its absolute profit may still enjoy a selective advantage over its competitors if its 'spiteful' deviation from profit-maximisation harms its competitors more than itself.

Thus, it could be alleged that airline's spitefulness has caused the immense industry losses during deregulation. The sign of reversal can be seen by the fact that the mega-carriers after years of losses in the early nineties retiring aircraft and exiting unprofitable markets increased contestability in the market by creating a vacuum that could be filled by smaller carriers. The purpose of such behaviour is to cash in on the short term 'spitefulness' by reducing over-capacity and stem away from fare-wars, cut costs and increase overall profitability.[68]

Entry risks and costs

The provision of entry in a market is one of the fundamental aspects of effective competition. However, one must distinguish between entry in terms of an extension of existing firm's operation and an entirely new firm's entry into a market. Thus, there are three facets of entry in deregulated air transport markets, namely the entry of incumbent pre-deregulation carriers into new routes, the entry of existing non-scheduled, intrastate or local carriers and finally the entry of entirely new carriers into the market. The risk level is in fact in the same order, being the least for well established large carrier, moderate for a carrier extending a similar operating base, but high for a new business entity in a new market. This can be clearly observed in the risk matrix in Figure 4.2. In addition to risk differences, there are different costs associated to entry depending on the new-entrant's relative industry position. Porter (1980, p.347) classified these costs into four groups: (i) the investment costs required to be in the new business; (ii) the additional investment required to overcome structural entry barriers; (iii) the expected cost from incumbents retaliation; balanced against (iv) the expected cash flow from operations. Thus, it is apparent that small airlines will an initial cost disadvantage when entering new markets, because of costs associated with overcoming 'resistance' or 'indifference' by the infrastructure authorities. Such costs are likely to be lesser for a well established large carrier starting to serve a community airport, contrasted to a new unknown carrier that may carry a higher perceived risk level. Furthermore, all new firms are bound to incur costs of being at the bottom of the 'learning curve.'

	New product	Existing product
New market	High risk	Moderate risk
Existing market	Moderate risk	Low risk

Figure 4.2 The market entry risk matrix[69]

Entry by new carriers is particularly viable in air transport when entry costs are low in terms of capital requirements for aircraft acquisition. This occurs when there is excess capacity leading to aircraft being available at favourable terms when the incumbents are financially weak and not prone to retaliate by fear of a market wide fare war, and likewise when the incumbents are exiting unprofitable markets during a recession or cost cutting.

Internal and external growth

It is important to realise that competition intensity increases when traffic growth declines because then the airlines will have to extract growth by attracting customers from the competitors.[70] As demand increases the airlines are faced with actual lack of capacity or projected lack of capacity, that is rectified by ordering aircraft that may have long order lead-time, usually years. This lead-time is sometimes extended during rapid growth and especially when major changes are occurring such as changed noise regulation that renders a portion of the fleet obsolete. When the new aircraft are delivered the growth period may be over and the new aircraft adding unwanted capacity, while the old planes can not be sold due to lack of demand. As soon as there is excess capacity there will be increase in rivalry because of the necessity to maintain growth and to cover the high fixed costs incurred by obtaining the new aircraft. The only way to reduce excess capacity in the airline industry is by growth and aircraft retirements.

The level of traffic growth is affected by a number of factors that can be divided into two distinctive groups, namely demographic growth and individual airline's strategic growth. The former group contains economic growth leading to an increase in disposable income, increase in tourism, population increases, increase in international trade and an increase in immigration. The latter group deals with sources of growth that are in the airline's domain to influence, namely fare reductions, addition of points served, marketing agreements and frequency increase. It is important to note that growth in air transportation is limited by bottlenecks in the system: ATC congestion and airport capacity. Figure 4.3 shows these possible sources of growth for an air carrier.

A firm's growth strategy can be divided into three different directions, to: (i) grow internally; (ii) grow externally; and (iii) determine the level of acceptable growth. PeoplExpress, for example, maintained the first strategy of growing only internally until 1985, when it acquired Frontier. The same was the case with Southwest that has avoided growth through acquisition but felt strategically unable to pass Muse Air and Morris Air into the hands of 'other' airlines. There is however a strange relationship between 'success' in terms of fast growth and 'failure' due to much success manifesting itself in too fast growth. Too fast growth will affect the company's cash flow in such a way that it can fail, although, it is making profit according to the books. Similarly, growth that is achieved, through a merger or acquisition can seriously harm the cost-structure of an airline in good condition through the inevitable addition of debt. Furthermore, the harmonisation of two entities into a larger entity can cost in terms of deterioration in company's working atmosphere and quality of decisions due to more time spent on 'merger' tasks rather than 'strategic' tasks necessary to maintain future profitability of the more complex corporation. Gialloreto (1986, pp. 41-44) suggested that the stress of rapid growth lead to enormous costs and structural stress of the airlines involved. He mentions the early Pan Am merger with National and North Central's merger with Southern and Hughes, that brought about detrimental effects on the two carriers. Both mergers were set astray due to severe cost increases after the pilots where brought up to the acquiring carrier's pay scales.

Aviation bankers (Airline Business, 1994, p.29) have argued that airline management should focus on keeping their share rather than adhering to bold strategic aims of 'pursuing growth for its own sake.' The argument is placed into context with the 'financial' institutions reluctance to finance poorly planned growth with no aim in itself but 'size.' With the airline business loosing billions on both sides of the Atlantic prior to 1994, bankers were understandable concerned. This belief has, however, ignored that growth as such is often related to factors such as competitors behaviour and the necessity of businesses to grow. First, all companies that have shareholders are prone to strive for growth in order to maximise their shareholders' wealth. That is the yardstick on which management performance is measured by the shareholders. This is especially so if the company is a corporation with large number of shareholders.

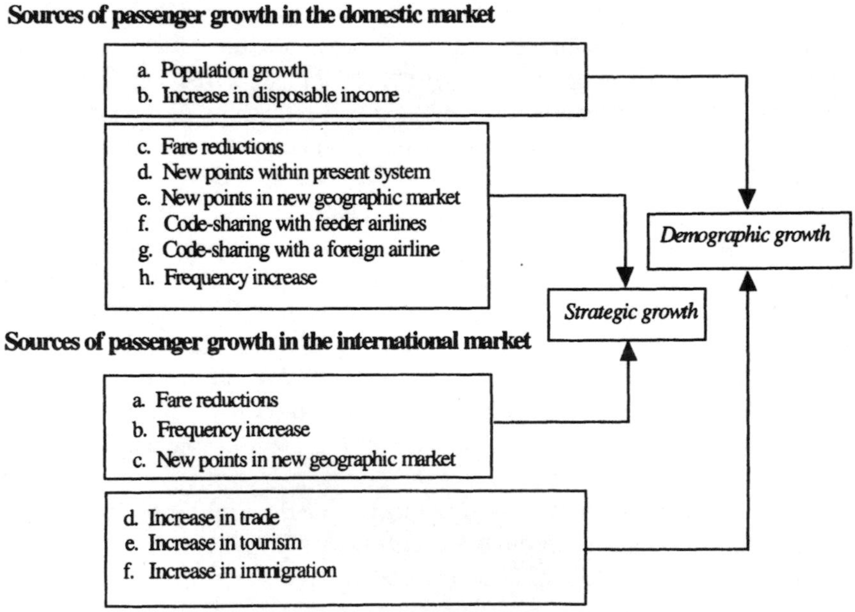

Figure 4.3 Sources of passenger growth for scheduled airlines

Growth associated with profits makes it easier for the company to raise capital through 'markets' both in terms of debt and equity. One can cite

PeoplExpress that was praised by most analysts until shortly before its collapse, even though the signs showed that the company's infrastructure and management practices were shaking as soon as 1983, but the 'light-speed' growth and profits were what the media was interested in.

Table 4.1 Yearly change in market share by airline based on enplanements: all airports, 1980 - 1991

*	1980	1981	1982	1983	1984	1985	1986	1987	1988	1989	1990	1991	Avg
Incumbents													
Alaska									0	9.1	8.3	-54	-9.2
Aloha	0	0	-10	-22.2	0	0	0	-43	0	25	0	-40	-7.5
American	-10	2.2	8.7	4.0	2.9	8.4	1.7	8.5	12.5	11.8	0	5.6	4.7
Braniff (I)	-8.7	-7.1											-7.9
Continental	-9.4	6.9	12.9	-2.8	2.9	28.6	15.5	78.8	-7.5	-5.8	-2.5	7.6	10.4
Delta	3.9	-3.7	-5.4	0	-2.5	-5.9	-6.3	20	9.5	14.5	-6.3	15.5	2.8
Eastern	0	-4.3	-3.8	-3.1	-3.3	-1.7	-6.8	-1.8	-21.5	-59.5	47.0		-5.3
Frontier	0	9.5	-8.7	0	4.8	-13.6	-36.8						-6.4
Hawaiian	0	9.1	0	-18.2	0	0	22.2	-27.3	0	0	-25	0	-3.3
Hughes Airw	18.7												18.7
Northwest	8.1	2.5	0	2.4	-2.4	0	26.8	59.6	-7.2	9.1	3.6	4.6	8.9
Ozark	0	15.4	6.7	0	0	0	-31						-1.3
Pan Am	76.7	-5.7	-12	6.8	-6.4	-15.9	-13.5	-25	16.7	10.7	0	-29	0.3
Piedmont	11.1	35	14.8	25.8	15.4	13.3	15.7	-6.8	5.4	-37.9			9.18
Republic	15.8	51.2	4.8	-9.2	-18.6	2.1	-22.4						3.4
Texas Intern.	7.1	-6.7	-14.3										-4.6
Trans World	-2.7	-5.6	-4.5	-3.1	-6.5	0	-12.1	11.8	0	0	-5.3	-9.3	-3.1
United	0	-6.2	11.3	6.8	15.9	-16.4	21.5	0	0.1	-3.8	0.1	9.4	3.2
USAir	11.1	0	6.0	1.9	-1.9	1.9	3.7	0	26.8	36.6	34.0	-3.8	9.7
Western	8.7	0	5.9	2.8	-10.8	0	-6.1						-3.1
New-entr.													
Air Wiscon.								33	-25	0			2.7
AirCal	10	30	-7.7	0	8.3	0	0						5.8
America W.					na	75	28.6	38.9	12	7.1	16.7	11.4	27.1
Braniff (II)									50	0			25.0
Midway									10	9.0	33.3	-25	6.8
People Expr.				70	120	68.2	10.8	-17.1					50.4
PSA	-25	9.5	13.1	3.8	-7.4	0	12.0	-17.9					-1.5
Southwest	41.2	20.8	13.8	9.1	5.5	-2.6	-10.8	0	9.1	100	-37.5	13.3	13.5
Tot. ind. enpl.	-7.7	-5.9	2.6	8.6	6.3	11.6	9.2	-10.8	1.1	0	1.4	-2.2	1.2
HHI	2.0	-3.1	0.8	2.6	-2.5	-4.3	3.7	17.2	3.9	11.7	1.4	10.8	

* Omitted squares are for years when an airline was not operating

Source: Based on Maldutis (1993).

One must conclude that endogenous growth along a planned long-term strategy that contains the growth level to a sustainable level in terms of debt addition and cash flow, is the most viable alternative for any business.

Rapid increase in market-share at airports appears to be related to failure as all the airlines listed in Table 4.1, having 8 percent annual growth or greater on the average have failed or been acquired, with the exception of USAir that was, nevertheless, having serious financial problems. It is only Southwest that has had more than 8 percent market-share and stayed profitable.

Carriers that have failed but had low overall average market-share increases, have nonetheless had sudden increases in market-share for one or more years. For example, AirCal increased its market-share by 40 percent in 1980-1981, Republic by 51.2 percent in 1981, Eastern by 47.0 percent in 1990, and Midway by 33.3 percent in 1990. Such sudden increases can often be explained by the airline in question, acquiring another carrier.

The general rationalisation of the alleged relationship between failures and fast overall growth or leap growth in market-share can be that the cost of gaining such an increase is greater than the benefit it provides. First, the acquisition of slots, terminal facilities and promotion costs of entering new markets can put a great strain on the airline's financial resources and cash flow in particular. The same can be said about the acquisition of another carrier in order to gain market-share, not mentioning the organisational strain it creates while staff functions and route networks are being merged.

Customer influence on competition

Sometimes it appears in air transport markets that the customer will accept most adversities in exchange for low price at the low-end and frequent flyer miles at the high-end. For example, why do passengers accept the indirect route through hubs to their destination? The reality is far from being so simple as to assume that passengers are indifferent about adversities at airports, in-flight or for any other aspect of their journey. In fact a passenger accepting hub flights might accept it, as there is nothing else available, but as soon as he or she has a choice of a direct flight at a similar fare the vote will be for the direct flight. The underlying framework is that airlines are offering a perishable commodity product that is basically the use of a seat while being transported from point A to B. In fact the product is highly standardised and viewed similarly by most buyers. As a result, price is highly important to the majority of buyers. In fact, the meaning of the time spent by the user in the seat is insignificant unless the airline violates his state of indifference or expectancy, be it to the negative or the positive. Accordingly, *Units of Satisfaction* (UoS) can be used in order to explain the nature of the airline's product quality interaction with customers.

The passenger moves from the *Indifference Contour* (IC) towards the *Positive Contour* (PC) if the airline scores enough UoS with the passenger. Moving to the PC will leave the passenger positive but not impressed, that is he will not press for flying with the airline but will happily accept it if convenient. If the airline scores into the *Loyalty Contour* (LC) the passenger will go out of his way to travel with the airline. For example, he or she will request to fly with the airline, pay higher fare than necessary or select less convenient flight schedule, in order to do so.

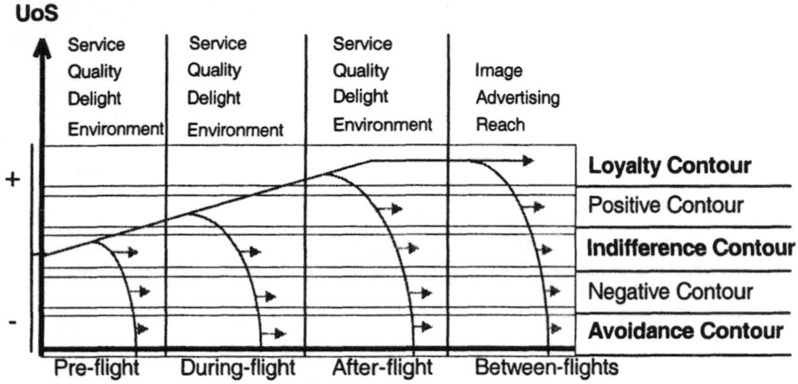

Figure 4.4 Customer Reaction Contours[71]

If the airline scores negative units of satisfaction it will cause the passenger to show signs of dissatisfaction with using the airline again, without direct objections though. A travel agent (TA) might pick up this feeling and select another airline without being asked to do so in order to maximise the customer's satisfaction. If the passenger's units of satisfaction fall within the *Avoidance Contour* (AC) the passenger will go into great lengths to avoid the airline, he may select less convenient flight schedule or/and higher fare just in order to avoid the carrier.

In the model it is assumed that new passengers enter at 0, i.e. in the *Indifference Contour* (IC). However, a passenger with prior experience or information (image) of the airline can enter in the negative area or the positive area of the model and stay there or shift towards indifference, increased disapproval or approval.

Figure 4.4, therefore, describes the interaction of the airline's product quality with passengers. It indicates how airlines lose market-share from below, that is if a new-entrant with higher quality and better service features enters a market with prevailing low quality, it will attract the passengers that have entered the AC and some of the passengers that are in the NC along with the innovators[72] in other contours. By the same token it can be risky to enter a market with competitors that have high proportion of passengers in the PC or the LC. Passengers of such airlines will only change airlines if the new-entrant offers something absolutely unique in the market and pushes the passenger into the positive or the loyalty contour immediately. In fact, a passenger will not accept being worse off, given that he or she strives for the maximisation of UoS.

A loyal or positive passenger will only remain as such until the airline fails to deliver what he or she expects or when something better is offered by a competitor. The fact is that a passenger who is inclined to maximise his UoS will not change carrier, unless he will gain more than he will lose by such a move. Frequent flyer programs (FFP) distort this relationship, making switching costs higher. Thus, a customer may decide to leave his FFP only if his loss of miles will be reclaimed partially or fully in the new program.[73]

Given what has been said above, one must recognise that airlines can never fulfil all passengers' needs, so there are always going to be customers in all the contours. The issue for a new-entrant is, therefore, how large a portion of the incumbent's total number of passengers is filling each contour on the average. If a large portion is filling the negative and avoidance contours, the incumbent is a weak competitor, if not, entry may not be viable.

Competitors' analogy

In some industries and markets there is constant infighting. In view of the frequent fare-wars in air transport markets it is important to analyse their possible causes in addition to those factors already mentioned. Henderson (*ctd. in* Kotler, 1988, pp.247-248) has explained this by a competitive equilibrium disruption, caused by the competitive relations of the market players. First, if competitors are nearly identical and make their living in the same way, then their competitive equilibrium is unstable. This is especially true for the larger carriers. Second, if a single major factor is the critical factor,[74] then the competitive equilibrium is unstable. If a carrier achieves a major cost differentiation and enters with low fare and achieves market-share at the expense of existing carriers, they will defend their market-share at all cost, causing a fare war.

The airline industry has been market-share driven since the pre-deregulation era, because the airlines were guaranteed a certain rate of return as a result of the General Passenger Fare Investigation (GPFI). Hence, large market-share would spell larger profits given reasonable cost-control. The same attitude prevailed after deregulation but for different reasons, namely that the airlines soon found out that fast expansion was not viable in light of high costs associated with initiating new routes, something Braniff (I) created an example of. It was, however, important to gain market-share in terms of gaining 'market power' and economies of scope, density and information. This is not to say that low market-share businesses can not survive in an industry, as it is generally accepted that low market-share businesses need to find a niche and gain large market-share within that niche. The problem of protecting that niche has, however, been clearly apparent in the air transport industry due to the commodity nature of the product.

The buyer's choice of airline will usually be first and foremost guided by fare and service quality.[75] Thus, it has been fairly easy for the incumbent to enter a market defined as a niche by a new-entrant and destroy the niche as such.[76] Third, if there are many critical factors, then it is possible for each competitor to have some advantage and be differentially attractive to some customers. The greater the number of critical factors that provide advantage, the greater the number of competitors that can coexist. Each competitor has his competitive segment defined by the preference for the factor trade-offs that he offers. Under this structure many differentiating opportunities exist and if customers value these differences differently the firms can coexist through niching. This coexistence lasts only as long as both carriers do not cross into each other's niche. Fourth, the fewer the number of critical competitive variables the fewer the number of competitors. Fifth, a ratio of 2 to 1 in market-share between any two competitors seems to be the equilibrium point at which it is neither practical nor advantageous for either competitor to increase or decrease market share.[77] It must be pointed out that the findings of Henderson and those of the *PIMS* (Buzzell and Gale, 1987, pp. 190-191) research program suggest that building market-share at any cost is not a viable strategy in itself. On the other hand, to improve service, reduce costs and improve quality in order to gain competitive advantage that leads to larger market-share is a viable strategy.

Competition strategy in air transport markets

Now that strategy has been covered in general terms, the definition of strategy leaves us with a question in mind, as to what a new-entrant's objective could be in a deregulated market? The U.S. Congress had an objective in this regard, by assuming that new-entrants would increase competition to the consumer benefit by lowering prices and increase service. The new-entrant, on the other hand, has a more down to earth objective, i.e., to: 'make a profit', 'provide employment', 'maximise the airline's size' or prove that a new-entrant airline 'can survive'.

The new-entrant airlines have made profit, some of them have actually benefited investors immensely if shares were bought early and sold during the new-entrant's peak. Some of the new-entrant airlines have grown very fast, indicating that their objective may have been rapid growth in order to reach large size. Perhaps in the belief that size was actually the only security for the carrier's long-term survival. Some of the new-entrants were established by former airline executives and staff possessing highly specialised knowledge, therefore, formed for the purpose of providing employment.[78] However, that as an objective can not stand on its own unless there is unlimited source of capital.[79] As a result, the profit motive has to enter the equation. Some carriers are actually established as 'rich' man's hobby. An example, would be MGM Grand Air that was owned by a well-heeled businessperson. Another motive is for retiring airline executives to have something to do in their retirement. The last item of 'proving that it can survive' may explain why new-entrants are constantly being formed against all odds. The challenge of proving that it can be done seems to attract an endless row of risk-takers willing to prove a point.

Due to the history of new-entrant airlines it must be concluded that new airlines (past 1986) can only be established with the grave objective of surviving, other objectives can only be secondary to that. Hence, each of the new-entrants must select a strategy to reach its goal of survival. Of course, this objective is an underlying rather than an stated objective of a new-entrant. As a result, past 1986 new-entrants' objectives may be 'carving out a defensible niche' or 'keep a low profile' in order to keep the incumbent indifferent. The problem with these goals, however, is that eventually the new-entrant will grow out of the limited niche. Furthermore, a carrier striving to keep the incumbent happy will eventually join the incumbent, if not peacefully then by force.[80] The early new-entrants had different goals, such as size maximisation that characterised PeoplExpress and America West or profit maximisation that has been the strategic trait of Southwest.[81]

The selection of an overall strategy focuses the sub-strategies in conjunction with the competition environment. In order to select the strategic alternatives the airlines will produce an intuitive or systematic opportunity analysis: strength, weaknesses, opportunities and threats analysis (SWOT). Figure 4.5 shows two sets of hypothetical new-entrant strategies, a very low cost airline and a high-cost premium service carrier. The former airline will exploit its cost advantage by offering low fares, and in order to do so it will not participate in a CRS but develop an in-house telephone booking system linked to an internal simplified CRS. Such carrier will offer on-board ticketing in order to save on ticket counters and staff, and unbundle services in order to charge for snacks and drinks on board. The image will range widely from being poor for fast growing carriers to being good for small niche carriers. Branding will be weak for the size maximisation carrier as it will emphasise fares in its advertising and save on costs associated with image building and brand creation. Service features will be as few as possible in order to save and quality may be lacking for the same reason. The carrier will strive for market-share maximisation, either in terms of overall market-share, city-pair market-share, airport market-share or some combination of those. The size maximisation carrier will sometimes enter niche markets to begin with but as the size gets larger and markets selected under the initial strategy run out, other segments will be added incrementally until most segments have been added.

The other example is a high cost carrier, offering premium service at business class fares (Regent, Air Atlanta, MGM Grand Air, etc.). Such carrier will participate in a commercial CRS system due to the smallness of the segment, requiring as large TA catchment area as possible. Backed by the fact that the CRS booking fee will be a relatively low proportion of the total fare.

The image will be emphasised strongly in order to create favourable attitude of the potential customer, lavish decor, many service features, superb service and dependability. Branding will be emphasised in conjunction with image by building up named service classes (i.e. Upper Class, SAGA Class, Flying Dutchman, etc.), but usually the airline's name becomes a brand in itself. Market-share is not an aim in itself nor emphasised as the market segment is very small. To reach break-even load factor is more important due to the high-costs involved with providing this sort of service. Quality is of a major concern as well as the service features. The service features are usually far more sophisticated than that of the incumbent carriers.

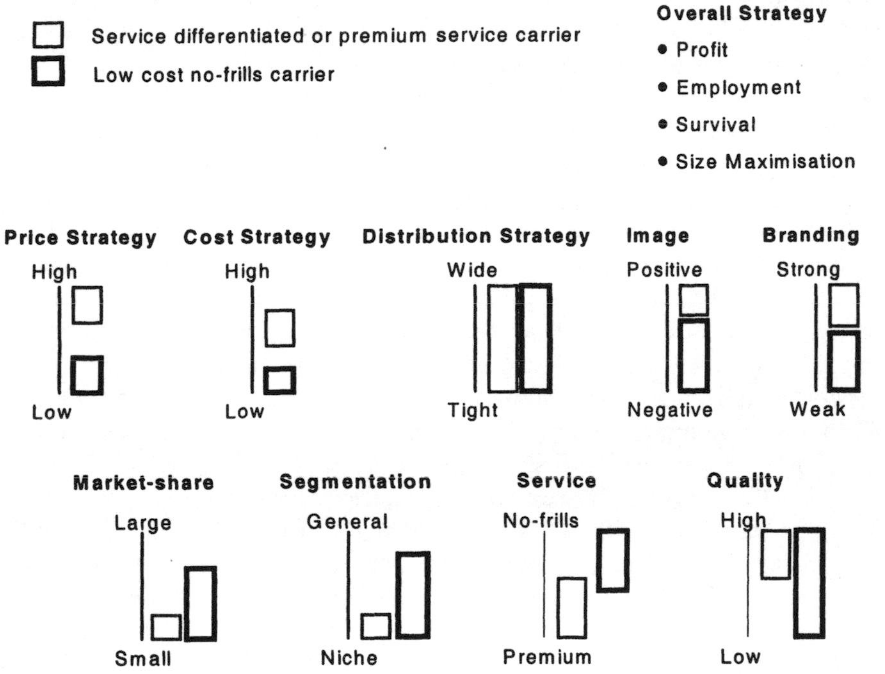

Figure 4.5 Strategy dimensions

New-entrants' strategies

The sophistication of the tools that firms can develop in order to outsmart the competitor distorts the traditional economic models of competition and has made the quantification of competitive reactions difficult. This has been quite clear in the deregulated air transport industry, with the advent of yield management, CRS bias, frequent flyer programs and the hub and spoke route systems, all of which had not been projected by economists prior to deregulation.

New-entrant strategies in the deregulated air transport market were usually a combination of the following: (i) low cost structure achieved through non-unionised staff with airline experience and low wage scales; (ii) high operating efficiency attained through fast turnaround at gates and efficient aircraft (B737, B727); (iii) highly motivated work-force, whose motivation is enhanced by stock participation programmes and flexible job tasks (cross-utilisation); (iv) market strategy geared to low fares by unbundling services, offering simple fare structure (peak, off-peak), non-participation in commercial CRS, high frequency, very low entry fares for promotion purposes (free coverage), no interlining, service differentiation (no-frills/extra frills), quality differentiation (high quality), niche identification, long haul/short haul and route differentiation (direct services/hub and spoke).

Meyer and Oster (1987) note that a new carrier has to be concerned with differentiation rather than with capacity in a market served. This is due to the fact that 'novelty' can make it harder for a carrier to achieve presence in a market. Thus if the customer has a choice among two identical alternatives, he will choose the one he recognises. Thus, the new carrier must create an 'unique selling proposition' that creates an advantage in the mind of the customer and the TA when choosing among two or more alternatives. A mere offer of an alternative service in a market can be advantageous if the existing service is in some way 'unpopular.'[82] This advantage can be overcome by an unpopular carrier through improvement of services leading to a situation where the new-entrant has no source of differentiation. An alternative airport constitutes a differentiation as is pointed out by Meyer and Oster (1984, p.42). Such was the case of Southwest's use of Dallas secondary airport Love Field that was actually closer to the City Centre than Dallas Forth Worth International Airport and less congested. However, the importance of capacity is not secondary in small to medium markets such as the Southwest example has proved. This is different, however, in heavily congested city pair markets, where demand for any service in the city pair market will exist.

Some of the new-entrants were wobbling with their base strategy. Braniff (II), for example, started out as a full service business carrier charging full fares. It became apparent within a year that such strategy did not work, thus, a 180 degree turn was taken, turning the carrier into a low-fare, low-service carrier. Such moves are bound to alienate both customers and travel agents. A similar strategy u-turn was attempted by Midway Airlines that wanted to reach the business market by establishing a separate carrier called Midway Metrolink but suffered a $22 million loss in 1984, as a result. Metrolink was abandoned but with the acquisition of Air Florida's assets the low-cost, low-fare Midway Express appeared from the company's design board. That carrier did not provide profitability so the carrier abandoned this differentiation strategy and returned to the name Midway again and full service.

If we compare Porter's (1980) theories on strategy with the new-entrants' situation we find that they do seem to apply in general terms. Porter pointed out, in his work on competitive strategy, that there are three basic strategic direction possibilities, which he calls *Generic Strategies*: *overall cost leadership*, *differentiation* and *focus*. The *cost leadership* strategy is based on the exploitation of scale advantages, cost control, cost reductions from experience and cost minimisation. The effect of this strategy is the ability of the cost-leader to extract higher than average yields in a highly competitive market, given that 'spiteful' behaviour[83] is not prevailing in the market place.

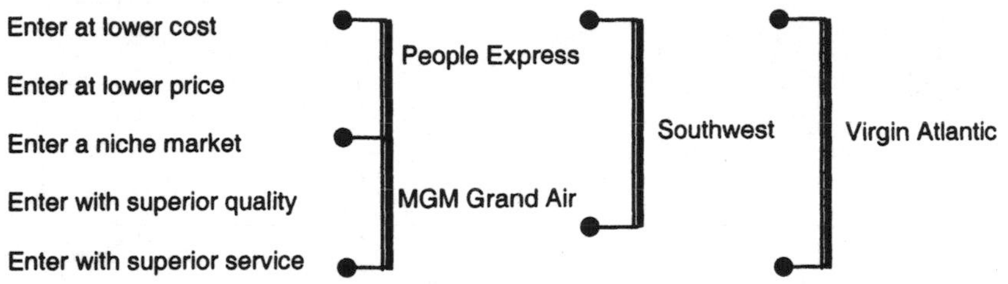

Figure 4.6 Five basic entry strategies

Differentiation, on the other hand, gives the airline an opportunity to exploit some unique trait of its product offering or location. Finally, focus strategy is when the airline targets a specific market, service or geographic segment. It is interesting to note that the most successful carrier in terms of profitability, Southwest Airlines (SW), has exploited all of these strategy alternatives in combination. It used a secondary airport, Dallas Love Field - differentiation, it achieved one of the lowest cost structures in the market - cost leadership, and it has focused on the 'sunbelt', as well as on direct flights and short-haul flights - focus (Porter, 1980, pp. 35-40). This unique ability of SW can be observed in Figure 4.6 in comparison to Virgin Atlantic and other less successful U.S. new-entrant airlines.

One could conclude that as more basic entry features are combined the greater the success of an airline, as the two airlines that can be termed as being successful have both combined, four or more basic entry strategies. The combination of high quality, high capacity but low service on short-haul routes where service features are not a major advantage in the customer's mind has worked well for Southwest, while Virgin adds superior service with a 'fun' element. Virgin does not imitate the U.S. 'premium' service carriers, but excels at traditional service features usually found at the incumbents, with a few 'extras'. One must also recognise that Virgin, unlike Southwest is a long-haul carrier, giving added weight to service features.

In Figure 4.7 we can observe three strategy dimensions on which three categories of new-entrants are charted. Categories 1 and 2 have proved to characterise failed new-entrants, while category 3 has proved successful so far. Quality and superior service in addition to low cost structure and low fares seems to be an important strategic advantage for new-entrants, as it is harder for the large incumbents to match the former two in conjunction with the latter two. A smaller carrier can introduce new services much quicker and better than large carriers due to the inherent flexibility of a small organisation.[84]

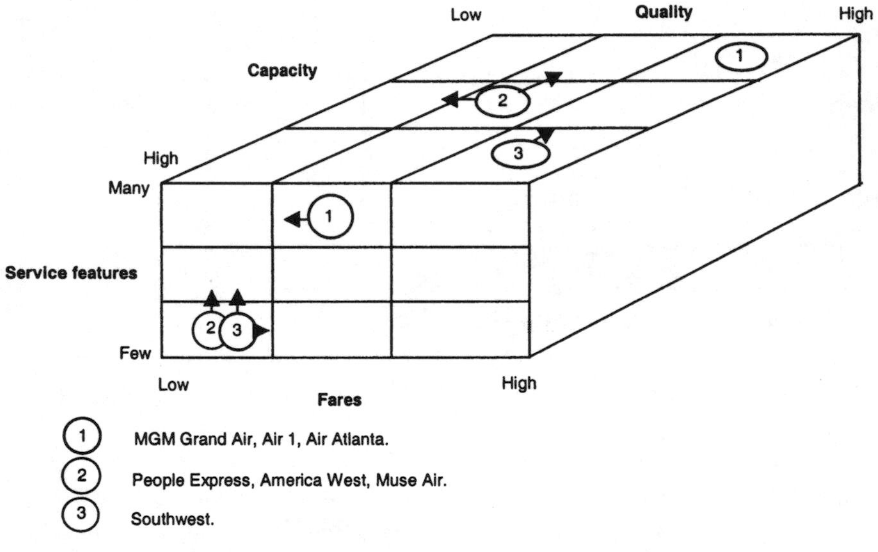

Figure 4.7 Strategy evolution of new-entrants

Table 4.2 shows in more detail entry strategies adopted by the new-entrants under deregulation. It is convenient to segregate the carriers according to service features as presented in the table. It shows well the main strategy directions adopted by the airlines.

The no-frills service strategy has been widely adopted by new-entrants in order to maintain their lower cost structure. The strategy has worked well for Southwest in conjunction with other factors already mentioned. The full-frills strategy has been adopted in order to gain access to the two main market segments leisure and business at once, such as most of the incumbents. That strategy as such has not secured any better survival chances for the new-entrants, although, America West has been around for longer period than most new-entrants. The so called 'superior service airline', including Air One, Air

Atlanta and MGM Grand Air, offered superior first class service at full economy or business class prices. The problem with this type of operations was the lack of frequency. This inference leads to a dilemma, as they may not have been able to reach break-even load factors at higher frequency due to lack of demand as the market segment is very tight. On the other hand, little frequency reduces the attractiveness of the service due to the importance it plays for the market segment. Can this strategy work then? The history tells us that it does not. Nevertheless, there are new carriers taking it up every once in a while. UltrAir, MGM GrandAir and Laker (II) being examples of carriers that have folded or abandoned the strategy.

Table 4.2 New-entrants' strategies

Airline	Fares	Capacity	Service	Quality *	Concept
No-frills					
PeoplExpress	Low	High	No-frills	Low	Low-fare, no-frills, low-cost, secondary markets, hubbing.
Southwest	Low	High	No-frills	High	Low-fare, no-frills, low-cost, secondary markets, direct service.
Full-frills					
Midwest Express	Full-fare	Low	Full	High	Full-fare, full-frills, one-class(business), direct, niche(Milwaukee)
Muse	Low-fare	High	Full	High	Low-fare, full-frills, multi-hubbing,
Florida Express	Low-fare	Medium	Full	na	Low-fare, full-service, hubbing (Orlando), incumbent avoidance, niche
America West	Low-fare	High	Full	Medium	Better than average service at a lower than average fare primarily for the business traveller through a hub and spoke system.
Premium					
MGM-Grand Air	Full-fare	Low	Premium	na	Premium service at competitors full-fare coach rate. Long-haul.
Air One	Full-fare	Low	Premium	na	Premium service at competitors full-fare coach rate. Medium-haul.
Air Atlanta	Full-fare	Low	Premium	na	Premium service at competitors full-fare coach rate. Medium-haul.

* Based on consumer complaint records.[85]

Source: Compiled from ATW 1979-1991.

Sequenced entry

In order to reduce risk a new-entrant airline may select an indirect route to achieve its goal. This is called 'sequenced entry', where the airline enters one market type or operation and then adds another. There are different types of sequenced entry in air transport: (i) low density routes to high density routes; (ii) extending one's geographic market area; (iii) entry from the leisure market into the business market; (iv) entry into international operations; (v) entry into another operation type (charter to scheduled, for etc.); and (vi) equipment upgrade (turbo-prop to jet operations). PeoplExpress sequenced entry strategy played a major role in its fast growth, entering first short-haul under-served markets, then long-haul (domestic and international) and finally with the acquisition of Frontier it entered a new geographical market instantly.

It is important to note that at every step of the way the carrier attracted retaliation on behalf of the incumbents, and as more entry segments were added the competition rivalry intensified. If the carrier builds a solid foundation, it can withstand the competition better, such as Southwest has done. PeoplExpress grew too fast to secure its foundation, failing to extract benefit from a sequenced entry strategy.

Table 4.3 Sequenced entry strategies

Sequenced entry strategy	Risk level	Entry barriers	Example
Low density route to high density route	High	Availability of slots and terminal facilities, development of market presence, retaliation of incumbents.	PeoplExpress
Entry from one geographical market to another	Moderate	High entry costs, availability of slots and terminal facilities, development of market presence, retaliation of incumbents, takes time during which the incumbents can recuperate.	PeoplExpress
Leisure to business market	High	High entry cost; brand conflict; retaliation of incumbents.	PeoplExpress, Virgin Atlantic, New York Air
Domestic to international	Low	Culture conflicts, route licenses, capacity and fare limitations.	PeoplExpress
Charter to scheduled	Moderate	High entry costs, availability of slots and terminal facilities.	Tower, World, MGM Grand Air
Propeller to jet	Moderate	Availability of capital, increased costs, increased route distances, incumbents retaliation.	Air Wisconsin, Empire
Short-haul to long-haul	Moderate	Increased costs due to equipment upgrades, retaliation of incumbents.	PeoplExpress

Table 4.3 shows the risk level associated with each of the entry possibilities in a deregulated market and what airlines have adopted the named strategy. The risk level is based on the extension of the risk matrix presented in Figure 4.2. The highest risk is associated with entering large markets where large competitors dominate, a market were the new-entrant will be a tiny player due to shortages of slots and airport facilities. The move from purely low-fare, no-frills service to offering business class is also regarded as high risk strategy due to the cost involved and the possible brand conflict that occurs because the no-frills carrier gains a strong image of low service and

sometimes poor quality. Furthermore, as the airline starts to advertise heavily to gather for the new business segment, the loyal low-end passengers may feel alienated as customers.

An example of a low risk strategy is adding international operations. This is due to the fact that most international routes are governed by bilaterals that reduces the risk as only few airlines are likely to be competing on the international route (this is changing rapidly through the U.S. Open Skies policy). Other entry strategies are classified as moderately risky due to their tendency to involve entry into new territory. The addition of jet equipment to turboprop operation is considerable risk due to the required changes in maintenance, operations, scheduling and costs (changing with the advent of regional jets). Charter carrier entering scheduled operations must establish its distribution, adapt to the inflexibility of scheduled operations compared to charter operations and harmonise the utilisation of its fleet for both charter and scheduled. This last item can be troublesome as charter requirements (long-haul) of flight equipment and that of domestic scheduled operations (short- to medium-haul) can differ dramatically.

Incumbents' reaction strategies

In any competitive market there is going to be competition between the small and large players in the market. The larger players do of course have more resources in order to protect their markets, but are usually more concerned with competitors of similar size. However, in the case of new-entrant airlines, small carriers have in many cases risen from being nuisance to becoming a serious threat. The words of Morton Ehrlich of defunct Eastern Airlines summarises well the reasons behind strong retaliation on behalf of the incumbents when a new-entrant enters their market (Business Week, 1981, p. 89)

> Successful aggressiveness begets more successful aggressiveness, and that leads to biggness[sic]. Then you've got a formidable competitor.

The immediate effect of the new-entrants' low cost structure was to focus the incumbents' management on labour costs. Re-negotiations and staff streamlining was the issue at the trunk carriers in the early eighties, that reached a peak when Continental Airlines declared Chapter 11 bankruptcy in order to get rid of its union attachment.[86]

In the course of deregulation it has become apparent that the airlines have adapted and developed schemes that protect them against the effects of new-entry to a degree. These are, yield management system, frequent flyer programs and hub and spoke operations. The yield management systems enables better management of the allocation of seats at different prices, which permits the incumbent airline to match the airfares of a new-entrant with lower cost structure, without risking too great a drop in yields. This is possible by offering few seats at a very low price subsidised by the higher revenue generating seats and, therefore, destroying the promotional force of the low price offered by the new-entrant.

The frequent flyer programs work as passenger retention force for the large airlines. This is due to the fact that business travellers have been able to redeem free holiday trips incurred during business travel. The business travel is 'less' price sensitive and, thus, the business passenger aiming for a trip to Hawaii with his family will use the carrier whose frequent flyer club member he is, even though a lower fare is available with another carrier. The third method, was the hub and spoke system, that increases the efficiency of the route network and boosts load factors on, otherwise, thin routes. It is, however, the power of the carrier dominating the hub that works as a buffer to entry on routes to and from the hub airport and permits premium pricing in the hub market.

A more detailed model of incumbent's historic strategic responses to entry was suggested by Williams (1990, pp.87-88)

(i) Reduction of operating costs through two tier wage structure, productivity increase, deunionization, staff reduction and re-equipment with efficient aircraft.[87]

(ii) Streamlining of operations through hub and spoke networks and downsizing of equipment.

(iii) [Innovative] marketing strategy through development of frequent flyer programs, commission overrides, frequency increases, code-sharing, development of CRS's, alliances with commuters, service increases, controlled fare matching, aggressive advertising and predatory tactics.

The most important items listed above are cost reduction and the development of the competitive tools. Although cost reduction has not provided the incumbents with comparable cost level to the new-entrants, the cost reductions have been, nevertheless, quite effective if one compares the U.S. majors with those of Europe.

To conclude, one can infer that during deregulation in a market competition intensity increases usually as the number of weak carriers increases. Carrier weakness is then escalated by poor management through too optimistic expansion or leveraged buy-outs that exceed financial resources. In such environment the larger financially strong carriers will attack the weaker ones in the hope of pushing them out of markets trying to secure faster growth.

Operations strategy

Routing

New-entrants' route strategies have been along four general types (Meyer and Oster, 1984, p.129): (i) turnaround; (ii) single hub; (iii) multiple hub; and (iv) independent markets. The difference between turnaround and independent markets is that the latter is enroute multistop itineraries while turnaround markets are served with frequent non-stop flights. The way of classification presented in this book is taking into account the route lengths and the market-sizes, as these have much impact on the overall strategy of the new-entrant and is in that regard a better indicator of the new-entrants' strategic characteristics. Figure 4.8 shows these route dimensions for a hub and a direct service carrier. The direct service carrier has to select along the same dimensions as the hub carrier, that is what its haulage segments are going to be as well as the market size segments. The difference between the two is that the direct service carrier has to determine whether it is going to emphasise non-stop or multi-stop strategy and whether it is going to operate route clusters or city to city strategy.

Route clusters are similar to hubs, except the carrier does not operate arrival and departure banks and has usually many clusters with relatively few nodes compared to hubs. An example of a carrier using this strategy is Southwest, while Air Florida was an example of the latter. The hub carrier has to select haulage lengths and market sizes that affects its aircraft selection and competition intensity that becomes greater as the markets get larger. In the figure the dotted circles depict a multi-hub strategy.

PeoplExpress altered its route strategy apparently to pursue its growth strategy. Its average length of haulage increased from 396 miles in 1981 to 630 miles in 1986. Route capacity changed from being relatively high in small markets to becoming very low in large markets. For most of its operating life the carrier operated a single hub at Newark. Then the carrier attempted to start a multi-hub operation, by acquiring Frontier, a move that failed due to incompatibility of the carriers and financial difficulties at the time of acquisition. The market size emphasis moved from small to medium size to large markets in the last two years of operations.

A different strategy was adopted by Southwest. Its haulage has remained short-haul through the years, although, the average stage length has increased slowly from 265 miles in 1979 to 378 in 1992. The carrier does not operate hubs although operations cluster around many cities.[88] In terms of strategy dimensions the carrier has maintained its emphasis on high route capacity, roughly one type of operations with some cargo service and no-frills service in terms of amenities on board, but free baggage.[89] It is apparent that Southwest has rooted its strategy on firmly grounded beliefs that it is not ready to drift away from. The strategic philosophy of Southwest is to grow slowly, stick to return services, avoid full-fledged hubbing, enter secondary markets and stay away from the big hub cities, offer high quality but few service amenities at very low fares.

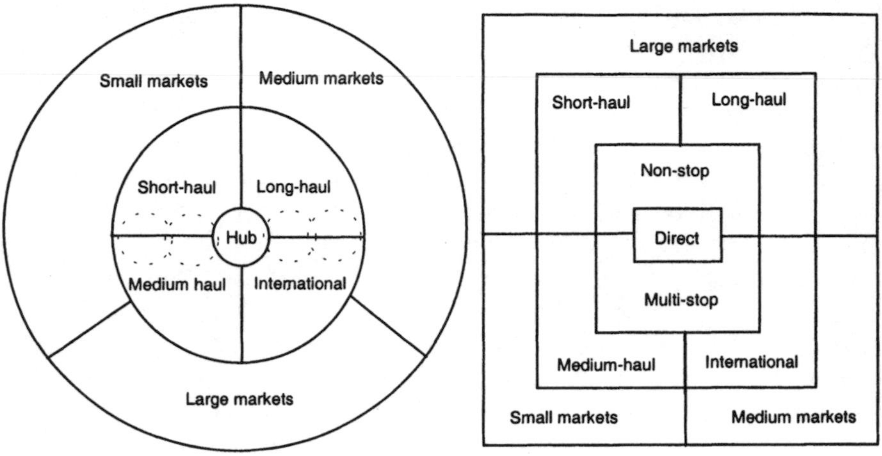

Figure 4.8 Route strategy decision dimensions

America West's route strategy was one of hubbing from the outset. The original hub was in Phoenix Arizona and soon other hubs at Las Vegas and Columbus, Ohio were added. The carrier entered routes usually with high capacity, although, its emphasis on entering large markets has limited the route capacity offered due to infrastructure limitations. The carrier offers cargo service and does some charter work.

It is important to realise that a carrier's strategic drift can be away from successful initial route strategy due to fast growth or goal change. Figure 4.9 shows in what directions three major new-entrants have drifted during their operating life. All the carriers drifted towards increase in average haul due to growth related segment additions, a conclusion supported by their tendency to move into larger markets. The carriers do, however, differ on the hubbing issue, the service dimension and the route capacity dimension. The trade-off by entering larger markets is that the carrier's market-share in terms of route capacity will be much less than that in secondary markets due to more competition and infrastructure barriers.

The important aspect of most new-entrants' strategies has been the emphasis on low costs and low fares. This emphasis has affected their route strategy because it requires the carrier to reach a high load-factor due to higher break-even seat-factor. In short-haul markets the new-entrants have often reached this target by enlarging the markets they have entered by luring people out of cars and buses, and by offering very high frequency and low-fares.

The new-entrants have been less successful on long-haul routes. In addition many new-entrants have avoided the densest routes to avoid incumbents retaliation as most emphasise long-haul domestic routes. Thus, one hears very frequently the new-entrant's CEO talk about avoidance of the incumbent's domain. Many new-entrants started out with this policy but changed it as they had reached larger size. This was what characterised America's West, People's Express and Southwest's route strategy. To begin with they entered under-served cities, with low fares and high frequency avoiding the major's hub cities and head on competition. As PeoplExpress and America West grew larger they altered their strategy and entered high-density routes served by the majors causing higher competition intensity.

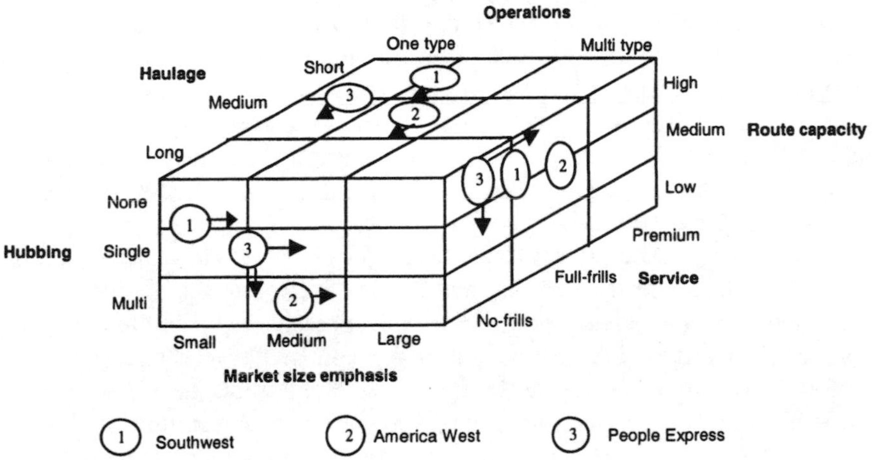

Figure 4.9 Route and service strategy dimensions

Southwest, although more reluctant to change its basic philosophy, seems to be doing the same by its 1993 entry into the Washington DC market at Baltimore that puts it head on with the financially weak USAir. America West moved into the incumbents' domain by entering the New York City market (JFK, La Guardia and Newark), Baltimore/Washington and Honolulu. Their resulting problem was not only increased competition but also a problem of gaining customer recognition in these larger markets.

PeoplExpress started off by serving secondary markets from the under-utilised Newark airport and then move on to initiate head on competition (1984) with the incumbents by entering Chicago O'Hare, Cleveland, Denver, Detroit, Los Angeles, Miami and Minneapolis. In the following two years more competitive markets were entered intensifying the threat to the major's even further. Similarly, America West selected secondary markets until 1987 when it entered Chicago O'Hare, Baltimore, New York's JFK, Philadelphia and Portland. Southwest, on the other hand, has been much more relaxed in entering primary markets. It entered Detroit in 1987, Denver in 1983, Indianapolis in 1989 and Los Angeles in 1984. True to its strategy the carrier entered Washington's Baltimore instead of Dulles and Chicago's Midway instead of O'Hare. Southwest and America West were main competitors on more than 50 percent of their routes in 1987. Perhaps that explains the reason for America West's decision to enter non-Southwest type of routes. Regardless of this America's West financial problems increased after the shift in strategy, just as occurred at PeoplExpress.

In the mid-eighties the notion was that the rule for new-entrant's success was to start a hub in an unhubbed city. This was clear at the time looking to the two most successful new-entrants PeoplExpress at Newark and America West at Phoenix. In the nineties the impression became that the costs associated with hub structures excluded the ability of an airline to gain an ultra low cost structure in order to be competitive with Southwest and similar airlines (Airline Business, 1993). Other carriers pursued this route strategy also with differing success: Midway at Chicago's Midway, Republic at Detroit, Memphis and Minneapolis and Air California at John Wayne airport in Orange County California.

When hub traffic increased inefficiencies resulted. These are primarily due to time lags between arriving and leaving banks causing lower aircraft utilisation and increased waiting time for passengers. This reduces the passenger's Units of Satisfaction opening a gap in the market that can be exploited by direct service airlines such as Southwest. In view of how profitable and strong Southwest has become as a competitor and hubs inefficient as a competition tool against such carriers, some incumbents like Continental have selected to establish their own Southwest clones (CalLite, now defunct) in order to protect their territory. This may be the main new feature of the incumbent's strategy in retaliation to new-entrant carriers. Another way would be to dissolve the bank concept of the hubs creating a more constant random flow to and from the hubs resulting in greater fleet efficiency. But such a strategy will not solve the passenger waiting time problem that will remain unresolved making the incumbent's market-share vulnerable to attack by the direct service carriers. Furthermore, such hub carrier strategy will cause a reduction in load-factors as fewer passengers will find it convenient to wait long hours for flights, making it necessary to shed flights to low density destinations. However, incumbent's exit from low-density routes can be kept in the network by allowing feeder carriers to take over the routes.

The majors are leaving more of their secondary markets to the feeder carriers, although the inefficiencies of small aircraft operations will not lead to the necessary reduction in fares to stimulate the markets to the same degree as Southwest has been able to do. Thus, leaving the incumbent's route system still vulnerable. As a result the most viable solution for the incumbent would be to establish a 'Southwest' clone tying together the short-haul nodes in the structure where it is viable for jet operations leaving no opening for Southwest. At the same time the incumbent can consolidate its route structure by concentrating on high density, long haul and international routes.

Equipment

New-entrants' equipment strategy can be divided into four main directions: (i) acquisition of older second-hand aircraft; (ii) leasing of second-hand aircraft; (iii) leasing of new aircraft; and (iv) acquisition of new aircraft. The strategies had much to do with their associated costs. The costs were usually analysed in terms of up-front capital needed, the terms at which such capital could be obtained and the availability of leased aircraft to the new-entrants (more if excess capacity is in the market). Furthermore, as practically all the new-entrants tried to minimise costs, fleet homogeneity was an issue. For some aircraft types it could be a problem to acquire enough aircraft of a type, as was the case with Fokker F28 and BAC1-11. The first strategy is the lowest cost and most viable on short-haul routes where the higher fuel consumption of older aircraft was less of a factor than on long-haul routes.[90] The buying strategy turned out to be useful for many new-entrants when it came to raising capital as their fortunes turned bitter, as debt could be secured on the equipment or it sold and leased back.[91]

The second strategy was to lease used aircraft. These were usually aircraft repossessed by leasing companies from bankrupt or troubled airlines or returned at the end of the leasing period by the original lessor. The new-entrant would then get a very good leasing rate, making it possible to keep the cost structure at a minimum. The third strategy of leasing new aircraft was not used very much by new-entrants, probably due to the leasing company's reluctance to place brand new aircraft into the hands of high-risk ventures. It was a totally different story when it came to return equipment whose usable-life had been mostly consumed. The fourth strategy to buy brand new aircraft has not been utilised much due to new-entrants' lack of capital or credibility in financial markets. This is of-course a different story for the established new-entrants such as Southwest that has been launching customer for some B737 types. Another carrier KIWI placed an order for 11 Rombac's BAC1-111's against an equity capital injection from the manufacturer of $1 million.

The most remarkable strategy and most influential in the nineties was ultra high aircraft utilisation on short-haul routes. This cost saving strategy has been mastered by Southwest Airlines by achieving fast turnaround at gates usually around 15 to 20 minutes compared to at least 45 minutes for the hub operating competitors. This allows Southwest to operate fewer aircraft to produce a comparable output of a competitor operating more aircraft. A low aircraft utilisation increases cost structure dramatically as more aircraft are required, crew, maintenance and management staff. Thus, if the airline can gain greater utilisation from aircraft it will achieve lower cost structure instantly, other factors remaining the same.

Code sharing/interlining/feeding

Many new-entrants avoided interlining in order to maintain as low a cost-structure as possible. Interlining was, however, highly important for the regional based new-entrants as they were already generating a large portion of their passenger flow by interlining with the large majors. Thus, it was only logical that they maintained this relationship after jet-operations started. These carriers kept, however, low profile in order to be able to work with the incumbent rather than against. Empire, for example, generated 42 percent of its passengers from interlining in 1981 and 38 percent were interlined from Empire to other airlines. Air Wisconsin had even higher proportion or seventy five percent in each direction. Midway generated only 8 percent of its traffic through interlining, while Air Illinois gained 65 percent (ATW, 1982c).

The general rule is that carriers operating to and from a hub airport dominated by a major carrier have high proportion of their passengers interlining with such a carrier. Thus, it is necessary for the new-entrant carrier to have an interlining agreement in order to maintain adequate load. A carrier such as Southwest, on the other hand, offering point to point service and operating only small hubs where it is the dominant carrier is not dependent on interlining. However, carriers mixing international and domestic operations need to offer interlining as large portion of the international passengers need to get on to other destinations. Hence, carriers such as Air Florida had to offer interlining, but thirty percent of their passengers interlined from other carriers and twenty percent to other carriers (ATW, 1982c).

After a change in CRS regulation on neutrality, feeder carriers that interlined with the incumbents experienced a drop in display priority on CRS. The result was increased emphasis on marketing agreements with incumbents in order to gain code sharing. Code-sharing is, therefore, effectively an accepted loop-hole in the regulation that resurrects the feeders that experienced dramatic drop in demand after the regulation change, but at the same time pushed the feeders into the arms of the incumbents that gained more power over them.[92] Code sharing has, as a result, brought immense problems to the code-sharing feeder partner. In fact it is stated that no code-sharing feeder will survive a sudden termination of a code-sharing pact. Thus the code-sharing agreement is comparable to the 'one big customer' problem frequently cited as one of the reasons for company bankruptcy.

In order to reduce the dependency on one incumbent major, some of the independent feeder airlines have made more than one code-sharing agreement. Air Midwest, for example, had code-sharing agreement with the Texas Air airlines and Trans World in 1988. The real meaning of code-sharing and the CRS bias regulation for a new-entrant is to foreclose a non-code-sharing new-entrant's ability to reach the majority of incumbent's passengers using a hub airport, due to the ease and convenience for the passengers to use a code-sharing partner. Furthermore, a flight terminating at a hub airport may actually be proportionally more expensive than a through flight, thus, reducing the passenger's fare incentive to use a non-partner's flight for the onward journey out of the hub.

The incumbents, in order to secure their feed, set the system up so that the feeder could not change partners. Through equity injection and outright acquisition the incumbents then set out to gain full control of their feeder airlines. Furthermore, it made sense for the incumbent to make initial agreements with more than one feeder carrier although the feeder's routes overlapped. Then as the feeder was depended on the code-sharing traffic the major could consolidate the traffic by either terminating the agreement and force the code-sharing partners it did not want to co-operate with into bankruptcy, or make an acquisition offer. The reason for such moves would be to control the feed in the hub area by eliminating independent commuter carriers and make it harder for other competing majors to gain foothold in the area. Code sharing, is viewed positively by the public and regulatory authorities as it does provide small communities with linkages to hubs, services that would not be viable otherwise.

Code-sharing agreements have led to frequent lawsuits, where the feeders claim that the incumbents are trying to push them out of business, often in an attempt to favour one partner over another or plainly to acquire the feeder carrier cheaply. Presidential, one of the noted start-up new-entrants, made code-sharing pacts first with Continental and then with United. The agreement with Continental 'wasted' management time as the carrier moved its operations from Dulles to Newark after the PeoplExpress acquisition. Harold Pareti Presidential's CEO estimated that the carrier's loss was in the vicinity of $30 million due to lost traffic centred around the Continental feed. In order to re-establish traffic, Presidential entered a code sharing agreement with United which it later claimed to have pushed the airline to bankruptcy. The reason, claimed by Pareti, was that United overtook some of the more lucrative routes in Presidential's route system (Airline Executive, 1990b).

Code sharing can be a factor in regional based new-entrant's demise especially if franchise-type marketing alliances accompany it. Although, it is not a one isolated cause of failure, it plays a large role in making the code-sharing feeder vulnerable due to the dramatic effect the cancellation of the code-sharing agreement has on the traffic levels of the smaller code-share partner. The regional based new-entrants did not have much choice, due to their mixed fleet and high costs, but to avoid competition with the incumbents. Thus code sharing was the only way to forge growth but at the same time the carrier's lost their identity. A carrier that looses its traffic and identity will not survive for long. The relationship with the incumbent is, therefore, a one way street full of risks, especially if the smaller code-sharing carrier is gaining from a marketing agreement that provides favourable slots and airport facilities that will be revoked if the agreement is revoked.

As some of the new-entrants became very large they needed feed such as any other major carrier. PeoplExpress, America West and Midway needed feed as they set out to be independent hub operators rather than feeder carriers, unlike most of the regional based new-entrants. PeoplExpress lacked feed to its Newark base, but gained from the vicinity of La Guardia and John F. Kennedy airports. In order to gain presence in other regions the carrier acquired Britt and PBA shortly before its demise. America West on the other hand started to feed itself from scratch by acquiring DHC-Dash 8s in 1986. America West did sign a feed agreement with Northwest Airlines in 1985 whose purpose was to provide the latter carrier with feed at Los Angeles for international flights to the Far East and at Phoenix for the Minneapolis hub, Detroit and Milwaukee (ATW, 1985a). The agreement was not in the spirit of traditional feeding agreements at the time as America West was not sacrificing any of its independence and Northwest was looking for feed to its international routes first and foremost.

Although, feeding is necessary for a large hub airlines in order to maximise their potential loads, new-entrants have usually not adapted the incumbents' strategy of creating a network of feeders carrying their name. New-entrants have rather been feeders themselves or fed themselves if necessary.

Marketing strategy

Pricing

Pricing strategy is important in air transport, but at the same time very restricted in terms of viable options for differentiation. Airlines can divide the aircraft into different product sections and the same product can be differentiated into price categories by attaching restrictions to the fares offered. Hence, a major differentiation becomes troublesome for individual airlines that are seeking to establish themselves on price or uniqueness. This is especially so for new-entrants because the basic airline product, the use of a seat from point A to point B, does not play any great importance to the passenger's ultimate benefit from a trip. Thus, it is no wonder that the PeoplExpress[93] low-fare, no-frills product became as popular as it did. The reason is that for the low-end of the market, price is the most important part of the decision to fly. However, if the full service competitor can match the fare and provide frequent and convenient departure times, the passenger will of course select to be pampered for no extra charge with 'free' meals and baggage allowance. Therefore, an airline can not assume customer loyalty to any degree if the passenger can buy a better or cheaper product elsewhere.[94] In fact a carrier can only assume customer loyalty as long as it provides consistent high quality product at similar or lower fare than the competitors, that is either superior or at least not of a lesser quality. Furthermore, the passenger has the short-term view of not considering the long-term effect of his decision, meaning that he will select the incumbent if it lowered its fares, although it will lead to the exit of the new-entrant causing an increase in fares again. It is the tendency of the higher cost carrier to raise its fares as soon as a lower-cost carrier has been pushed out of the market. This erroneous consumer behaviour will always be present due to imperfect information and the tendency to get as much for the money as possible although that will be a short-term privilege.

The early new-entrants attempted to provide low fares, peak and off-peak, as their primary differentiation feature. Such fares had proved to be highly advantageous for pre-deregulation intrastate carriers such as PSA and Southwest that were small low-cost carriers. Such fare structure was simple enough for the passengers to know what his approximate fare would be next time they travelled and the travel agents would not have to find the fares in the CRS, but could refer to the airline's tariff with confidence. A schedule listed in the CRS that included the tariff was usually enough. Southwest and PeoplExpress are the most noteworthy carriers that used this fare strategy and Southwest still does. These were, however, not the only fare strategies adopted by new-entrants.

Other fare strategies adopted by the new-entrants, were: (i) low overall fare regardless of prevailing fares; (ii) fare adjusted to the competition in each market; and (iii) 'normal' fares for premium service. If capacity and product characteristics enter the fare equation the strategy becomes something along these lines: (i) low fares, high capacity relative to market size and homogeneous but reliable product;[95] (ii) similar fares as the competition and low capacity in the market;[96] and (iii) marginally lower fares, low capacity in the market and high quality product.[97] America West, PeoplExpress and Southwest all followed the low-fare, low-cost, strategy and initial entry into secondary markets that are overcharged, under-served or both and served by higher cost carriers. Air Florida altered its fares according to the competition in each market leading to less market stimulation than Southwest and PeoplExpress generated with their comparatively low entry fares. Air Florida's strategy was among other factors due to its higher cost structure compared to PeoplExpress and other comparable start-up new-entrants. The low fares of PeoplExpress and Southwest reflect their low cost structures, while Air Florida and Midway, with higher cost structure, had to maintain higher yield in order to account for their higher costs. Due to Midway's high market-share at Midway airport an uncongested Chicago airport, it was able to charge higher fares, especially, due to the airport's easy reach from Chicago compared to O'Hare. This may be one of the reasons why Midway survived longer than PeoplExpress under deregulation despite the lower cost structure of the latter. The pricing strategies of the former intrastate carriers were, however, derived from pre-deregulation

Taking account of the intrastate example most start-up new-entrants took the stand of being price leaders. What is more they entered secondary markets and avoided primary markets dominated by the incumbents. Regional new-entrants, on the other hand, serving the incumbent's hub airports took the stand of keeping a low profile in terms of pricing and capacity in the hope of avoiding retaliation by the incumbents.[98] Whose ultimate peace keeping was to secure a marketing agreement with the incumbent.

Meyer and Oster (1984, p.134) concluded that there were three basic incumbent pricing strategies in retaliation to a new-entrant threat during early deregulation: (i) introducing a new matching low-fare category; (ii) adjusting the range of an existing fare category; and (iii) streamlining the fare offerings. The first strategy often resulted in a fare that was below cost for both the new-entrant and the incumbent. As the incumbent had usually much larger market-share its relative loss was much higher, as the new fare was usually offered for all capacity on the route. Then the new-entrant tended to raise fare levels until it was profitable for it but not for the incumbent because of its higher cost structure. The second strategy was to allow the new-entrant to build market-share until it became substantial and then match its fare. The third strategy was to match or under-cut the new-entrant but only for limited capacity restricted to the leisure market. In view of the fact that the incumbent had usually much higher frequency it could easily offer as many seats at partial capacity at the same fare as the new-entrant at full capacity. Furthermore, the incumbent often added frequency in order to leave as little incentive as possible for the consumer to travel with the new-entrant, and to pick up the extra demand that resulted from the fare reductions. The only reason a new-entrant carrier would survive such a strategy was if substantial portion of the incumbent's passengers were in the *Avoidance Contour* or *Negative Contour* of the model presented in Figure 4.4. A fourth reaction strategy, capacity controlled fares managed by yield management systems, became the norm after 1986. The system allowed the incumbent to adjust fares weekly or even daily according to the projected sales to higher paying passengers. One more reaction strategy by the incumbent was to match the new-entrant's fare without reducing the service. This became the 'unique selling point' (USP) in the mind of the customer that preferred full service over limited service at the same fare. Yet another fare strategy was to increase service without increasing the fares.

The advent of the yield management systems (YMS) caused a major change in fare strategy after 1985. American Airlines had developed their in-house CRS system to such an extent at that time that they had produced a highly advanced competition tool that allowed them to compete with other carriers by offering multiple fares on a single aircraft, sometimes up to 10 different capacity controlled adjustable fares. PeoplExpress could not compete effectively with this new development due to its unsophisticated computer reservation system. The off-peak and peak pricing was not effective anymore as American could undercut such fares easily for limited seating, generating high demand that would sell the low-fare seats easily and generate further sales at higher prices. People's Express chairman Donald Burr stated in an article (CIO, 1989) that the development of the sophisticated yield management system at American was the final bite into his airline, causing its collapse due to dramatic reduction in demand.

The picture for a new-entrant competing solely on price was, consequently, rather bleak after the advent of YMS, unless there was a strategy that counteracted the incumbents ability to match fares. The only strategy that appeared to have worked in the deregulated environment is that of Southwest Airlines whose simple fare-structure was, in combination with other factors, successful. As mentioned before, its strategy is basically to enter under-served medium to high fare routes, with direct service, high frequency, high quality and very low fare.

Service

The new-entrants selected three main strategies regarding service: (i) no-frills service in order to keep fares down; (ii) full-frills service in order to match service at lower fares; and (iii) premium service at 'normal' fares. The first strategy was important in order to keep costs down and being able to offer very low fares. The service amenities missing in such cases were usually hot meals, interlining and ticket offices. All of the airlines offered, however, meals although very low-cost carriers such as PeoplExpress charged the passengers for it. Such strategy, unbundling of the service features makes the advertised ticket price very low, but most passengers have to add the cost for checked baggage and meals if those service features are used.[99] The second strategy was to keep costs down but match the incumbents in terms of service features. Carriers following this strategy attempted to offer all the same features as the incumbent but at a lower price due to lower costs achieved through leaner organisation structure and lower pay scales. Thus, lower fares were the way they intended to eliminate the customers' incentive to select the incumbent for the sake of more service. However, when price equilibrium formed, particularly after the advent of capacity controlled fares, passengers would rather select the incumbent due to its name recognition and extra service for the same price. The third strategy, premium service, is costly for the carrier but is usually offered at first or business class prices. Again, the problem with that strategy is its segment, the business passenger, requiring high frequency in order to build loyalty. Furthermore, carriers depending on only one market segment, experience large weekly and seasonal fluctuations in demand.

To the contrary of what may be believed People's Express service levels may not have been the reason for their collapse as much as their explosive growth. Of course the quality of service suffered as a result of the fast growth, especially at the crowded terminal in Newark. Nevertheless, it must be taken into account that the customer segment PeoplExpress aimed for originally was ready to sacrifice traditional airline service amenities in exchange for low fares. The problem was very real when the incumbents offered the same fares but full service. In that case the passenger would of course maximise his benefit and choose the low fare and full service carrier. One of the reasons why America West has survived longer than PeoplExpress was that the carrier gathered for business passengers as well as the leisure passenger, avoiding weekly and seasonal traffic cycles to some extent. In 1987 the year PeoplExpress was absorbed into Continental, 50 percent of America's West passengers were business travellers (Fenger, 1987).

If we look beyond service features, at quality, new-entrants seem to have reached fairly good marks by their passengers if DoT complaint rates are used as an indicator. This conclusion is reached by excluding charter based new-entrants, having very high complaint rates. Fast growth does not seem to have been particularly harmful in terms of service quality, although, PeoplExpress complaint level is relatively high. Conversely other fast growing carriers had low complaint levels, carriers such as Muse and America West.

Market penetration

The matrix in Figure 4.10 shows the cost associated with CRS participation and TA emphasis. There are four combinations possible: (i) emphasise TA and participate in a CRS; (ii) emphasise TA but not participate in a CRS; (iii) de-emphasise TA but participate in a CRS; and (iv) de-emphasise TA and not participate in a CRS. For a low-cost, low-fare new-entrant it would become a major cost as percentage of total ticket price to pay both booking fees and TA's commission. The new-entrant will, therefore, have to decide what distribution strategy it wants to select on the basis of distribution costs. The lowest cost new-entrants tried to circumvent CRS use. For example, PeoplExpress did not use commercial CRS until after its Frontier acquisition in 1985. Furthermore, Southwest[100] was only listed on CRS, meaning that travel agents could check its flight schedules but bookings had to be made with Southwest directly through the phone system. Such strategy allowed the carriers to avoid booking fees that added on TA's commission amounted to a considerably greater proportion of their ticket price than that of the large majors were fares tended to be higher and better controlled through yield management systems.

It is clear that the new-entrants will have a problem surviving with only their own distribution system (phone-reservations, Internet reservations) as the newest action by the commercial CRS is to refuse carriers to be only listed on their CRS. Meaning that new-entrants using this feature pay for lowest-level participation or disappear from the system. This move alone will raise the new-entrants' cost structure unless other strategies are adopted. So in the future it is hard to see that new-entrants will be able to avoid the CRS and circumvent the TA to any large degree as their size increases.

		Commercial CRS Emphasis	
		Yes	No
TA's Emphasis	Yes	High	Medium
	No	Medium	Low

Figure 4.10 Travel agent and CRS cost matrix

PeoplExpress, Southwest and Air Florida depended almost entirely on the phone system, employing a large force of telephone-sales people. The systems worked adequately to begin with, but the problem starts when the growth level is high and special promotions occur causing major peaks. This causes excessive demand on the telephone reservation system leading to frustrated customers and a 'bad service' mark. This became the single greatest customer barrier at PeoplExpress, as well as at Air Florida during the latter part of their life-cycles. Attempting to circumvent this problem, PeoplExpress had a stand-by option for passengers creating an independence of booking systems from both CRS and telephone reservations.[101] PeoplExpress, nevertheless paid commission to travel agents if passengers wanted to use them, but the necessity was at a minimum. This sort of a service was no problem for students and tourists on flexible schedule but less desirable for business travellers and passengers interlining with other airlines.[102]

Another important issue of the new-entrants' distribution strategy is TA commission level (*see* Table 4.4). The commission level can work as a tool to make the airline more attractive to the TA by offering higher commission than the competition or more free travel, which the TA can use to reward their best customers, or use for staff. Those new-entrants that are not emphasising TA as their primary distribution outlet are consequently paying less commission as can be seen from the level of commission paid as percentage of revenues by Southwest Airlines.[103]

Table 4.4 Airlines' travel agent commission as percent of revenues

	Commission as percentage of revenues				
	1982*	1983*	1989	1990	1993
New-entrants					
America West			7.6	7.9	8.5
Air Wisconsin			8.4	8.1	
Empire			7.7	10.7	
Horizon			7.4	7.1	7.7
MGM			7.6	7.7	
Midway			8.8	8.2	
Southwest	4.99	4.22	6.3	6.3	6.5
Air Cal	6.57	6.48			
Capitol	8.11	3.28			
PSA	6.36	5.90			
World	15.66	8.58			0.6
Incumbents					
American	7.08	7.72	9.6	9.9	10.1
United	7.35	7.56	14.7	16.8	19.6
USAir	6.33	6.23	7.6	7.5	8.8
Northwest	8.54	8.84	17.3	17.9	19.6
Delta	5.72	7.00	10.7	10.4	11.3
Eastern	6.34	6.98	10.2	9.3	-

* Domestic commission only, while 1989 and 1990 levels include international. Northwest pays, for example, much higher commission on international travel than domestic, causing inflation in the percentages shown.

Source: Compiled from Air Transport World 1983 - 1994.

Customer retention

The origins of frequent flyer programs (FFP) can be traced to American Airlines launch of the American Advantage Scheme in 1981. The purpose of the program was to reward business flyers that flew frequently, often in economy class but paying higher fares compared to passengers using discount fares. In order to distinguish these passengers and retain their loyalty American developed the named program. The FFP have become a major strategic tool in maintaining passenger loyalty in a customarily low loyalty business. Furthermore, the programs have enabled the airlines to identify an important target group for promotion purposes.

Figure 4.11 shows clearly the importance of frequent flyers to an airline in terms of number of trips. Those undertaking twelve or more trips per year, although being only 1.7 percent of the total number of flyers, generate 31.6 percent of the total number of trips. Not only do these passengers fly more, they also pay higher fares. Thus, it is natural for any airline to try to maintain their loyalty.

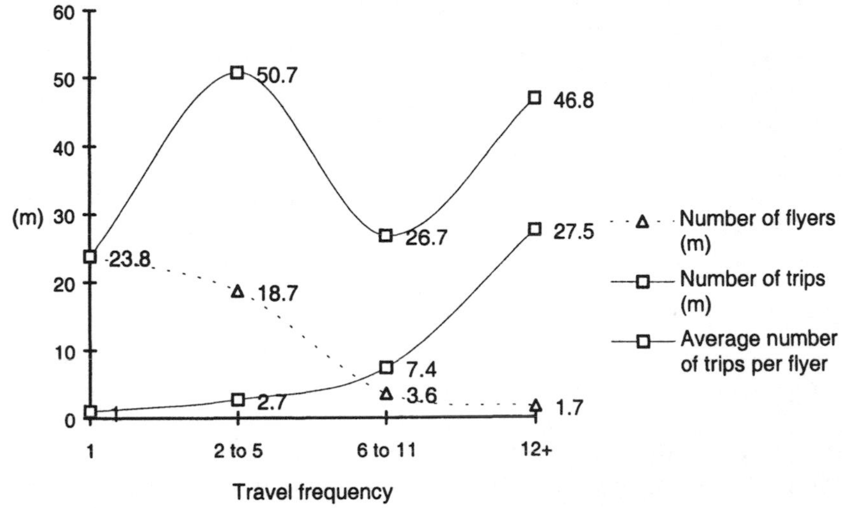

Figure 4.11 U.S. Travel frequency by air in 1985

Source: Compiled from Lloyds Aviation Economist, February/March 1986.

Frequent flyer programs (FFP) are often cited as one of the obstacles to effective competition by smaller carriers and new-entrants. This is embodied in the fact that a passenger is prone to select a carrier that is included in his or her FFP often without checking if lower fares or more convenient schedule exists, all for the purpose of earning 'mileage' points flying on behalf of the employer, to be claimed as personal 'rewards.'

Thus, the higher the mileage the more lavish destination and class of travel can be selected, making exotic holiday destinations important for the carrier in order to increase the popularity of its FFP. This fact alone makes the FFP of new-entrants unappealing to the business passenger. As a result, it is of a primary importance for new-entrants to gain access to a link-up with the FFP of larger airlines, by securing a 'joint marketing agreement' and include a tie-in with the larger carrier's FFP, reducing the disadvantage of small size. Table 4.5 shows examples of such tie-ins in the past between new-entrants and incumbent carriers. Frequent flyer programs of larger carriers are obviously of greater benefit to the user, supporting further the stronghold of large-market share carriers.

Table 4.5 New-entrants' FFP tie-ins in 1987

New-entrant/Regional	Program tie-in
Midway	Canadian International Airlines and Air New Zealand
Air California	American Advantage/Northwest Orient Free Flight Programme
Mid-Pacific Air	Continental One Pass/Northwest Orient Free Flight Programme
PeoplExpress	Continental One Pass
Air Midwest	-
New York Air	-
America West	Northwest Orient Free Flight Programme
Business Express	Delta Automated Mileage Programme
Express One	-
PSA	TWA Frequent Flight Bonus Program/USAir
Air Wisconsin	United Airlines Mileage Plus
Aspen	-

Source: Compiled from Travel & Tourism Analyst (1987).

Market-share

The airline industry has placed market-share strategy high on the agenda, based on the assumption that 'survival' as well as profitability depended on large proportional market-share. However, it can be argued that market-share strategy will lead to cut throat price competition leaving the whole industry worse off. Another argument is that building market-share for the sake of market-share, can not work, simply because the resulting increase has to be substantiated by other factors such as relative product quality, niche-marketing or cost leadership. In order to cast some light on what argument is nearest to the actual fact in air transport markets, the U.S. General Accounting Office (GAO, 1991) performed a detailed study on the impact of market-share on fares. A general finding associated with the arguments produced above, was that market-share actually affects pricing in such a way that a 23 percent market-share advantage due to a rise in enplanements was associated with 2 percent higher fares on the average.

The GAO (1991, p.6) produced an econometric model on the *Effects of Airline Market Concentration and Barriers to Entry on Airfares*. The model showed that a 65 percent increase in an airline's average enplanement shares at the airports on a route was associated with 21percent higher market share. Furthermore, if the largest competitor of a given airline increased its enplanements share by 45 percent it caused a 6 percent decline in market-share on a given route. The model implied as well that an airline's market share tended to be higher if it owned a computerised reservation system that was dominant at the endpoint cities and had a large proportion of the gates in the same cities (GAO, p.6). However, if the largest three carriers increased their enplanement share by 65 percent it would lead to 15 percent higher fares on the routes involved, compared to a non-significant increase in fares for the other airlines (GAO, p.7). Comparing the GAO findings with the *PIMS* (Buzzell, Gale and Bradley, 1987, p.76) one can see that there is a similarity, supporting the GAO results. Market leaders (largest three) in the *PIMS* database were enjoying average return on sales of 12.7 percent, compared to 4.5 percent for firms that ranked 5th or less in market-share. This indicates that market-share leaders enjoy a price premium compared to the smaller share businesses.

Table 4.6 Comparison of incumbents and new-entrants market-share in excess of 10 Percent at airports

Airline	1981				1986				1991			
	Market-share intervals in percent (number of top 50 airports)											
	10-30	31-50	51+	Tot	10-30	31-50	51+	Tot	10-30	31-50	51+	Tot
New-entrants												
Southwest	3	0	2	5	3	2	1	6	6	1	3	10
America West	-	-	-	-	3	1	0	4	2	2	0	4
Midway	0	0	1	1	0	0	0	0	0	0	0	0
PeoplExpress	0	0	0	0	2	1	0	3	-	-	-	-
PSA	3	0	0	3	5	0	0	5	-	-	-	-
Republic	7	0	0	7	1	1	1	3	-	-	-	-
Incumbents												
United	14	3	0	17	9	3	0	11	11	3	1	15
American	18	1	0	19	11	2	1	14	18	2	4	24
Delta	14	3	1	18	11	2	1	14	11	3	3	17
USAir	7	1	2	10	5	2	1	8	8	2	7	17
Trans World	10	3	0	13	1	0	1	2	1	0	1	2
Continental	4	1	0	5	1	1	1	3	2	2	2	6
Eastern	11	7	0	18	12	4	0	16	5	1	0	6

Source: Compiled from Maldutis 1991.

Referring back to Porter's theories, he stated that rivalry would increase as growth levelled off and companies started to strive for growth by snatching customers from each other. Hence, the airlines invite intense 'rivalry', as high fixed cost is a characteristic of airlines creating strong pressure to fill capacity, in other words to maintain high utilisation. If excess capacity is present as has been in the airline industry from 1990, fare war will occur if one competitor disrupts the fare equilibrium. This is because the reacting competitor can not stay inactive under the threat of loosing market-share. In addition, if firms are many or quite similar they tend to enter intense rivalry in order to win market share, battling for the same customers, especially if the industry has low customer loyalty. If there is an undisputed leader, he can induce discipline if there is an attempt by the weaker player to disrupt the fare equilibrium. Such discipline can be in the form of threat to dump prices in a hub city of major importance to the disciplined player, hence, initiating a fare war.[104]

When looking at the new-entrants in terms of market-share one can quickly assess that large market share at airports is important in order to fend of retaliatory action on behalf of the large incumbents and also in order to maintain higher yield. In fact new-entrants that gained dominant market-share at one or more airports tended to survive longer and enjoy greater overall success over those that did not.[105] This is clearly apparent if one examines Southwest, Midway, PeoplExpress and America West, which all gained large market-shares at secondary airports near to large cities. In view of this finding it is apparent that market-share as such does matter in the overall ability of the airline to earn higher returns. Yet, it is also apparent that high city-pair market-share is important in addition too high market-share at the airports on each end. This is exactly what Southwest has practised in its route strategy, to cluster their operations at many secondary airports aiming for substantial market-share at each airport served.[106]

Then the question of the impact of relative quality on market-share remains. Namely whether high quality carriers are gaining market-share for that reason rather than building market-share entirely on price cuts and use/abuse of dominant position. Southwest had an average complaint rate of 0.70 complaints per 100.000 passengers from 1981 until 1991, while America West had 1.73 from 1984 to 1991, and Midway 2.47 from 1984 to 1991. The average for all jet-operating airlines from 1981 to 1991 was 3.22 and 3.63 for new-entrants, and from 1984 to 1991 it was 2.95 and 2.4 for new-entrants. All of the airlines are better than average except Midway that was slightly worse. Unfortunately exact complaint data was not available for all the operating years of the airlines involved, making comparisons and conclusions indicative. Still, there seems to be a relationship as no airline with complaint rate worse than the median (based on the average) survived for a substantial period of time with the exception of World (charters have been in and out of scheduled operations). The same goes for market-share as none of the carriers having worse than average complaint rates reached major status or near major status, except PeoplExpress.

The linkage between market-share and profitability has been established by Buzzell and Gale (1987) in their work on 'Profit Impact of Market Strategy' (*PIMS*). The causal link behind the relationship is not fully known, but they mention four possible underlying factors (p.73): (i) economies of scale; (ii) risk aversion by customers; (iii) market power; and (iv) a common underlying factor. A common underlying factor between ROI and market-share could be competent management. It is fairly well established that economies of scale are limited in air transport although other scale efficiencies are more prevalent. Risk aversion is based on the customer's tendency to select a product he or she firmly knows and feels comfortable with, while market power is nested in the ability to bargain more effectively with suppliers of services and products. These findings do hold in air transport as large market-share at one airport has usually created strong bargaining position of an airline.

Airports that have become 'hub' airports usually experience downgrading of their bond ratings as risk is considered to have increased (Doganis, 1992). This is based on the fact that if a dominating hub airline leaves the airport or fails, the airport will be seriously harmed. As a result the airport authorities may go into great lengths to avoid any such disastrous developments by giving concessions to the dominant carrier in the form of protection from competition and airport fee reductions under special circumstances. This ability of US airports is based on their private or county rather than government ownership. Market power is, therefore, conclusively a major force in the US air transport market.

The link between ROI and market share does not exclude small market-share businesses. Studies in the *PIMS* database (Woo and Cooper, 1982) show that such businesses can reach high ROI if they offer high relative quality narrow product lines and low total costs. Maldutis (1993) showed that the market-share of the largest six carriers went from 45.7 percent in 1979 to 78.0 percent in 1991. This is a considerably concentration, creating an effective barrier to entry at major airports.

Promotion and advertising strategy

In the early days the new-entrants gained considerable free promotion by being newsworthy. Carriers such as Southwest and Muse knew from the outset the importance of maintaining high profile in the media and integrated into their image a 'fun' element in order to keep the airlines in the news. Another method of gaining free media coverage was to offer a comparatively very-low promotional fare that would attract major media coverage, treating the new-entrant as the low fare saviour from the high fare incumbent, contrasting incumbent as the 'bad guy' exploiting the community (Levine, 1987, p. 480). The result, was an immediate presence in the market reducing substantially promotional and advertising costs. As entry by new carriers became more commonplace, new-entrant carriers began to exit markets and incumbents gained experience in dealing with the new-entrants, free media coverage played a lesser role in entry as well as in maintaining good-will for the new-entrant. As a result entry costs increased and new-entrants had to look very carefully on their promotion schemes.

New-entrant's promotion schemes are usually much weaker than those of the incumbents due to the smaller size of the new-entrant. Thus promotion has to be highly targeted in order to be effective. Braniff (II) for example emphasised personal visits by company sales people to travel agencies in destination cities in order to explain the company's plans and assure the agents that the new Braniff was a different story from the old Braniff. Such promotion is, however, very difficult for any airline due to the very many TA operating. As a result, such strategy can only work in a very concentrated fashion, for example, in a city market, which the airline is entering.

Promotion strategies have varied as much as the carriers involved. In order to give some examples one can name Braniff's (II) 1986 promotion 'Penalties Stink' in order to battle with American Airline's fares that had 50 percent penalty on date changes on their 30 day advance purchase fares. The promotion increased Braniff's load factor allegedly from 56.3 percent to 66.7 percent during the month following the campaign. The fare strategy had its cost, as yields dropped as a result (ATW, 1984b, p.47). This move by Braniff against the competitor's actions gives an example of a promotional strategy that became effective and met expectations of a segment of the market that wants to pay low fares but needs the flexibility of changing ticket dates. In fact marketing at new-entrant airlines, demands constant creativity without sacrificing profitability in order to stay ahead of slower moving incumbents.

Advertising by the incumbents soon battled the low-fare oriented advertising of the new-entrants, a diversion in strategy from the pre-deregulation emphasis on service. The incumbents were often able to rebuff an advertising campaign by a cost efficient low-fare new-entrant, by engaging in low-fare advertising. Often citing fares that did not actually resemble the real cost to the passenger due to imposed black-out periods, low seat offerings or continued advertising after the low-fare seats were sold out or black-out period in effect. As a result the new-entrant did not receive the market attention it should and the incumbent carrier had the opportunity to divert passengers to the higher fares on offer, knowing that a certain percentage of callers would actually accept a higher fare.

Branding and image

Airlines have had considerable difficulty creating an image that is unique and defensible, competing on service features for business or first class, but on price when it comes to economy class. How do the airlines then create their image and brand their products? New-entrants have allegedly placed less importance on image creation than crude advertising to stimulate demand. However, the low-cost structures geared toward low fares has not allowed the new-entrants' to spend much on image advertising per se. This has led to poor passenger retention as soon as a competitor matches or under-cuts the new-entrant's fares as large part of customers are bargain hunters. Having said this one can cite Southwest Airlines as an exception, a carrier that has considered its image carefully, just as its former competitor Muse Air did. These two airlines carefully created an image of 'fun,' as mentioned before. Such image, apparently, fits new-entrants quite well as the older established airlines will hardly follow suite. The image of 'fun' is geared towards the younger people and the 'baby boomers' that are entering the top layers of society and those that are bored with the 'sameness' that characterises airlines' image in general. Muse Air used in its inauguration advertising, airline 'personification' to position itself among the competition (Airliners, 1993, p.26)

> ...Southwest, with its irreverent approach, would be Bo Derek. Braniff International, projecting a grand dame, high fashion look would be Sophia Loren or Princess Grace. Texas International's zany peanut fares advertising made it a Suzanne Sommers or Goldie Hawn. American would be Dallas Cowboy football player turned business man Roger Staubach - confident, stable and almost too serious, while Delta could be the no-frills, humorless and literal coach Tom Landry. If this were accurate, then Muse Air was to be the Urbane, classy and smooth Peter Graves, Bill Blass, or even George C Scott.

The quotation above shows one aspect of Muse Air's image creation, namely that it was going to be humorous, as well as classy, such as its aircraft paint scheme portrayed with its signature style name. The interior was to begin with a single class layout with high profile leather seating and three lounge areas, designer made harmonising with flight and ground crew uniforms, and airport and boarding decor (Airliners, p.26). Legroom was generous, seating was pre-assigned and there was unique no-smoking policy on all flights. Whether the careful image creation was effective in differentiating Muse Air from the competitors spelled into greater demand is not clear. In the inauguration year load-factors were only 36 percent, rising to 47 percent in 1985, with 1983 peak of 51 percent. That is perhaps not poor in view of the carrier's emphasis of offering full service.

Strangely enough, PeoplExpress had originally a strong image as the 'peoples friend' that was on a crusade to beat the high fares of the big 'unfriendly incumbents,' but soon developing into an image of poor quality service. The created image worked enormously well for the carrier as long as it was able to offer a substantial price differential, despite the negative service image it soon earned. As soon as PeoplExpress started to enter other market segments such as the business segment, he initial concept of serving the low end of the market, 'People' became a liability and the 'old' image caused a conflict in the customers mind as to what the carrier stood for. Advertising was suddenly geared towards the business person, whose image of the carrier was rather poor in terms of quality, and the leisure traveller got the notion that the carrier was going up-market, cutting down on the fabulous offers it had been geared towards in the past. In this way the carrier endeavoured for something it could not get and alienated its old customer base in the process (Davidow and Uttal, 1989).

Financial strategy

Costs

Gialloreto (1988, p.50) proposed a model of 'U.S. industry airline carrier types' whose basis is very much grounded on cost strategy. *Type 1*, is high-cost, full-service; *Type 2*, low-cost, low-service; and *Type 3*, is low cost, low to medium differentiated service levels. The first type was the pre-deregulation type, while the second type was the opposite and characterising many new-entrants. The third type is low-cost as the second type but offering a differentiated product based on *Type 1*, full-service or 'premium service,' offered by Air Atlanta, Air One and similar. The fact of the matter is, however, as Gialloreto states that no airline selects the *Type 1* strategy in the deregulated environment and those that started out as *Type 1* tried to approach the *Type 2* concept. Thus, there are only two basic viable cost strategies available to new-entrants, to enter at low-cost and low service, in order to keep fares at a minimum, or to enter at low-cost but with differentiated product. The latter strategy is, of course, higher cost but the relative cost of producing the 'premium' product is relatively low compared to the *Type 1* incumbents. Some of the new-entrants went back and forth between *Type 2* and *3* strategies. Midway started Midway-Metrolink and became a *Type 3* carrier as a result, just as New York Air that increased service in order to match that of Eastern. In addition, PeoplExpress, the *Type 2* carrier, started to become a *Type 3* carrier by stepping up its service in order to gather for business travellers. America West started out by providing comparable service as the incumbents, thus, being classified as *Type 3* from the start. The model as such is useful for classification purposes of airlines, but it does not make a clear distinction between ordinary low-cost full service carrier and the quite different 'premium' service carrier. The operating costs, operating characteristics and marketing is different between the two groups, to such a magnitude that they should not be classified under the same group. Furthermore, the ordinary full-service carrier has enjoyed considerable success but premium-service carriers have had difficulties, so far.

As Meyer *et al.* (1984), have observed, the cost advantage that many new-entrant carriers have had over the incumbents is not as important as it may seem at first. The reason being that the new-entrant is likely to base pricing on the fully allocated costs, whereas, the incumbent is more likely to base it on the marginal costs. However, what needs to be observed as well is the importance of the incumbent's capacity in a market were a new-entrant appears. If the new-entrant offers a seat at a price of 50 and the incumbent has an average price of 70, the incumbent may be selling, lets say, 10 per cent of its capacity based on marginal pricing of 30. The problem for the new-entrant in this situation is that 10 per cent of the capacity sold at this very low price may be greater than the total capacity provided by the new-entrant in the market. Therefore, the new-entrant's pricing strategy falls 'between' at the price of 50 and the airline looses the potential price advantage. One apparent way of preventing this is for the new-entrant to select secondary routes served by a weak carrier where fares are relatively high and capacity low. Therefore, as the new-entrant enters the market it gains immediate superiority by offering lower prices and relatively high capacity. Thus, the incumbent will have problems immediately, as further increase in capacity will reduce load factors. Moreover, 'spiteful' behaviour by the incumbent will not pay unless the incumbent has greater staying power and reduction in fares by the higher cost incumbent, will harm the new-entrant's profitability.

Mergers

Airline acquisitions and mergers are usually costly for firms in terms of capital and management time. Especially if an acquisition deal does not materialise as happened when SAS was bidding for British Caledonian in the eighties. Another example was Horizon's unsuccessful attempt to merge with Cascade that was claimed to have cost Horizon $4 million during the process (ATW, 1986b). Furthermore, costs involved with bringing together different company cultures can drain the new entity, manifest in the incompatibility between PeoplExpress and Frontier, a highly unionised high cost carrier acquired by the former. Furthermore, an acquisition often brings with it problems in merging different strategies that are costly to change. If we keep to the Frontier example, the carrier had a strategy of full service that was not only costly to change in terms of alterations in operations (to no-frills) but also in terms of lost business when passengers used to the full service flocked into the arms of the competition, expecting a lower quality product from Frontier - PeoplExpress.

Southwest Airlines acquired the full service carrier Muse Air in 1985 and turned it into a separate entity called TranStar, but maintaining the full service characteristics of Muse Air. The carrier lost money and became a liability on Southwest that lost $9.2m in the first six months of 1987, after 55 quarters of straight profitability (Avmark, 1987b). As a result of these losses Southwest dissolved the carrier in 1987.

Mergers are usually justified in terms of reaching new markets, neutralising a competitor or achieving the 'necessary' critical mass in order to become profitable. These aims of the merger are usually fraught with contradictions as the shear increase in problems that are created by a merger sometimes leave the acquirer in a worse situation after the merger. Herbert

Kelleher of Southwest opposes the need for large size in order to be competitive (ATW, 1987, p.51)

> It is said you have to be a certain size to survive these days,...but we haven't been able to determine what that size is. [Southwest] tries to achieve mass in individual markets rather than on an overall basis,...

The importance of the already mentioned mergers was first and foremost strategic for the new-entrants involved. The benefit was, however, at large meagre, causing sudden increase in debt and increased vulnerability to failure.

Table 4.7 Acquisitions by new-entrant airlines

Airline	Acquisitions		
Southwest Airl.	Muse Air ('85)	Morris Air ('94)	
PeoplExpress	Frontier ('85)	PBA ('86)	Britt ('86)
Air Florida	Attempt for Air California		
Air Wisconsin	Mississippi Valley ('85)		
Braniff (II)	Florida Express ('87)		
PSA	Attempt for Braniff ('83)		
Midway	Air Florida assets ('84)	Fisher Brothers ('87)	Eastern's assets in Philad. ('89)
America West	Attempt for Eastern's Shuttle ('89)		
Horizon Air	Air Oregon ('82)	Trans Western ('83)	Attempt for Cascade ('85)

Source: Compiled from Air Transport World 1980 - 1994

In order to throw some light on the meaning of the Frontier, Britt and PBA acquisition for the downfall of PeoplExpress a detailed account will follow. One has to have in mind, though, that the acquisition was not the actual cause of PeoplExpress problems that led to its failure, it was rather one of the symptoms. PeoplExpress acquired Frontier in 1985 after a relatively short courtship. The carriers financial procedure for acquiring Frontier was by providing $95 million of the $307 million purchase price, while the rest was funded by cash and short-term investments of Frontier and Frontier Holdings. The acquisition of Frontier was accomplished by securing a bank approval to form a holding company. PeoplExpress Airlines the subsidiary then raised $125 million through joint extendible term securities and used $100 million of it to buy Frontier stock through PeoplExpress Holdings. The acquisition of the securities caused considerable uneasiness among People's banks. As a result, PeoplExpress made a public offering of Secured Equipment Certificates valued at $115 million (Lloyd's, 1986a). The results were used to pay off the banks that refused the redrawal of a revolving loan after PeoplExpress offered to pay it down given that the carrier could redraw in the third quarter of 1986. PeoplExpress acquired both Britt and PBA. The price for Britt was not disclosed but could have been in the vicinity of $25 million according to a SEC filing for $35 million public offering that was supposed to be loaned to PeoplExpress to restore funds, with the exception of $6.5 million, used for other purposes. PBA was acquired for $10 million (Airline Business, 1986, p.23).

The mergers undertaken limited unnecessarily PeoplExpress financial flexibility and increased the carriers perceived risk in the eyes of its financiers and customers. Soon afterwards PeoplExpress disappeared from the scene such as so many new-entrants before as well as after.

Summary

Air transport appears to be first and foremost market-share driven, which explains the reason for the low profitability and the intense rivalry. If Porter's Competition Model is examined, one finds that the threat of new-entry has been minimised by the development of various competition tools by the incumbents, while the bargaining power of suppliers and buyers is little and the threat of substitutes small. Although the four forces mentioned in the model do not explain the intense rivalry in air transport, other factors do such as: excess capacity, commodity nature of the product and the importance placed on market-share. The learning curve is not a main barrier to entry in air transport markets. Of greater importance are entry strategies and the identification of a sustainable niche.

During deregulation incumbents have learned effectively to compete with low fare, low cost new-entrants by price matching or undercutting for limited capacity only, optimised by sophisticated yield management systems. The only way for a new-entrant to compete is then to form an alliance with the incumbent or to enter a niche market that is defensible. Both of these options are difficult for the new-entrant as the co-operation with the incumbent is potentially dangerous for the new-entrant and to find a defensible niche market is difficult. The experience shows that new-entrants can operate without commercial CRS systems, as has been proven by Southwest, PeoplExpress and Morris Air. The problem starts when peaks occur in demand and the system can not handle the incoming calls. In such cases a CRS system accessible by TA would preserve the airline's good will.

The risks associated with entry are different depending on the background of the new-entrant, being highest for a start-up carrier and the lowest for an intrastate based new-entrant. Growth plays a major role in new-entrants' strategy. Many early new-entrants tried to maximise their size in the hope of becoming more competitive. This strategy was not proven to be useful. Successful new-entrants would rather try to identify a niche market and survive.

Growth can come from two sources: growth in demand from exogenous sources, or from strategic moves that transfer customers from one carrier to another. The latter source of growth is bound to increase rivalry in the market during stagnation or declining demand.

Darwin's Theory of Evolution explains well the tendency of the stronger airlines (spiteful incumbents) to harm themselves (fares below total costs) in order to harm others (new-entrants) more. The optimum end-result for the spiteful player would then be the death of the weak carriers, allowing the spiteful carriers to restore to strength (higher fares). This alternative theory approximates developments in the deregulated air transport market, although the underlying reasons behind the losses in the late eighties and early nineties may have a much more complexity behind it than this theory implies.

The prisoner's dilemma explains forceful reactions of incumbents to a new-entrant, moving all players to a worse financial state. This analogy provides for a similar line of thinking as the Theory of Spite, where a strong carrier may decide to forego short-term profitability for a long-term market power.

Customers do influence competition, although, their role is sometimes overlooked or ignored by the airlines. A model of Customer Reaction Contours is presented in order to explain how airlines ignoring service quality will lose market-share as a competitor with superior relative quality enters the market at a similar price.

The Henderson's 'market equilibrium disruption' analogy is used in order to explain a market's tendency to enter a condition characterised by 'price war.' It was found that in order to create a reasonable stability, niche marketing has to be possible. Researchers have stated that new-entrants should be concerned with differentiation rather than with capacity in the market. The problem with that is, however, the limited ability of a new-entrant to differentiate in any meaningful way.

There are five basic entry strategies mentioned: (i) at lower-cost; (ii) at lower fare; (iii) a niche market; (iv) with superior quality; and (v) with superior service. The combination of the first four seems to be the common trait of 'successful' new-entrants. The competition intensity apparently increases as more entry segments are added. Sequenced entry where the financial basis of the carrier is build before the next entry segment is added makes the carrier better prepared to fight the increased competition intensity associated with each added segment.

There are four general route strategies available to airlines. Two are most common after deregulation 'hubbing' and 'direct service'. The only 'successful' pre-1990 new-entrants' were direct service carriers. A strategy of short-haul, non-hub, no-frills service, seems to work well if the carrier sticks to the basic underlying philosophy. America West and PeoplExpress changed their successful basic philosophy and failed (America West emerged from Chapter 11 bankruptcy), while the successful Southwest has not done so in any marking way.

New-entrants have usually selected two pilot, fuel efficient, short-haul aircraft. Such airlines have also tried to maintain a homogenous fleet in order to minimise maintenance and training costs. In short, fleet strategy has been geared towards cost savings first and foremost.

New-entrants that have become feeding carriers for the majors have in most cases lost their identity and eventually been acquired by the incumbent. The change in the CRS regulation harmed the ability of feeder carriers to stay independent, thus, lessening their survival chances. New-entrants have found it difficult to cash-in on their lower cost structure due to the incumbents sophisticated yield management systems. The simple fare system is, nevertheless, in full swing at the successful carrier Southwest. Thus, it is apparent that the simple fare strategy is route dependent (short-haul, secondary markets) rather than unworkable as frequently cited by those looking at PeoplExpress collapse.

The new-entrants have selected three basic service strategies: (i) no-frills; (ii) full-frills; and (iii) premium service. The last type of service has not worked for the new-entrants in any form. The other two concepts have worked better with Southwest being an example of the former and Midwest Express of the latter. With regard to market penetration the new-entrants have had to decide whether to participate in a CRS and emphasise TA. The low-cost new-entrants tried to circumvent both of these options by setting up telephone booking systems. Such systems harmed the carriers' image and were inadequate as the airlines got larger.

New-entrants targeting the business segment have been at a disadvantage due to the majors' FFP that have secured the loyalty of business passengers. New-entrants' programs are usually smaller and less appealing in terms of exotic destinations to cash-in rewards. Furthermore, the new-entrants' route systems are more limited making it harder for the frequent flyer to build up mileage unless he travels to few destinations within the new-entrants' system. In order to account for this some of the new-entrants have entered into marketing agreements with other larger carriers where the two FFP are joined.

Market-share is important for new-entrants, especially, to gain a dominant share at a niche airport near a large catchment area or to gain dominant share on secondary routes. The low-cost new-entrants have emphasised prices in their advertising, making image building troublesome.

Two new-entrants, Southwest and Muse made fun a part of their image, which seems to work well for the new-entrants due to the reluctance of the majors' to follow suit. The early new-entrants got the image of being the people saviours from high prices, an image that soon changed into an image of poor quality. The free media coverage many new-entrants enjoyed at first disappeared, making entry costs higher and community exposure lower, especially when large markets were entered. Branding is concluded to be little used by airlines, although, names for business classes have been adopted. The sameness and limited differentiation possibilities make branding in air transport problematic. A change in basic strategy is a cause of brand conflict that occurred at PeoplExpress when it attempted to gather for business passengers.

Most new-entrants decided to offer lower fares than prevailed in order to exploit lower cost structure than the incumbents had. Simplicity in fare-structure and non-participation in CRS lowered costs and directed the passenger away from the travel agents that further reduced costs. Most new-entrants redirected their strategy towards using the CRS and travel agents as their size got larger and the craving for further growth overpowered their fundamental operating philosophies. The simple fare-structures worked well until American and other incumbent airlines initiated a highly efficient yield management systems that enabled them to manage their capacity in order to undercut or match the new-entrant's fares for limited capacity without lowering yields as much as before on new-entrant's competition routes.

Large market-share at large airports, is linked to new-entrant's longevity. This is especially important in terms of governing a secondary airport to a large city. New-entrants enjoyed free media coverage in the early days that reduced their entry costs in new markets. As deregulation progressed they had to spend more to make their presence felt. This was not as much of a problem in small cities but was a major problem when the new-entrant began operations to large cities dominated by the incumbents. New-entrants had very little to offer in primary markets besides fares. As a result they have not fared well in such markets at all, due to the incumbent's hard felt presence.

Code sharing has been highly troublesome for the regional based new-entrants due to their loss of identity and control over strategy. Many code-sharing new-entrants have been acquired by the incumbent partner indicating that the new-entrants may have had the 'big customer' problem often associated to failures. If the incumbent partner severs the relationship the feeder looses the majority of its customers overnight and is likely to fail as a result: one example being Air Wisconsin and another Presidential. To conclude, the customer is both better and worse off with code-sharing and feeding depending on how one views it. In terms of making equipment change and ticketing smooth the customer benefits but if the customer likes to know whether he has to change planes en-route he can not detect such equipment change under code-sharing unless he is informed, but that is often omitted by TA. The new-entrant, however, is in a similar situation as the customer, it needs the association with the incumbent to survive in the hub environment but that very co-operation is usually fatal in the long-term.

The effect of the merger strategy is discussed with detailed reference to the PeoplExpress case. The conclusion is that mergers are highly risky endeavours for new-entrants and unlikely to be successful unless the acquired airline is smaller and offering a similar product. It is concluded that internal sustainable growth, based on a long-term plan, is superior to the merger strategy.

To conclude, the *PIMS* (1987) showed that a superior product's effect was more important for lower-share businesses in terms of ROI. Thus, it is likely that a strategy of a superior product may be important for new-entrants. Not only that but also that superior perceived quality is necessary if market-share increase is to generate increased ROI. Thus, it is evident that new-entrants are unlikely to survive without the two, especially if one cites the successful new-entrants, Southwest in the U.S. and Virgin Atlantic in Europe.

---

63 The US Congress held hearings on a number of occasions that have resulted in regulation change concerning CRS and advertising in order to increase competition in an alleged 'concentrated' industry, by neutralising anti-competitive tools of the large carriers.

64 For such equilibrium to form, it seems that a ratio of 2 to 1 in market-share between the two competitors has to exist.

65 Furthermore, the second part of Southwest' strategy, to enter secondary markets, will soon be saturated as there are only so many markets available.

66 The best known application of this concept was by Milton Friedman, The methodology of positive economics, in: Essays in positive economics, University of Chicago Press, Chicago, Ill., 1953, p.22.

67 Market power is the ability of a firm to control market prices and other terms and conditions of supply, usually through dominant market-share.

68 In 1993 Delta retired 20 aircraft and lay-off 600 pilots, United made an agreement to defer and convert to options 49 aircraft orders, American cut 900 jobs and reduced its operation at unprofitable San Jose hub, which created an immediate opportunity for Southwest Airlines (*see* US cuts win confidence, *Airline Business*, May 1993, p. 10).

69 Based on Ansoff's (1987) 'Product/Market Expansion Grid.'

70 Saturation of the U.S. domestic market has definitely led to an intensification of competition and led the airlines to increase emphasis on international routes. Furthermore, the pressure on the government to provide 'deregulated' bilaterals has increased as a result, thus, leading to increased pressure on the international community to liberalise air transport policy in terms of access, fares and capacity restrictions. In such liberalised international markets US airlines are very competitive in terms of low unit costs.

71 It is assumed that all passengers enter at 0 or in the indifference contour or if with previous experience of the airline, in the expectancy contour, which two are in fact the same in the model. A passenger with prior experience of the airline can enter in the NC or the PC of the model and stay there or shift towards indifference, increased disapproval or approval.

72 Innovators are those that have to try new products early, regardless of their happiness with present product.

73 It is important to offer mileage exchange in order to break a passenger loyalty with a competitor.

---

74 A critical factor could be market-share, profitability, growth, etc.

75 It is an over generalisation that the business market is price inelastic. This market can in fact be segmented into the size of businesses the business passenger represents and the smaller segment is likely to be highly elastic, while large corporations use their bargaining power to gain volume discounts off air travel, either directly or through their travel agent.

76 Presidential identified a gap in the market out of Washington, but shortly after initiation of services both New York Air and United entered the market, thus, eliminating any advantage Presidential may have had.

77 Henderson is the Chairman of Boston Consulting Group and the list was derived from number of articles he has written. The list was composed by and appeared in Kotler,1988, p. 247 - 248.

78 This is the case for some past 1990 new-entrants, with KIWI being formed by ex-Eastern pilots that put up most of the start-up capital, and Reno being formed by ex-Midway staff.

79 One may allege that the fundamental objective of Air France and similar government owned giants was to provide employment, to which all other goals were secondary, including profitability, efficiency, service, quality and so on.

80 Examples include most of the independent feeder carriers and Empire, Air Wisconsin, etc.

81 The stated goal of Southwest is to get people out of their cars on short-haul routes.

82 This was the case with Braniff at its main base causing little loyalty of the community regardless of a long period of service, creating a gap for other carriers to fill.

83 In an economic system where behavioural freedom is almost limitless in economic terms, meaning that predatory behaviour is allowed or antitrust laws poorly enforced, there is going to be what is termed as 'economic natural selection'. The framework is important as a crude way to explain the behaviour of large powerful airlines in a market with weak airlines. The framework gives also simple explanation for the poor overall profitability in the US airline industry for the past decade. The theory derived from evolutionary biology,[83] uses the act of *spite* to explain the behaviour of firms that have market power in a competitive market of few. Spite is the behaviour trait of harming both oneself and another, in the belief that such an act will only lead to short-term loss but long-term gain as the competitor will be harmed more (*based on* Schaffer, 1989)

84 Branson has made uniqueness and quality of Virgin Atlantic his main priority. That airline is in fact the only new-entrant in the world combining all the features successfully. His philosophy comes clearly accross in the following quotation, where he compares his airline with a restaurant: 'If you run an independent restaurant, the way to beat McDonalds is to make sure all the little details are right - to make it unique and so special and friendly that people will go out of their way to go there.', (Independent, 1991).

85 It is assumed that airlines with consumer complaints less than 1 per 100.000 passengers are 'high' quality, while those having 1.1 to 5 to be 'medium' quality and those having 5.1 and greater to be 'low quality'. Note that quality does not indicate the level of service offered as Southwest is a high quality low service carrier!

86 For an interesting account of Frank Lorenzo's union busting, see: Jennings (1989); and Bernstein (1991). See especially pages 14-20 in Bernstein's book.

87 Fuel efficient, lower maintenance, two pilot aircraft. Many airlines tried to increase the homogeneity of the fleet.

88 In this regard a hub is defined as an operation where aircraft are scheduled to and from an airport in 'banks.'

89 Southwest Airlines' Flight Schedule, 31 October, 1993.

90 Many of the used aircraft acquired or leased by the new-entrants were less fuel efficient than newer aircraft at the time: Boeing 727-100's, B737-100's and similar. The cheap used long-haul types acquired by new-entrants were usually very fuel inefficient: DC-8's, B707's, B747-100's, L1011's and DC-10-10's.

91 This was a major factor in PeoplExpress financial strategy.

92 A code-sharing agreement is usually part of a marketing agreement between a major carrier and a feeder carrier at a hub. Under such an agreement schedules are integrated and airport facilities shared. The schedule integration involves the use of the same flight code for an entire trip from city A to a hub and on with the code-sharing airline to a city B. So on the ticket the flight is shown as flight XXX from city A to city B and no mentioning of change of planes or the hub in between. The present regulation says, though, that upon booking the passenger must be informed that he/she is buying a code-shared flight. The origin of code-sharing can be attributed to the regulation on CRS bias that pushed interlining flights as third priority on CRS displays. This led to serious difficulties for feeder carriers that had marketing agreements with incumbents as their flights would suddenly be pushed from the first screen to perhaps the third or fourth screen. Given that TA's have a tendency to book from the first screen, carriers lost immediately substantial part of their traffic after the change was effected. Thus, the interlining carrier had only one way of beating the system and maintaining its traffic level, that was to make an marketing agreement with the major involving code-sharing.

93 PeoplExpress was granted a certificate by the CAB to offer scheduled passenger service between Newark and 27 major cities in 1980 and got its operating certificate April 1981. The airline offered unbundled service, that is no-frills, where the passenger had to pay for a picnic basket on board, pay for checked baggage and for the ticket on board. As a result the company offered comparably very low fares and high frequency. The employees were shareholders and everyone was a manager. This seemed to give the staff a greater feeling of responsibility and flexibility, as most staff members could attend to more than one staff function. The airline grew very fast and ran into financial difficulties that resulted in an acquisition by Continental in 1987.

94 This was one of the things that Freddy Laker discovered and mentioned to have surprised him when the incumbents matched his fare and the passengers flocked away from Laker Airways. But this was no wonder as the incumbents provided a higher frequency and more convenient distribution system. Only a small portion of their trans-Atlantic capacity at the low fares would easily eat up Laker's market-share.

95 In this case the airline might enter the markets of weaker incumbents and drown them with high frequency at low fares and when the airline has gained enough critical mass it will go for the trunk routes of the 'big' carriers. This was the strategy of PeoplExpress and America West.

96 Here the airline maintains low profile, basically hoping the customers will select it although having no unique selling proposition. This strategy is basically defunct as the passenger not having any incentive such as low price, will select the more

'reputable' carrier unless that carrier is providing 'terrible' service compared to the new carrier.

97 Highly competitive strategy, but can be low growth oriented. The carrier usually pursuing low profile hopes that the incumbent wont bother with it in view of its low market share. Furthermore, it may be dangerous for the incumbent to retaliate if such carrier is able to skim most of the more lucrative markets, as fare war will harm the incumbents more than the newcomer, given that the newcomer can break-even at a much lower fare levels than the incumbents. This type of strategy facilitates a strong USP by achieving outstanding and highly flexible product, such as Virgin Atlantic.

98 For a small new-entrant entering primary markets the story was entirely different as it certainly doesn't make sense for an incumbent to cut fares in a lucrative market to force out a new-entrant having negligible market share. Air Atlanta was one such carrier operating out of Atlanta in competition with Delta and Eastern. Their strategy was based on premium service at standard prices: 'Anybody can match a price strategy. But I know that the major airlines are too musclebound to react to a service strategy that affects only a small part of their system' (Neil Effman, Air Atlanta). If the new-entrant intends to grow fast in the market and has the facilities and means to do so, such as PeoplExpress and America West did, an entirely different stand may be taken by the incumbent. An example of such entry was when New York Air started service to Detroit from New York's La Guardia offering a $69 and $49 off-peak fare where Republic offered a $128 fare. Republic, true to its policy of matching any fare offers in its markets, dropped its fare to the same level, and when New York Air dropped its fare further to $39, Republic did the same and offered passengers 50 percent bonus coupons on some routes. The move nullified New York Air's attempts and fares rose again as a result. This is a typical Bertrand Duopoly situation.

99 In 1985 PeoplExpress charged $3.0 per bag, $3.0 for light snacks on afternoon and night flights. Furthermore, the carrier offered meals on transcontinental and international flights.

100 Southwest started to participate in a CRS system in the early nineties allowing bookings on a low level.

101 The system was organised in such a way that the passenger would list, upon arrival at the airport, on first-come first-served basis instead of booking through a TA or the phone. A booking through the phone was actually no warranty of a seat due to the heavy overbooking practised by the airline. Furthermore, payment was collected on board reducing further the necessity for extensive sales-offices or the use of TA's.

102 That explains the serious problems the carrier had with building an image for the business segment during the latter part of its life-cycle

103 New-entrants that do not emphasise TA usually run a phone-reservation system, but no new-entrant carrier known of, has refused commissions to TA's using the phone reservation system. In fact some of the new-entrants have provided TA's with separate reservation lines.

104 Porter's theory may not apply to air transport as the increase in entry occurs when there is excess capacity reducing the 'financial barrier' to entry and the incumbents weak due to a recession. According to Porter the airlines should be having intense 'rivalry' at that time. The fact of the matter is, however, that this rivalry occurs only for a period of time during the downward swing but seems to fade off as the economy passes the bottom of the curve, creating opportunities for new-entrants.

105 One must recognise that some of these carriers turned these airports into major airports by serving them.

106 Southwest's routes centre at following cities: Reno, Sacramento, Oakland, San Francisco, Los Angeles, Phoenix, Albuquerque, El Paso, Dallas Love Field, Houston Hobby, San Antonio, Midland/Odessa, Kansas City, St. Louis and Chicago Midway.

PART II

AIRLINE SUCCESS AND FAILURE ASSESSMENT: THEORY AND APPLICATION

5 The question of success or failure

Continued adaptation mean continued pain,..And it could hardly be otherwise, because pain is one half of the power to form judgments. Any form of life which insulates itself too successfully against pain fails to notice any change in its environment until it is too late.

Hermann Korn (Martin, 1970)

Introduction

Knowledge on corporate failure can be divided into four parts: (i) findings based on manager's 'hands on' experience of success or failure; (ii) case studies of successful or failed companies; (iii) construction of theoretical models of failure; and (iv) empirically derived prediction models of failure or non-failure.

Definition of failure

There are many different definitions of corporate failure. Altman (1971, p.2) proposes this definition

> ...the situation where the realised rate of return on invested capital, with allowances for risk considerations, is significantly and continually lower than prevailing rates on similar investments.

Weston and Copeland (1986) make an important distinction between economic and financial failure. The above definition would, according to their distinction, fall under the economic criteria. In their view, failure in economic terms, means that the firm's revenues do not cover its costs. They go further and say that it can also mean that the rate of earnings on its historical cost of investment is less than the firm's cost of capital. A financial failure, on the other hand, can be divided into two types. First, *technical insolvency* that constitutes a situation where the firm can not meet its current obligations, even if the assets of the company exceed its total liabilities. Second, *bankruptcy* that constitutes a situation where total liabilities exceed the assumed value of the total assets.

This account can not exclude Dun and Bradstreet, who publish annually the 'Failure Record', that has to do with statistical analysis of corporate failures. Their definition of corporate failure is as follows,

> Business failures include those businesses that ceased operations following assignment or bankruptcy; ceased with loss to creditors after such actions as execution, foreclosure, or attachment; voluntarily withdrew leaving unpaid obligations, were involved in court actions such as receivership, reorganization, or arrangement; or voluntarily compromised with creditors.[107]

The definition is more practical in terms of identification of failed firm from statistical sources, while Weston's and Copeland's is more financially oriented. Beaver (1967) suggested even broader definition of failure, while constructing an empirical failure prediction model. He defined failure as a situation where any of the following events have occurred: bankruptcy, bond default, an overdrawn bank account, non-payment or a preferred stock dividend. This definition is very broad as an overdrawn bank account is a frequent occurrence in the course of doing business and most firms have fixed overdraft permissions used as short-term loan-facility. Slatter (1984), on the other hand, observes a decline stage prior to failure. [108] Such decline state is important in terms of failure as during the decline-state the symptoms of failure become apparent. Slatter (p.19) has defined this decline state in terms of a turnaround situation where a firm whose real profit before tax has declined for three or more successive years.[109] For the purpose of this book a new-entrant airline is considered failed: if it filed for bankruptcy under Chapter 11 or 7, or was overtaken as a result of poor financial record.

The legal framework of bankruptcy

Bankruptcy law in the United States

In the United States there are different types of bankruptcy filings possible, Chapter 11 and Chapter 7. Chapter 11 is for cases initiated on voluntary basis and deals with reorganisation of the company involved. The latter route on the other hand is for involuntary filing, usually by a creditor. When Chapter 7 is initiated the company is liquidated and the proceeds distributed among the creditors. The process is as follows: (i) the judge issues automatic stay, so creditors can not press suit for repayment, debts are frozen, secured creditors can ask for hardship exemption from debt freeze; (ii) unsecured creditors form a committee who can ask the court to appoint an examiner to investigate possible fraud or mismanagement, usually leading to the appointment of a trustee to run the company; (iii) the committee and company negotiate a reorganisation plan that contains among other things a repayment for frozen debts; (iv) creditors approve the plan following negotiations that can run from few months up to years, but the approving is based on the majority voting in favour of the plan by creditors owning more than two-thirds of the debt; (v) bankruptcy court judge approves the plan; (vi) the reorganised company emerges from bankruptcy having to meet the terms of the agreed repayment plan.

Under both types of bankruptcy filing, the debtor continues to operate the company unless the assigned bankruptcy court decides otherwise. Such a decision usually involves the appointment of a trustee that has broad powers according to a court order. He may bring in new managers and replace existing ones. His role is basically to run the company, to minimise losses and sell it or parts of it as a going concern to maximise the returns from the liquidation. Although, the debtor can regain control from the trustee by filing a bond as required by the court. Reorganisation on the other hand, has the specific purpose of protecting the company from its creditors in order to return the company to profitability.

Having discussed the U.S. bankruptcy procedures, it appropriate to point out that such procedures differ around the world. For example, in the United Kingdom the Company's Act of 1893, 1948 and 1981, made it possible to appoint a receiver and a manager instead of a liquidator, which was the only alternative before the Companies Act of 1893. The receiver's role is to realise the assets of the company for a client who is usually a creditor and in doing so he has to keep the interest of other creditors in mind. When the receiver has collected for his client he leaves the company and normal business resumes, or the liquidator is called in to distribute the remaining assets to the creditors and shareholders (Slatter, 1984).

Bankruptcies and exogenous influence

Bankruptcy is often explained by adverse influence from the exogenous environment. The most frequent contributors cited have been recession, change in government policy, high interest rates, labour disputes and acts of god, etc. Furthermore, it is common to see statistics that show company age as contributor to failures, that is the 'liability of newness.'

Environment's influence

Goudie and Meeks (1991) found a relationship between the effects of exogenous macroeconomic shocks on the failure rate. Their research shows that a variation in the exchange rate can cause failures among large companies. It is known that exchange rates can influence a company's ability to compete in international markets where the dependency on such markets is considerable. This is a certitude for companies that have a limited domestic market but incur a large part of their costs in the domestic currency, such as the international airlines to name but one industry as an example. Desai and Montes (1982) support this analogy further reporting findings showing that changes in the interest rate and the growth of the money stock (M1) influenced the failure rate among companies.

Altman (1993, p.14) concludes that a selection of exogenous reasons attest to the increase in failure rates among US businesses despite the overall expansion of the economy (GNP): (i) chronically sick industries; (ii) high real interest rates; (iii) increased international competition; (iv) increased leveraging in corporate America; (v) deregulation of key industries (aviation, financial services, etc.); and (vi) relatively high business formation rates.

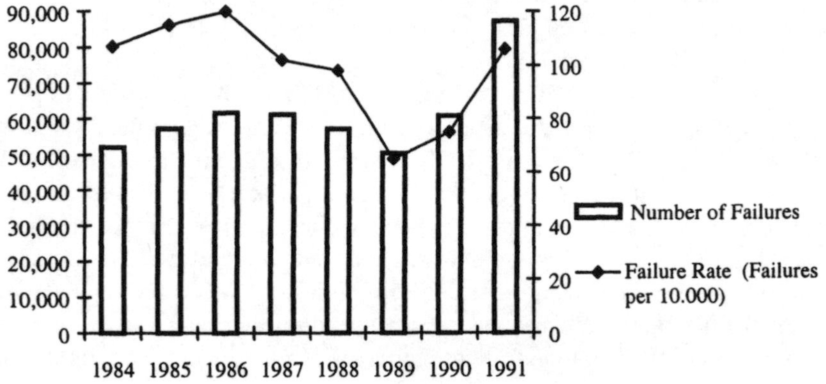

Figure 5.1 Number of failures and the failure rate in the US (1971-1991)

Source: Based on Altman (1993).

The increase in failure rate from 1984 to 1986 and in 1991 is blamed on recessions during the periods. Thus, recessions appear to conquer the weak companies lacking financial flexibility to account for set back in revenues.

Liability of newness

Lane and Schary's (1991) study on business failures found that the age of a firm is highly correlated with its susceptibility to failure. The predicted probability of failure by age of the firm showed that for the period from 1984 to 1990, the probability of a two year old firm to have failed within one year was .94, three year old .84, four year old .70, five year old .60 and for a ten year old firm it was .40. The probabilities in this study are based on bankrupt firms only not all firms, leading to inflated probabilities. Furthermore, the same study showed through regression analysis that the age effect is twice as large as the macro effect for three year old firms, but declining gradually until the firm reaches the age of nine when it is about equal. Dun & Bradstreet (*see*

Altman, 1993) the leading source of bankruptcy statistics have reported findings showing fewer failures in the first year but an increase in the following two to three years and then decrease for each consecutive year thereafter. However, the total number of failures, based on all firms in a 10 year period from establishment, reaches 70 to 80 percent. Comparing 1990 to 1980 showed that failures in early years are increasing, especially in the first year of operations. The increase seems to be related to deregulated industries having more new-entrants.

In conclusion, it is important to recognise that the age factor as such is not a causal factor of failure at all. The underlying reason for the failure of a younger company, can be founder's inexperience, lack of financial resources, marketing of a product that is not needed and therefore lacks demand, inability to sustain a low income period while the company is penetrating the market, and so forth. Pointing clearly to a higher risk associated with novelty, a rather obvious relationship, although the answer to the question 'why' is less obvious.

Causes and symptoms of failure

John Argenti (1976) stated that it was necessary to make a distinction between the causes and symptoms of corporate collapse. As a result there have been a number of attempts to come up with causal factors that explain why companies fail. It is apparent from the literature that there are a number of factors that differ from one research to another although there are certain similarities. A survey by D&B in 1980 has indicated that over 44 percent of all corporate failures are linked with inexperience, unbalanced experience or incompetence (Altman, 1993, p.17). In fact one can infer that success or failure will always be crystallized around the management factor. It seems that there are layers of contributing factors to failure: (i) management ability; (ii) management actions; and (iii) the symptoms of management actions. An elementary finding calling for research into what constitutes 'good' management and how such a property is integrated into the organisation and reacting to endogenous and exogenous forces. However, based on supposition the causes of corporate decline and failure can not be attributed to few variables only.

The question of failure

Argenti (1976) observed that corporate failure prediction models were not good indicators as to what has gone wrong in bankrupt companies although such models could predict corporate failure for up to three years in advance with fairly high certainty. Hence, Argenti came up with a three-part sequence of decline: defects, mistakes and symptoms. His observation was that corporations can have defects in their system, if we think of the corporation in terms of a holistic system. Then he assumes that there are only three mistakes that can lead to failure, overtrading, the 'grand project' and excessive financial gearing. He alleged that companies making these mistakes were virtually doomed to failure and the result would be the appearance of the symptoms. The 'symptoms' can present themselves as creative accounting or deteriorating financial ratios (*see discussion in* Lane and Schary, 1991). Further to this, there are trajectories to failure and one characterising successful companies. Argenti (1973, p.148) concluded that *Type One* firm would never really take off in terms of performance and fail soon after formation. While the *Type Two* firms would take off very rapidly reaching high performance and receive much attention, but then decline rapidly and fail. The *Type Three* firms would, according to Argenti's analogy, grow to excellence and then decline gradually until failure. Finally, the *Type Four* firm a successful company would achieve success along the 'S' curve and stay successful. According to the concept (p.123) accounting information was lacking in failing companies especially in terms of ineffective budgetary control, non-existent cash flow forecasts, lack of costing systems and incorrect asset valuation. Furthermore, failing companies lacked vision in terms of forecasting change, due to deficiencies in the top team. The concept has been criticised due to its lack of research backing. D'Aveni (1989, p.577) concludes that Argenti's findings may not necessarily be defective but nevertheless, needing confirmation and further explanation.

Clutterbuck and Kernaghan (1990) surveyed most of the groups of people associated with company failure to derive lessons for success. Their questionnaire was sent to 300 organisations, resulting in a reply rate of just over 15 percent. The most frequently cited causes for failure were in the order of intensity (pp.79-80): poor financial information (40),[110] lack of control in general (34), insufficient working capital (33), management inexperience (33), lack of strategy (30), poor understanding of the market (29) and insufficient margins (27). The survey concluded that the aggregated main causes of failure were: (i) inadequate information and controls; (ii) poor understanding of the market and the product; and (iii) inadequate strategic vision and implementation. Although the study is based on a small portion of the total sample it is not uncommon when executives are surveyed.

One source of failure and success elucidation is company 'doctors' or 'recovery' specialists. These are usually brought in to try to return the corporation to profitability after insolvency or when the directors find no other way or are pressured to do so by banks. In 1991 the three leading British insolvency specialists David James, Roger Cork and Adrian Lickorish had a panel discussion on the subject (Director, 1991). Their discussion revealed that the role of the non-executive directors is crucial in decline and failure as their purpose is to guide the company's direction. Furthermore, they found that a good banking relationship based on trust and loyalty could benefit a company running into problems, although, this does not have to be so in all circumstances.[111] The bank that is asked to furnish a rescue loan needs to know the company in detail in order to analyse the recovery changes. In fact the company insolvency specialists often provide security to the banks if they have a string of successful rescues. Furthermore, they mentioned that over-enthusiastic funding of growth out of proportion to the company's real value frequently causes corporate problems. Similarly, the management buyouts have added immensely to the corporation's debt, often during periods of low interest rates, making the companies vulnerable during rising interest rates. According to the three insolvency specialists, directors of troubled companies are prone to run into a 'siege' mentality and fail to admit their need of rescue until very late in the downward spiral (Director, 1991). The company insolvency specialists' discussion reinforces further the findings presented in this section placing much responsibility and blame with the company directors. They just as Argenti draw the attention to the importance of the board of directors and especially the non-executive directors that can 'distance' themselves from the day to day operations in order to see the 'big' picture.

Clutterbuck and Kernaghan (1990, p.79) point out, however, that insolvency specialists are usually brought in late in the decline process gaining only 'second hand' knowledge on the actual causes. The authors claim that venture capitalists do possess more information on the real causes of decline and failure due to their participation in the corporate saga from the outset. In fact a survey conducted by Gorman and Sahlman (1989) concluded that venture capitalists saw shortcomings in general management as the main cause of failure in their portfolio companies. Venture capitalists, themselves, are cited as a cause of corporate failure by Gorman and Sahlman (p.238) due to: (i) their aid to capitalise highly uncertain ventures; and (ii) provide less capital than necessary to minimise own risk.

In order to give a comprehensive overview of frequently cited 'causes' of failure in the literature, Table 5.1 was constructed from a number of studies. The most frequently cited reasons for failure, according to the aggregated table are: (i) improper pricing with regard to cost structure; (ii) high gearing; (iii) insufficient working capital; (iv) over dependence on one customer; (v) management inexperience; (vi) unbalanced top team; and (vii) inadequate control systems. Thus, the aggregate of these studies is backing most of the findings proposed by Argenti.

The question of success

Many books have been published that take a set of successful companies and derive lessons on why they are successful. The book by Peters and Waterman

Table 5.1 Causes of failure

Financial *	Marketing	Management	Organisation	Strategy	Operations	Environment	Information
Improper pricing with regard to cost structure (5)	Over-dependence on one customer (4)	Management inexperience (4)	Unbalanced top team (4)	Overexpansion (3)	Poor facilities and machinery (1)	Change in demand (3)	Inadequate control systems (5)
High gearing (5)	Failure to adapt to new market circumstances (3)	Inadequate leadership (3)	Combined chairman, chief-executive (1)	Overdiversification (2)	Obsolete or easily overtaken technology (1)	Competitors actions (3)	Inadequate accounting systems (2)
Insufficient working capital (4)	Lack of marketing effort (1)	An uninvolved board (2)	Failure to change (1)	Wrong choice of strategy (1)	Maintaining inventories that are too large (1)	Increase in material costs (2)	Poor financial information (1)
Lack of credit control (3)	Poor marketing or sales management (1)	A dominant executive (2)	Organisational structure (1)	Poor implementation of strategy (1)	Poor operations management (19	Changes in the physical environment (1)	Insufficient awareness of competitive activity (1)
High cost structure (2)	Poor product quality (1)	Dissension in the management team (2)		Lack of strategy (1)		Poor state of the local economy (1)	
Undercapitalisation (2)	Obsolete product (1)	Inadequate management (2)		Big projects (1)		Government restraints (1)	
Lack of volume (2)	Too narrow or too wide product line (1)	Loss of vital personnel (2)		Playing follow the leader (1)		Technology advances (1)	

Financial	Marketing	Management	Organisation	Strategy	Operations	Environment	Information
Weak finance function (2)	Lack of sales (1)	Poor planning (2)		Acquisition (1)			
Spending excessively as earnings begin to rise (1)	Over-emphasis on sales (1)	Theft and dishonesty (2)		Getting too big for your britches (1)			
Poor management accounting (1)	Poor location (1)	Ignorance of the wants, needs and expectancy of the stakeholders (1)					
Declining margins of profit (1)	Fat marketing organisations (1)	Arrogance (1)					
Underutilisation of assets (1)							
Short term liquidity (1)							
Costing not able to show the fixed cost contribution provided by incremental sales							
Lack of financial control (1)							
Poor asset management (1)							
Overtrading (1)							
Financial policy (1)							
Failure to analyse financial statements carefully (1)							
Bad debts (1)							

* The numbers in the brackets indicate the frequency of each factor's appearance in the literature.

Source: Clutterbuck and Kernagahn (1990); Argenti (1976); Slatter (1984); Boyle and Desai (1990); Mesdag (1988); Buccino (1991); Wood (1989); McQueen (1989); Gruhn (1990).

(1982), *In Search of Excellence*, provides insight to the reasons behind specific companies' successes.

The authors do not put forth a sustainable theory of success according to Varadarajan and Ramanujam (1990, p.466), who criticise the Peter's and Waterman book on various accounts. They claim that the generalisations of the book are not timeless, that it omits factors such as proprietary technology, market dominance and control of raw materials, and finally that the definition of 'excellence' is faulty. A similar book was written in the UK, titled *The Winning Streak*, by Goldsmith and Clutterbuck (1985). The *Winning Streak* cites factors that distinguish the successful from the unsuccessful, such as: leadership, autonomy, control, involvement, market orientation, zero basing, innovation and integrity. These items are similar to the items cited in Table 9.4, reinforcing further the general ideas on what constitutes success. The Profit Impact of Market Strategy (*PIMS*) database of the Strategic Planning Institute is a large research project linking success with strategy. The *PIMS* (Buzzel and Gale, 1987, p.36) claim to have established that performance is related to investment intensity, relative product or service quality,[112] labour productivity, and vertical integration.

The *PIMS* research (p.190) has also indicated that market leaders are more prone to lose market share than gain, this is in direct proportion to their market-share. Thus, it is clear that smaller businesses gain from leaders on the basis of an ability to be innovative in ways, which the leader is most reluctant to follow.

Table 5.2 shows an overview of factors cited in the literature as success factors. Most of the articles found on the issue tended to provide rather generalised if not superficial words of advice. The aggregated findings according to the popular literature is that successful businesses are characterised by leadership in terms of quality, price and any other way that distinguishes the company from the rest. Such businesses do careful planning in all aspects, but especially in the financial and market aspects. Furthermore, successful businesses know the competitors well in order to plan moves. Finally, they stay in touch with the customer and know his needs and wants. However, the first item, high relative quality, appears to be the most important item of all and the key to success if one has in mind the articles examined. One of the main defects of the studies and opinions voiced in the articles is the lack of systematic research and theory on the subject of success. One might conclude that the construction of theory on business success is impossible due to the inherent dynamism of the firm. In fact the authors of the book on the *PIMS* Principles (Buzzel and Gale, p.2) shy away from attaching their findings to any underlying theory or principles.

Success contrasted to failure

Krüger (1989) examined 96 successful and unsuccessful companies in Germany to determine what factors explain corporate success and failure, as well as to assess the implication of the identified factors for managers. The COMPASS (A Concept for Multidimensional Planning and the Analysis of the Strategic Components of Success) project was divided into causal segments, which were further divided into 21 components of success. In order to distinguish the 'successful' and 'unsuccessful' companies, they were selected on the basis of extremities in performance measured through financial ratios. Then Krüger analysed reports on the companies in the various business magazines, to determine to what extent the various components were responsible for success or failure. The components were grouped into people responsibility, culture, strategy, structure, systems and implementation potential.

The most important groups in terms of unsuccessful companies according to the research (Krüger, p.109) was strategy (51%), people responsibility (50%), structure (45%) and implementation potential (37%). On the other hand, the most important groups in terms of success were strategy (48%) and then far behind, implementation potential (31%), systems (30%) and culture (28%). The potential contribution of this study is to uphold that failure as such is due to interaction between a number of factors. The surprising conclusion is that success, according to the findings, is attributed to much fewer factors. In fact, it is primarily one factor, product/market concept, with profit and revenue orientation and marketing/distribution/market research trailing far behind. However, a word of caution, as the study is based on the literature (business magazines) there is a potential bias in what is considered 'newsworthy' or fashionable at each time. Furthermore, the management of a successful company is hardly criticised for incompetence in the business press regardless if the firm may have landed such a profitable industry niche that the company makes profit in spite of obvious poor management.

Success as a failure factor

Success can lead to failure according to a number of industry observers. The cause of this predicament is the inertia caused by the positive strokes of success, leading to resistance to change. Miller (1990) carried out a study to explain why outstanding organisations bring about their own failure. The relevance of his study to new-entrant airlines is that many were very successful in terms of growth but failed as they matured, a behaviour of successful companies previously identified by Argenti (1973) as mentioned before.

Table 5.2 Success factors: literature review

Hall (1991)	Graham (1991)	Maren & Rose (1991)	Ray (1991)	Berg (1991)	Douchesneu and Gartner (1990)	Dahl and Sykes (1989)
Company reputation	Saying "yes" rather than "no" to customers	Target marketing efforts where the current customers discovered the business	Managers must overcome the myopic bottom-line syndrome and instead be visionaries	Make it clear that the company welcomes creative ideas and behaviour	Entrepreneurs that are successful are more likely to be raised by entrepreneurial parents	Develop a goal orientation
Product reputation	Raising standards to increase sales	Know the competition	Managers must be global strategists	End evaluation pressures, competition and excessive supervision	Have broader business experience	Understand how viewpoints influence the ability to achieve
Employee know-how	Staying in touch with the customer after the sale	Monitor every customer complaint	They must be masters of technology, especially information technology	Tolerate unconventional, troublesome behaviour and ideas	Have more business experience	Clarify values
	Doing everything possible to distinguish an organisation from its competitors	Emphasise point-of-contact service	They must be motivators	Emphasise informality and minimise long meetings	Seek to reduce risk	Identify wants and needs
	Generating sales leads	Enlist the sales force	They must be excellent politicians		Work long hours	Set achievable goals
	Working to develop a reputation of being the leader	Co-opt the competition	They must not become the intellectual prisoners of the period of time in which they live		Have personal investment in the firm	Develop strategies and tactics for accomplishment

Hall (1991)	Graham (1991)	Maren & Rose (1991)	Ray (1991)	Berg (1991)	Douchesneu and Gartner (1990)	Dahl and Sykes (1989)
	Keeping priorities straight	Be a predator			Good communicators	
		Watch cash flow and receivables			Have clear broad business idea	
		Have a plan			Engage in broad planning efforts that considered all aspects of firm and industry	
					Spend considerable time on planning	
					Use outside professionals and advisors during start-up	
					Use advice and information from suppliers and customers	
					To be flexible, participative and adaptive organisations	
					Sought to become larger firms	
					Sought to increase market-share	

Miller's (1990, p.5) study identified four trajectories, which he named: *Focusing*, *Venturing*, *Inventing* and *Decoupling*. The first trajectory characterises companies emphasising engineering culture, orderly structure, quality as a goal and leadership. Success reinforces these characteristics to the extreme leading to inflexible technocratic culture, perfection, eventually ending in technical tinkering that alienates the customers with perfect but irrelevant offerings. The second trajectory converts growth-driven companies managed by resourceful entrepreneurs into impulsive greedy 'imperialistic' companies. The strategy of building becomes over-expansion, the goals of growth, grandeur, the culture of entrepreneurship, gamesmanship, and divisionalised structure becomes fractured. The third trajectory causes innovation to become high-tech escapism, the goals of science for society becomes 'technical utopia', the culture of R&D becomes think-tank and organic structure becomes chaotic. The fourth trajectory turns a strategy of brilliant marketing into bland proliferation. The goal of market-share becomes quarterly numbers, the culture becomes insipid and political, and the structure oppressively bureaucratic. The study gives strong indication that positive reinforcement has occurred due to extreme success leading to too much emphasis on key 'success' factors. Therefore, guiding the company away from the very balance of resources, products and marketing that generated the success in the first place.

Growth

One other aspect of success is fast growth, a contributing factor to failure. In the chapter on deregulation we found that most of the new-entrant airlines experienced high growth but failed nevertheless. This is according to popular view, due to the company outstripping its human, production and financial resources (Stockton, 1989). Many rules of thumb have been assigned to what constitutes healthy vs. unhealthy growth, one suggested by (*qtd. in* Stockton, 1989, pp.18-19) Clemens of Durkee/Sharlit Associates was that yearly growth in excess of 40 percent was 'trouble'. The trouble associated with too fast growth is the increased receivables and inventories relative to sales, reduced cash flow and increase in debt servicing.

Aragon (*ctd. in* Stockton, 1989, p.19) proposed the following formula (*see* formula 5-1) based on: (i) profit after taxes earned on each dollar sales; (ii) percentage of net income reinvested in the business; (iii) maximum amount of liabilities available or desired on each dollar of equity; and (iv) the dollar amount of assets needed to support one dollar of sales

$$\text{Growth} = \frac{(\text{M})(\text{R})(1 + \text{D/E})}{(A) - (M)(R)(1 + D / E)} \qquad (5\text{-}1)$$

Where: M - Ratio of net income to sales, R - Ratio of reinvested income to income before dividends, D/E - Ratio of total liabilities to net worth, A - Ratio of assets to sales.

A different formula (*see* formula 5-2) was proposed by Weston and Copeland (pp. 233-234) based on the idea of sustainable dividends

$$\text{Sustainable growth rate} = T \times m \times L \times b \qquad (5\text{-}2)$$

Where: T - asset turnover, m - margin on sales, L - financial leverage, b - retention rate.

Both formulas are supposed to capture the full range of the underlying management decision making relating to growth potential of the corporation.

Human capital and corporate mortality

The single most frequently cited reason for a firm's failure is poor management. Poor management can be defined as: (i) incompetence, that is combined by lack of education, experience and success relaxation (arrogance); (ii) single-mindedness, made up of problem denial, too much self-reliance and quick decision making that lacks analysis (high risk taking); and (iii) personal constraints or ignorance composed of poor environmental realisation, lack of delegation, poor identification of relevant information and over emphasis on central control.[113] Argenti concluded that poor management was the main cause of failure, characterised by (1973, p.123): (i) 'one-man' rule where one person dominated his colleagues rather than to lead them, making decisions despite their hostility or reticence, not allowing discussion or listen to advice; (ii) non-participating board composed of individuals not participating in discussions unless it affecting their own vested interest; (iii) unbalanced top team, composed of individuals from similar backgrounds (all engineers, all finance background, etc.); (iv) weak finance function and inadequate control systems; (v) lack of management depth; and (vi) combined chairman and chief executive.

There are a number of warnings of imminent business failure that can be observed in management behaviour, according to Sharlit (1990): isolated, obsessed, angry, indecisive, capricious and workaholic manager. Hickey (1991) confirms these observations through his consulting but identifies the signals as: denial, bad-luck, lack of balance, high life-style, follower attitude, impulsiveness, lack of values, harmful relationships and old age. Clarence Farrar (1990) concluded after having experienced the bankruptcy of his own company, that the early warning signals of failure were: management complacency, lethargy, egotism and greed. Then he found that sales deteriorate causing a chain reaction due to the central function of sales in the business survival. The relationship being decline in sales, increased inventory and payables, leading to expenses becoming higher percentage of sales, thus, leading to cash-flow problems.

It is obvious from the review so far that managers have quite varying styles that do affect their performance. According to Nahavandi and

Malekzadeh's (1993, p.414) Strategic Leadership Dimensions (SLD) there are four types of leaders, charted along two dimensions, challenge and control. Low challenge-seeking leader who avoids risk and seeks to maintain the current state of affairs, accomplished by initiating only strategies that require minimal change. A challenge-seeking leader, on the other hand, is risk taking, entrepreneurial and future oriented. The other dimension, control, indicates that a leader exercising low control will emphasise employee involvement tolerance and encouragement of diversity. In contrast, if a leader maintains high control he maintains high centralisation and little delegation. Such high centralisation will reduce employee participation and diversity. These management types can obviously provide a very effective generalised way of classifying executives of firms into four groups. However, it could be that different company situations crave for different 'types' of managers. For example, a highly innovative technology firm may need *Type II* manager in order to unleash the staffs' creativity in order stay competitive. Another type of firm could be that of a financially distressed company in air transport needing to turn-around. In such a situation a *Type I* manager would be needed in order to force cost cuts through and necessary changes to return the company to profitability. In fact it could be an option in some situations to alter the types of top leaders according to the situation at hand, given the constraints of necessary stability.

Another dimension in the leader influence on success or failure of a company is experience, often represented by age. Preisendörfer and Voss (1990) researching German registrations and de-registrations found that there is a convex relationship between founders' age and company mortality.

Organisational life-cycle theories

The organisational life-cycle concept

The life-cycle concept assumes that organisations have the same traits as organisms, there will be birth, maturity and eventual decline leading to death. Researchers have found that organisations seem to follow this trait in most aspects, although the lifetime span is very different from living organisms. In fact the firm can extend its lifetime, in theory, indefinitely if it adapts to its environment perfectly. However, inefficiencies are created with age due to the rigidity of 'old ways' and employee shielding[114] that limits the efficiency of the organisation leading to its inevitable decline.

It is possible to hypothesise that organisation decline is also linked to its market decline rather than its endogenous decline solely. The *PIMS* program has features in order to chart the life-cycle of markets and concludes that markets show life-cycle characteristics. According to the program (Buzzel and Gale, 1987, p.54) markets show erratic behaviour of growth in infancy and instability in technology, market structure and competition strategy, followed by rapid growth after a company shake-out. Then there is a period of maturity and stability that can last for long or short period depending on the characteristics of the product. Finally the markets will decline because of the introduction of new products, superior technology or changing life-styles (needs). One would of course expect that responsive management would, through innovation, offer new products in order to reduce the impact of declining markets on the organisation. That is precisely one of the factors that effectively differentiates between successful and declining firms according to research conducted by Miller and Friesen (1983). They concluded in the study, based on the life-cycle concept,[115] that steady increases in information processing and decision making sophistication occurred at least until the revival phase, that successful companies have more decision-making complexity, especially in analysis, multiplexity and integration, and successful phases had higher level of innovation-related activity with the exception of risk taking. Their study showed also that in the successful periods there is high level of risk-taking during the birth-phase, but the opposite is true for the decline-phase where the unsuccessful companies are more prone to risk taking.

In addition to the research mentioned already, one can not exclude Flamholtz (1990), that uses the life-cycle concept to explain why firms run into problems as they grow. He concludes that many firms develop an organisational development gap, which he names 'growing pains'. The gap can occur for two reasons, namely too fast growth or poor adaptation of infrastructure to size increases. His findings list the five 'most common organisational growing pains' as (p.53): (i) employees' feeling of being unable to cover their daily tasks; (ii) constant fire-fighting; (iii) lack of communication; (iv) lack of vision; and (v) few good managers being around.

Summary

There is a correlation between a firm's novelty and likelihood of bankruptcy. There also appears to be relationship between macroeconomic variables such as interest rate, deregulation of industries, recession and increased competition intensity with failure. Most researchers on failure as well as specialists, such as venture capitalists and company 'doctors' agree that management appears to be the main contributor to the failure of firms. The literature provides, however, few established systematically researched conclusions on what constitutes poor management, although Argenti provided explanations that unfortunately lacked adequate confirmation by empirical research.

The most frequently cited causes of failure according to the literature are: (i) improper pricing; (ii) high gearing; (iii) insufficient working capital; (iv) over-dependence on one customer; (v) management inexperience; (vi) unbalanced top team; and (vii) inadequate control systems. Company insolvency specialists have cited inadequate participation of non-executive directors as a leading cause of company problems escalating out of hand. A number of studies have been conducted on what characterises successful companies. Such studies usually lack rigour in research design making their conclusions obsolete as soon as some of the 'successful' companies become 'unsuccessful' although they still apply the apparent 'successful ways'. This implies that researchers have not discovered any underlying principles of success.

The *PIMS* program has come up with number of findings, but the most important one is that high relative quality is one of the foundations of low market-share businesses earning adequate profits. Furthermore, the program does not look at market-share as cause of profitability on its own, but rather that a combination of features such as high quality and low cost will bring about increases in market-share, which in-turn will increase profits further. Growth plays an important role in failure, because very fast growth will outstrip the company of resources. Manager's personal traits are an important factor in company failure. Personal factors such as lack of education, lack of experience, too much self-reliance, jumping to conclusions (lack of analysis) and problem denial, are all factors that contribute to failure. A German study found a convex relationship between founder age and de-registrations. Corporations seem to go through a life-cycle, although, decline can sometimes be avoided or companies revitalised.

The life-cycle concept is important as it shows that fewer and fewer companies exist in a population established at a given year, as time passes. However, the theory does not substantiate that *all* companies or organisations will eventually die. In fact a company having perfect ability to adapt to its environment will survive indefinitely, although, such company may not necessarily exist in reality. Furthermore, an adaptable company may be engaged in a totally different business after 50 years from foundation.

---

107 D & B do statistical analysis of corporate failures (*see* The Failure Record (Annually), Dun & Bradstreet, New York.)

108 Of course this is not true in all situations, as companies can run into sudden catastrophic problems.

109 Slatter referred to '1970 prices' in his definition, this has been omitted here for obvious reasons.

110 Numbers in parenthesis denote frequency of cause marked by respondents.

111 The Laker case was a point, as the bank called in the receivers over relatively small default compared to the total turnover of the company. That decision, however, could have been based on a long-term view of the company's destiny.

112 The *PIMS* (Buzzel and Gale, 1987) methodology uses relative quality measurement, which is based on a questionnaire where respondents are led through a 'quality profiling' where they identify the key product and service attributes that count in the

purchase decision. These attributes are then rated on a summation scale totalling 100. Followed by rating of own performance compared to the performance of leading competitors for each attribute on a scale from 1 to 10.

113 This last item is sometimes a cause of under-financing because share-capital will not be sought unless it will not dilute the founder's control.

114 Layoffs are sensitive in organisations so if the organisation does not provide for constant education and training of employees it will accumulate ineffective staff that are pushed into non-productive roles, while others have to be hired to do what needs to be done. Thus, the organisation will suffer from employee 'inflation' with age.

115 In their study they divided the life-cycle into the following phases: Birth phase, growth phase, maturity phase, revival phase and decline phase.

6 The survey research

Introduction

The questionnaire was divided into three parts, with the third part acting as means to classify respondents into various groups. In Part I (45 statements), respondents were asked to state the degree of agreement or disagreement with statements on various aspects of organisation and management on a five point Likert scale (*see* Part I data descriptive in Appendix A). In Part II (75 factors), the respondents were asked to indicate on a scale of 0 to 10, the importance placed on various factors: in the past, at the present and as expected in the future (*see* Part II data descriptive in Appendix B). The reason for emphasising the rating of 'importance' of each factor was to distance the respondent from the term 'failure'. This was done in order to prevent the manager judging his own performance as such measurement is subject to bias, especially, in the face of poor performance or bankruptcy.[116]

The statements in Part II were divided into categories of statements based on Cowan (1990): personnel-human resources, strategic, operations, marketing (18 factors), management, MIS-data processing, external-environmental (6 factors) and communications, financial (10 factors) and production-manufacturing. Personnel-human resources was collapsed into *management and organisation* (18 factors), MIS-data processing and communications was combined into *information- and communication system* (9 factors) and production-manufacturing became *operations* (14 factors). Cowan came up with 17 additional categories that are excluded because their occurrence is infrequent. The statements in Part I were in the first instance based on the concepts of Hall (1992), but during the course of development these statements underwent changes and adaptation to the task at hand. The factors presented in Part II were developed on the basis of intuition, literature research and comments on early pilot questionnaires.

Both of the rating methods are common in social research but subject to controversy as most attitude scales are. Hoinville and Jowell (1989, p.35) conclude in a widely used book on survey research practice, that much literature is available on the advantages and defects of attitude scaling methods, but

> ...since a rating scale is not an absolute measure of attitude but a way of placing people in relative positions on a dimension, there is no particular way of presenting scales that is intrinsically better than others. The object should be to find the way that discriminates most effectively between respondents.

Having this in mind and the characteristics of the task (discrimination) the selected scales were considered to suit their purpose well. The questionnaire includes mostly factors that could not be measured by other sources in order to add dimension to numerical data, deemed necessary due to the conformity in the literature that the main cause of failure is the management of the failed organisation. As a result, it must be the importance that the management has placed (a function of decisions) on various factors that makes or breaks a company. The questionnaire research is based on this presumption and the hypotheses that there is difference between the management as contributing factor and other possible contributing factors of failure such as that of the environment.

The length of the questionnaire was a considerable issue, as a major pilot study for item reduction would take too much time and reduce the sample available for the final survey. Thus, it was decided to go ahead with the questionnaire in the form it was. The questionnaire can be considered to be of medium length, although, the answering process may have placed considerable demand on the respondent's attitude to various issues. However, no statement or factor required information that was necessary to search for in company records. Due to the possible sensitivity of information provided by respondents much emphasis was placed on confidentiality and to identify the questionnaire with a reputable organisation in order to facilitate security for respondents.

The population

A sample was not considered adequate in this research due to the various backgrounds and the diversity associated with the new-entrants. Thus, all known new-entrant airlines fitting a criteria were included. A division of the population was necessary in order to recognise the differences in the operating and life-cycle status of the jet-operating[117] new-entrants, resulting in the identification of three populations of new-entrants and one of expert observers. These identified populations were as follows (*see* Table 6.1): (i) failed new-entrants (11), an airline that has failed totally or called in the receivers or filed for Chapter 11 or 7; (ii) recently established new-entrant (6), an airline with operating life of less than three years before the survey, i.e., established in 1991 or later; (iii) established new-entrant (23), a carrier that has been operating for more than three years when the survey was conducted, i.e., established before 1991; and (iv) specialists (44), that are observers of new-entrants, i.e., journalists, academics or consultants associated with aviation in general and/or new-entrant airlines. The four populations required four different questionnaire formats. Reason being that 'recent' new-entrants could not answer questions on the past, 'failed' new-entrants on the present and industry specialists on the airline specific questions in Part I of the questionnaire. Furthermore, the questions in the questionnaire for 'failed' new-entrants had to be worded in the past tense. In other word all statements and factors were the same facilitating combination of populations.

New-entrant airlines included in the survey and associated managers were derived from two main sources, the Air Transport World's World Airline Report and the Flight International's World Airline Directory. Airlines included in the population were jet-operating airlines established or expanding operations after deregulation of domestic market or bilateral route. This allowed cross-sectional analysis of new-entrants, meaning that the survey gave indications as to different importance of factors along the new-entrant's life-cycle. One executive was selected from each functional area within each airline. This was a non-random selection of subjects, guided by the pre-set requirement of every subject being a member of the executive team of the airline. This led to the inclusion of all such managers listed in the named sources for most airlines. In few cases, where there was an alternative the more senior executive was chosen. As a result, the likelihood of at least one response from each airline was raised. By using this method each airline received 3 to 16 mailings to various individuals within the airline (the average was 7). The specialists were, however, selected on the basis of their association with issues relating to new-entrants, an association derived from written articles and listed specialisation in the World Aerospace Directory.

The problem of small population

The small number of respondents is first and foremost the result of the small population of airlines fitting the project's aim. In that sense the number of responses received from airlines was deemed satisfactory. The problem of interpretation then arose: Are the results reliable? To answer this it has to be recognised that due to the high proportion of responses from the overall population being researched one has to conclude that the results are reliable for that particular population.

Response statistics

The total number of respondents was 61, but two responses were rejected: one on the basis of being heavily positive biased compared to other responses from the same airline, and another for being very incomplete. Fourteen responses were received from specialists that got a shorter version of the questionnaire containing only Part II, and 45 responses were received from airline managers at 26 airlines in the United States and Europe.

The average response rate for all four populations by individuals was 27.9 percent while it was 67.7 percent by airlines. This means that subjects from 67.7 percent of the airlines in the population responded. To gain fairly good overall response rate from airlines was actually one of the main objectives of the survey. Effective mailings that is mailings that actually should have reached the persons involved was high for most strata with the exception of failed new-entrants, where little information was available about the strata.

Table 6.1 Survey response statistics

Population	Survey	Number of mailings	Effective mailings	Responses by individuals	Number of airlines	Responses by airline
Established NE	Whole population	136	129[a]	33 (26%)[d]	23	16(70%)
Recent NE	Whole population	30	25[b]	8 (32%)[f]	6	5(83%)
Failed NE	Whole population	32	Unknown c	5 (15%)	11	5(45%)
Specialist	All linked with air tran.	44	44	15 (34%)[e]		
		242	na	27.9%	40	67.7%

[a] One airline went bankrupt just before the questionnaire was sent out, unknown to the researcher. [b] Two airlines went bankrupt during the survey execution period. [c] Present residence of ex-managers of failed airlines was inferred from International Aerospace Directory. As it was difficult to track these managers, poor results were anticipated. [d] One response was seriously positive biased and was rejected on the basis of two other responses from the same airline. [e] One response was incomplete and was rejected. [f] One airline went bankrupt in 1994. [g] The 59 effective responses were received after taking into account notes [d] and [e].

The pilot survey

The initial pilot survey was conducted by distributing the questionnaire to three airline specialists. This resulted in changes in question wording, improvement of cover letter, a change from a 100 point to a 10 point numerical scale and segregation of factors into groups. The scale alteration was performed due to the tendency of subjects to rate in ten point intervals making the scale inadvertently equal to a 10 point rating scale.[118] In the second pilot survey of the questionnaire, ten airlines in Europe and the US, were selected. Of those, three had actually gone out of business shortly before the mailing, resulting in no responses from those airlines. The pilot was tested on turboprop operating new-entrants in order to avoid cutting into the actual population.

In total 29 questionnaires were sent out addressed by functional title. Of the 29 questionnaires sent five were returned undelivered and three responses (10%) were received. However, a reminder was not sent to non-respondents due to time constraints. No serious faults were found with the questionnaire based on the responses except the low response rate that was deemed a fault in itself. The low response rate was attributed to the following: (i) lack of identification with a recognised organisation; (ii) pilot performed on a non-representative sample; and (iii) the use of titles instead of actual names of receivers. Changes were made accordingly leading to an increase in response rate.

The survey management was according to a standard process. Following alterations from the pilot survey, the first questionnaires were sent out, along with a cover letter. Approximately one month after the initial mailing a follow up letter was sent. Two months after the initial mailing a second follow up letter was sent. This applied to all populations except that of the failed new-entrants, where a search letter was sent to all 'names' identified as possible ex-executive of a failed airline. The letter asked if the person would be willing to provide the names and addresses of colleagues that worked for the failed carrier. The response was very limited or only two in total. After further checks of the name lists in the International Aerospace Directory the questionnaire was mailed to the identified names. The results were disappointing as only five responses were received. However, a number of bankruptcies occurred during the research process raising the number of failed carriers. Nevertheless, it was deemed necessary to change the original intentions and segregate the carriers into distressed (*D*) and non-distressed carriers (*ND*) on the basis of past performance.

Subjects versus airlines

In the analysis of the questionnaire most of the results are based on the subjects rather than the aggregated results of airlines. This is due to the necessity to analyse the dependability of individual respondents in a qualitative prediction model. In order to examine the dependability of this approach the agreement of respondents from same airline was analysed and displayed in Table 6.2.

As the table shows there was a significant positive correlation ($p<.05$, or better) between respondents from the same individual airline for all airlines having two or more respondents, except airline 114 and 122 that were slightly negatively correlated. In 55 percent of the cases for Part I the positive correlation among respondents is >.5, in 82 percent cases it is >.3. For Part II the correlation for all valid cases was >.3 and for 38 percent of cases >.5. The overall agreement of respondents from the same entity can therefore be judged to be satisfactory (*see* Table 6.2).

Responses by category and geography

The questionnaire responses fell almost evenly between U.S. and EU carriers. The largest discrepancy was unfortunately in the 'failed' category, where the U.S. is over-represented. The critical factors were, therefore, verified by constructing a separate category of distressed and non-distressed airlines as mentioned earlier.

Table 6.2 Agreement among respondents within the same airlines: questionnaire Part I and Part II

Airline	Number of respondents	Correlation among respondents: Part I	Number of respondents	Correlation among respondents: Part II
206	2	.6260	2	na*
204	2	.5749	2	na
203	2	.5024	2	na
122	3 (2)	-.0174	3 (2)	.4123
118	3	.6763	3 (2)	.7053
117	2	.4555	2	.3215
114	2	-.0641	2	.3737
108	3	.5980	3	.5496
106	2	.3984	2	na
105	5	.3442	5	.4619
104	4 (2)	.5637	4 (3)	.6370

* Could not be calculated due to missing values. Numbers in brackets indicate that correlation is calculated for less than the actual number of respondents due to missing values. Only airlines having two or more respondents are shown.

Table 6.3 Responses by category and geography

Area	Established	Recent	Failed*	Specialist	Total responses	Percent
US	14	4	4	7	29	49.0
EC	18	4	1	7	30	51.0
Total	32	8	5	14	59	100.0

* Five responses counted in the Established column and one in the Recent column were classified as failed in the analysis, as the former respondents were employees of an airline operating under Chapter 11 and the latter was an airline that failed shortly after the survey was conducted.

Responses by functional category

The number of responses by functional category varied from 6 to 13. As expected fewest responses were from top managers and financial managers or six responses from each. Upper management response to surveys is usually poor due to time pressures and the reluctance to provide information that could prove sensitive or useful to competitors.

Furthermore, in a survey dealing with failures the probability of non-response is escalated due to the sensitivity of the issue. The distribution of responses according to function was as follows: eleven marketing managers (18.6 %), nine operations managers (15.3 %), six financial managers (10.2 %) and six top managers (10.2 %), i.e., chairmen or CEO. Managers that could not be classified clearly into the traditional functional areas, were thirteen (22.0 %), while specialists were fourteen (23.7 %). The distribution of responses is fairly good across the functional areas, although, a higher response rate for financial managers would have been advantageous.

Table 6.4 Responses by functional category

Functional category	Frequency	Percent
Top managers (Chairman, CEO)	6	10.2
Marketing managers	11	18.6
Operations managers	9	15.3
Financial managers	6	10.2
Other managers	13	22.0
Specialists (consultants, journalists, academics)	14	23.7
Total	59	100.0

Responses by education

Most of the respondents had at least undergraduate education (BSc. or BA) or 83.4 percent. It was expected that more of the managers would have a pilot license as primary qualification, but only two did. The general conclusion is that managers of new-entrant airlines are educated professionals.

Table 6.5 Responses according to education

Education level*	Frequency	Percent	Valid percent
Graduate	12	26.7	28.6
Undergraduate	23	51.1	54.8
Some college	2	4.4	4.8
High school or equivalent	3	6.7	7.1
Pilot license	2	4.4	4.8
Missing cases	3	6.7	-
Total	45	100.0	100.0

* Specialists were not asked to specify their education

Age distribution of respondents

The largest number of respondents was in the age group 40-49, as expected. But during this age-interval most people peak in their work career. The age span of 30 to 59 contained the majority of respondents or 90.7 percent.

Table 6.6 Age distribution of respondents

Age group[a]	Frequency	Percent	Valid percent
20-29	2	4.4	4.7
30-39	12	26.7	27.9
40-49	17	37.8	39.5
50-59	10	22.2	23.3
60-69	2	4.4	4.7
Missing cases	2	4.4	-
Total	45	99.9 [b]	100.0

[a] Specialists were not asked for their age. [b] Does not add up due to rounding.

Factor importance along the time dimensions

From Table 6.7 it is apparent that *employee's productivity* and *employee relations* are regarded as highly important along with the related factors *of flexible job descriptions*, *company culture* and *union free operations*. *Aircraft utilisation* that affects unit cost is rated as highly important. A factor that is influenced by fares, passenger load-factors and cost. The strategic factors *expansion into new markets* and *price leadership in served markets* are rated fairly high as well. Which indicates a level of strategic aggressiveness being regarded as important in the past.

Price leadership is usually related to low cost structure so it is no surprise to see cost control among factors highly emphasised by new-entrant's management. Senior executives of new-entrant airlines have placed less importance on alliances, mergers, code sharing, feeder airline agreements, diversification into other industries and hub and spoke operations. This result is surprising in view of all the emphasis on these issues in the media. Frequent flyer programs are among the least important factors, probably because of new-entrant airlines' inability to offer attractive programs in competition with the large carriers, usually offering attractive holiday destinations in their programs. It is likely that managers of established major carriers such as American and United, would rate this factor higher than new-entrant managers. The basic results looking at the importance rating of the factors is that factors relating to efficiency, aggressive marketing and image, are rated high; information, distribution and company vision are rated in the middle; management, employee motivation, and non-core aspects of airline commerce are rated low. The issues that show solid increase in emphasis in the future are costs, image building, information systems, distribution and company vision. One more factor involving external co-operation (code-sharing, feeding and alliances) was identified as becoming more important, while its overall emphasis was low.

Table 6.7 Factor means for questionnaire Part II: past, present and future

	Past	Present	Future	Overall mean
Financial factors				
Cost control	7,36	8,79***	9,28*	8.48
Fuel costs	6,69	7,53**	8,03**	7.42
Cost reduction	6,64	8,58***	8,88	8.03
Increase margins	6,73	7,82**	8,42**	7.66
Turnover growth	5,43	5,73	5,73	5.63
Off-balance sheet financing of aircraft	5,65	6,21	6,50	6.12
Achieving critical mass	5,50	5,34	5,72	5.52
Long-term rather than short-term profits	5,48	5,63	6,70**	5.94
Debt reduction	5,35	7,35***	7,61	6.77
Reduction of labour costs	5,52	7,33***	7,21	6.69
Marketing factors				
Service quality	7,33	8,12*	8,85***	8.10
Passenger load-factors	6,69	7,39**	7,82*	7.30
Expansion into new markets	6,82	7,06	7,79**	7.22
Price leadership in served markets	6,33	6,91*	6,97	6.74
Brand image	6,52	7,55*	8,27**	7.45
Promotion	6,15	6,64	7,09	6.63
Media advertising	6,15	6,45	7,15**	6.58
Business passengers	5,94	7,00**	7,33	6.76
Market-research	5,12	6,67***	7,45**	6.41
Distribution network	5,55	7,06***	7,74***	6.78
Avoidance of price wars	5,63	6,36*	6,48	6.16
Market-share	4,94	5,55	6,06**	5.52
Weight load factor	4,57	4,75	4,82	4.71
Commission overrides	4,48	5,75***	5,97	5.40
Frequent flyer program	3,42	5,45***	6,33**	5.07
Alliance with the incumbents	3,03	4,35***	5,35**	4.24
Merger/acquisition to gain market-share	2,71	3,29	3,90*	3.30
Diversification into other industries	1,71	1,29	1,68*	1.56
Information and communication factors				
Computer reservation system	5,63	7,21***	8,00***	6.95
Inter-departmental communication	5,64	6,45*	7,54***	6.54
Market-intelligent information system	5,22	6,25***	7,48***	6.32
Contol systems	5,19	6,84***	8,19***	6.74
Planning systems	5,09	6,54***	7,94***	6.52
Motivation systems	5,03	5,97***	7,33***	6.11
Logistics systems	5,00	6,09***	7,34***	6.14
Yield management systems	4,36	6,94***	8,09***	6.46
Simplification of information system	4,63	6,06***	7,09***	5.93
Management and organisation factors				
Employees' productivity	7,33	8,36***	8,94***	8.21
Employee relations	6,91	7,33	8,28***	7.51
Operations without unionised staff	7,29	7,23	7,22	7.25
Flexible job descriptions	6,67	7,15**	7,54**	7.12

	Past	Present	Future	Overall mean
Company culture	6,67	7,39	8,24***	7.43
Business strategy	6,15	7,15***	7,72***	7.01
Managements' external contacts	5,94	6,90**	7,52**	6.79
Shared company vision	6,15	6,94**	8,03***	7.04
Company mission	5,94	6,91*	7,58***	6.81
Management teams	5,38	6,22***	7,09***	6.23
Delegation	5,34	6,53***	7,69***	6.52
Employees' autonomy to take decisions	5,47	6,50***	7,40***	6.46
Managers' incentive programs	4,63	5,12	6,30**	5.35
Employees' incentive programs	4,64	5,06	6,24***	5.31
Job rotation	3,89	4,38	4,75*	4.34
Union relations	3,63	4,50**	5,16**	4.43
Staff reduction	4,27	6,06***	5,67	5.33
Decentralised organisation structure	4,38	5,06*	5,90***	5.11
Operations factors				
Aircraft utilisation	7,68	8,25*	8,88***	8.27
Matching aircraft size with ...	6,25	7,34***	8,06***	7.22
Homogeneous aircraft fleet	6,30	7,12	7,42	6.95
Frequency in served markets	5,61	7,18***	7,81***	6.87
Acquisition of airport slots	5,64	6,06	6,54	6.08
Acquisition of new aircraft	6,79	7,18	7,24	7.07
Quality of terminal space	5,85	6,94***	7,54***	6.78
Interlining agreements	4,85	5,85***	6,63***	5.78
Operation on trunk routes	4,97	5,70*	5,83	5.50
Hub and spoke operations	3,15	4,21***	4,63	4.00
Long-haul routes	3,48	3,33	3,94*	3.58
Freight operations	2,94	4,30***	5,13**	4.12
Feeder airline agreements	2,75	4,63***	5,64***	4.34
Code sharing	2,06	3,91***	4,97***	3.65
Environment factors				
Investors' attitudes towards the airline	5,56	7,18**	7,72*	6.82
Favourable attitude of travel agents	6,14	7,48***	8,30***	7.31
Competitor analysis	5,00	6,75***	7,91***	6.55
Reduction of CRS bias affecting the airline	5,45	6,09	7,13**	6.22
Forecasting adverse effects of the environment.	5,56	6,94***	7,28*	6.59
Influencing government policy	5,54	6,90**	7,18	6.54

Note: *** = $p < .001$; ** = $p < .01$; * = $p < .05$; Ψ = $p < .1$. Factors were rated on a scale from 0 = no importance to 10 = most important.

A noticeable finding was that all factors relating to information systems are rated high in the future. It may also indicate that this aspect of airline management needs overall improvement.

A factor showing negative change from the past into the future, surprisingly enough, is *service quality*. The factor scores very high in comparison to other factors meaning that the managers view this factor as one of the most important ones in running their airlines. Thus, the reduction may not mean that less emphasis will be placed on *service quality*, rather that they find little scope to increase emphasis on an already highly emphasised factor.

Other factors showing little change or negative trend are *achieving critical mass*, *weight load-factor*, *diversification into other industries* and *long-haul routes*. All of these factors receive relatively little emphasis by respondents, especially the last two. Although *long-haul routes* is not emphasised much by the respondents, the fact of the matter is that average stage length increases gradually over the life-cycle of the new-entrant airline. This means that airlines will increasingly enter medium and long-haul routes to maintain adequate growth. However, the respondents may not have seen this factor as one of unavoidable necessity and definitely not of strategy. It has also been stated in this book that charter-based new-entrants emphasising long-haul routes have fared poorly.

The basic message read from the questionnaire responses is that new-entrants intend to stay in their core business, transporting passengers as the factor on diversification into other industries shows. This last statement was rated very low by the respondents and of decreasing importance in the future. This is perhaps not surprising in view of the high degree of specialisation involved in air transport. In fact, the idea advocated by some airlines in the past, notably SAS, was that 'airlines were in the travel business'[119] and should as such operate 'total travel' service, involving ground transportation, hotels, business services, travel agencies, car rentals and travel information services. The concept has failed for most airlines just as it has for many companies trying to enter industries that involve different concepts from the one they are in. Of course, there are success stories, but for airlines they are few and far apart.

Analysis of the means for the dichotomous failure variable

Management attitudes: failed vs. non-failed carriers

Analysing the means for the dichotomous failure variable for Part I of the questionnaire lead to the results presented in Table 6.8. Again the statements in this section were rated on a Likert scale (1 = strongly disagree, 5 = strongly agree).

Marketing factors. Examining the marketing variables it becomes apparent that customer service variables appear to distinguish well between the two groups. This includes a number of statements. First, *our service has a range of features that make it distinctive* that is rated higher by non-failed carriers (4.4 vs. 3.2, $p<.01$). Implying that service differentiation is important critical factor. Second, *we are innovators in customer service* also rated higher by non-failed carriers (4.1 vs. 3.2, $p<.05$). A statement that is clearly linked to the previous statement but emphasises the leader's aspect of customer service. Third, *our customer loyalty is strong* that is agreed more readily by respondents of non-failed carriers (4.3 vs. 3.3, $p<.1$). Fourth, *we plan and allocate sufficient resources to developing new markets* having a higher mean by respondents of non-failed carriers (3.6 vs. 2.4, *p*<.01). This indicates some constraints in terms of resources or it might represent poor planning function at the airlines involved.

Table 6.8 Significant differences between failed and non-failed carriers: questionnaire Part I

Statement	Group	Mean
Marketing		
We fulfil our customers' needs well	F	4,000 **
	NF	4,559
Our service has a range of features that make it distinctive	F	3,182 **
	NF	4,412
We are innovators in customer service	F	3,200 *
	NF	4,118
Our customer loyalty is strong	F	3,273 Ψ
	NF	4,324
We plan and allocate sufficient resources to developing new markets	F	2,364 **
	NF	3,647
Finance		
Lack of capital will not limit our growth	F	1,818 *
	NF	2,853
We usually have enough resources to plan for the future	F	2,364 Ψ
	NF	3,235
Environment		
The airline's success is largely dependent on factor out of its control	F	3,545 ***
	NF	2,088
Management		
Everyone in our airline understands our long term aims and objectives	F	2,091 **
	NF	3,500
The airline has a vision of the future shared by all the employees	F	2,636 **
	NF	3,824
Our staff provide us with a competitive advantage	F	3,636 Ψ
	NF	4,353

Note: *** = *p*< .001; ** = *p*< .01; * = *p*< .05; Ψ = *p*< .1. Failed *n* = 11, non-failed *n* = 34. Five point scale was used: 1 = disagree strongly, 5 = agree strongly. Italicised statements are significantly different for both non-failed/failed and non-distressed/distressed.

Financial factors. Respondents of failed carriers were less secure about their airlines' ability to secure capital for growth, *lack of capital will not limit our growth* (2.9 vs. 1.8, *p*<.05). The general finding is that capital is not readily available to either group. The statement *we usually have enough resources to plan for the future* is disagreeable to respondents of failed carriers (3.2 vs. 2.4, *p*<.1), indicating resource constraints leading to weak planning function within failing airlines.

Environment factors. The environment related statement, *the airline's success is largely dependent on factor out of its control* shows that failed airlines are in more agreement (3.5 vs. 2.1, $p<.001$), but the difference between the two groups is highly significant. This implies that managers of distressed carriers are more prone to feel out of control.

Management factors. Statements falling into the management group were three, two of which showed highly significant difference between the two groups. These were *the airline has a vision of the future shared by all the employees* having higher mean by respondents of non-failed carriers (3.8 vs. 2.6, $p<.01$), and *everyone in our airline understands our long-term aims and objectives*, which had also higher mean for non-failed carriers (3.5 vs. 2.1, $p<.01$). A slightly more agreement shows for both groups for the statement, *our staff provides us with competitive advantage*, with higher mean for non-failed carriers (4.4 vs. 3.6, $p<.1$).

Factor importance: failed vs. non-failed carriers

Only questionnaire Part II, past is analysed for differences between failed and non-failed carriers (see Table 6.9) as respondents of failed carriers were not asked to rate the factors for the present. The italicised statements are significantly different for both failed/non-failed and distressed/non-distressed carriers. Highly significant difference was found between the components of the dichotomous failure variable, for following elements: *hub and spoke operations* (7.7 vs. 2.3, $p<.001$), *yield management system* (7.3 vs. 3.6, $p<.001$), *delegation* (7.6 vs. 4.8, $p<.001$), *operations without unionised staff* (9.4 vs. 6.7, $p<.001$) and *achieving critical mass* (8.4 vs. 4.9, $p<.001$). It is interesting and worth noting that the factors showing highly significant difference of the means are distributed evenly between all the categories represented in the table. All of these factors are rated higher by the subjects of failed carriers indicating that there may be some underlying factor interfering with the results. One possibility is that during attempt to turnaround a scenario of 'increased activity' (*see* The Increased Activity phenomenon, p. 228) takes place.

Analysis of the means for the dichotomous distress variable

The reason for using distressed (D) rather than failed airlines only, is the fact that the response rate of managers of failed airlines was low, besides being important issue for research. Thus, a self-evident assumption was made that operating loss has a string of causes that are the same as that related to failure. As a result, airlines making operating losses for number of years will show the same or similar characteristics as airlines that have already failed. However, loss-making airlines can reverse the situation, making losses less reliable for

Table 6.9 Significant differences between failed and non-failed carriers: questionnaire Part II, past

Statement	Group	Mean
Operations		
Hub and spoke operations	F	7,727 ***
	NF	2,269
Code sharing	F	3,909 *
	NF	1,769
Matching of aircraft size with route requirement	F	7,818 *
	NF	5,923
Long haul routes	F	6,455 *
	NF	2,889
Frequency in served markets	F	7,546 *
	NF	5,370
Quality of terminal space and ground facilities...	F	7,000 *
	NF	5,407
Interlining agreements	F	6,818 *
	NF	4,519
Management		
Delegation	F	7,600 ***
	NF	4,846
Operations without unionised staff	F	9,364 ***
	NF	6,680
Job rotation	F	5,800 *
	NF	3,308
Managers' incentive program	F	6,364 Ψ
	NF	4,222
Marketing		
Market-share	F	6,818 *
	NF	4,444
Finance		
Achieving critical mass	F	8,364 ***
	NF	4,885
Fuel costs	F	7,909 *
	NF	6,269
Environment		
Competitor analysis	F	6,700 *
	NF	4,741
Information		
Yield management system	F	7,364 ***
	NF	3,593
Computer reservation system	F	7,000 *
	NF	5,482
Market-intelligent information and communication system	F	7,000 *
	NF	5,000

Note: *** = $p < .001$; ** = $p < .01$; * = $p < .05$; Ψ = $p < .1$. Failed $n = 10$, non-failed $n = 27$. The statements were rated on a 10 point rating scale: 0 = no-importance, 10 = most important. Italicised statements are significantly different for both non-failed/failed and non-distressed/distressed groups.

bankruptcy prediction. Nevertheless, there were number of identical factors showing significant differences of the two groups both for the dichotomous failure and distress variables (*see* italicised statements in Table 6.9).

Airlines were only selected into the distress category if they had made operating losses in 1992 or 1991 and during three of the last five operating years counted from the last available financial data. The assumption is therefore that losses for three out of five consecutive years can not be due to environment's influence or catastrophic events alone. All the failed airlines were included in this category as well.

Management attitudes: distressed vs. non-distressed carriers

The results of the survey (*see* Table 6.10) show that managers of new-entrant airlines feel that their airlines are performing well overall. If each factor is examined separately, we discover that there were seven factors that showed significant difference between distressed and non-distressed. *Lack of capital will not limit our growth* had as expected higher mean for non-distressed carriers (2.1 vs. 3.2, $p<.01$). The general finding on this issue, is that capital is a limiting factor for new-entrants' growth prospects.

Non-distressed carriers felt marginally stronger about their ability to *fulfil customers' needs* (4.6 vs. 4.3, $p<.1$). Non-distressed airlines showed slightly higher mean on the statement *we plan and allocate resources to developing new markets* (3.7 vs. 3.0, p<.1). This must be viewed as one of the fundamental processes for reducing the risk of growth, as entry into new markets can be viewed as high risk due to the costs and uncertainties involved. Careful planning must therefore be viewed as highly important. The finding therefore supports the notion that distressed carriers are more prone to allocate less resources to this function, leading to greater costs and somewhat poorer route network than that of non-distressed carriers.

Table 6.10 Means for questionnaire Part I: the dichotomous distress variable

	D	ND
Management		
Group consensus is the usual way we make decision	3.63	2.90Ψ
Everyone in our airline understands our long term aims and objectives	2.79	3.57*
Finance		
Lack of capital will not limit our growth	2.08	3.19**
Marketing		
We fulfil our customers' needs well	4.29	4.57Ψ
We are innovators in customer service compared to our competitors	3.57	4.29*
We plan and allocate sufficient resources to developing new markets	3.00	3.71Ψ
Environment		
The airline's success is largely dependent on factors out of its control	2.83	2.00*

Note: *** = $p<.001$; ** = $p<.01$; * = $p<.05$; Ψ = $p<.1$; Five point scale was used: 1 = disagree strongly, 5 = agree strongly; distressed $n = 24$, non-distressed $n = 21$.

The respondents of distressed carriers feel that *the airline's success is somewhat out of their control* (2.8 vs. 2.0, $p<.05$). Respondents of non-distressed new-entrants agree more readily that their airlines are *innovators in customer service compared to the competitors* (4.2 vs. 3.57, $p<.05$). It is clearly apparent that innovation is an important critical factor, in view of its relationship with other management factors. This stems from the fact that innovation in customer service has to be employee supported to work, hence needing resourceful personnel management. Furthermore, because of the commodity nature of the product it is probably important to come up with some distinguishing service features for competitive advantage. An other factor, supports this view, as respondents of non-distressed carriers feel stronger about *everyone in our airline understands our long term aims and objectives* (3.6 vs. 2.8, $p<.05$). This supports the notion that employees of non-distressed airlines are better guided towards a common aim.

Respondents of distressed new-entrant airlines agree more readily with *group consensus being the usual way to make decisions* (3.6 vs. 2.9, $p<.1$). This is the only additional statement to the ones identified in the failed/non-failed group. The reasons for respondents of distressed carriers seeking greater consensus on decision making are numerous. One of the likeliest explanations is that the individual airlines having experienced losses for years are putting an extra effort into turning the airline around. This will involve among other things increased team effort, involving consensus on action plans and individual decisions. Another totally opposite explanation is that group consensus is actually slowing down the decision-making speed within the organisation. Such situation could develop in an organisation where risk aversion is prevailing to the extent that all major decisions are avoided by attempting to gain group consensus. A highly political environment where the consequences of 'errors' are high for the individual would also lead to an environment of consensus seeking management.

Factor importance: distressed vs. non-distressed carriers

As mentioned before Part II of the questionnaire involved the rating of factors on the scale from 0 to 10 according to the importance placed on a factor at the airline. The following coverage will deal with factors that showed significant differences between distressed and non-distressed new-entrant carriers.

Operations factors. Respondents of non-distressed carriers emphasise more *aircraft utilisation* (8.9 vs. 8.0, $p<.01$). In fact the factor has been emphasised greatly in the last few years as a result of the success of Southwest Airlines, that emphasises *aircraft utilisation* very much in its strategy. Distressed carriers show (*see* Table 6.11) higher emphasis on *hub and spoke operations* both in the *past* (6.0 vs. 1.4, $p<.001$) and *present* (5.4 vs. 2.8, $p<.05$), indicating a possible relationship between such operating strategy and poor results, although causality needs to be researched more closely than possible here (*see* Routing, p.115).

Management factors. Decentralised organisation structure was significantly different only at *present*, with distressed carriers placing more importance on this factor (6.3 vs. 4.3, $p<.05$). Here there appears to be a contradiction with widely accepted beliefs that decentralised organisation structure is positive for the firm. However, the relationship of this factor with performance may be complex meaning that either the carriers are emphasising this factor in order to turnaround or that it is actually a contributing factor to distress. More research must be performed to establish the link accurately. Another interesting result was the persistent difference in the emphasis on *job rotation* in all three periods, with respondents of distressed carriers emphasising this factor more in the *past* (5.2 vs. 2.7, $p<.05$), at the present (5.8 vs. 3.2, $p<.001$) and in the future (5.8 vs. 3.6, $p<.01$). It is possible that highly emphasised *job rotation* policy creates inefficiencies (instability) that are linked with the airline's overall profitability or that this practice is highly used as a tool for turnaround.

Marketing factors. Respondents of non-distressed carriers show higher emphasis on marketing items such as *media advertising* at the present (5.5 vs. 7.3, $p<.01$) *service quality* in the past (8.2 vs. 6.4, $p<.05$),[120] and *brand image* in the past (7.3 vs. 5.9, $p<.1$). These items are usually regarded as playing large role in airline success today. The survey further substantiates that belief and supports the *PIMS* findings discussed in Chapter 4. *Expansion into new markets* was also emphasised more by non-distressed carriers both at *present* (6.5 vs. 7.6, $p<.1$) and in the *future* (6.8 vs. 8.3, $p<.01$) implying growth emphasis. However, there were two factors showing higher emphasis by distressed carriers, *merger and acquisition to gain market-share* in the past (3.9 vs. 1.9, $p<.05$) and *alliance with the incumbents* in the *past* (4.2 vs. 2.4, $p<.05$), at *present* (5.3 vs. 3.5, $p<.05$) and in the *future* (6.4 vs. 4.7, $p<.1$). This factor is strikingly different from what was expected as alliances would usually be associated with non-distress (proactive marketing), but again it is difficult to establish its causality with distress.

Finance factors. The factor *achieving critical mass* was rated more important at distressed carriers in the past (6.9 vs. 4.8, $p<.1$). Here again we may have further backing of the *PIMS* as high importance on critical mass could indicate market-share building at the cost of quality and image, rather than the other way around. Aircraft acquisition is a highly important factor in the overall cost structure of a new-entrant and distressed carriers seem to have placed more importance in the *past* on *off-balance sheet financing of aircraft* (6.7 vs. 4.8, $p<.1$). This finding does raise important questions such as whether the distressed carriers were also having cash-flow problems, etc. However, it was not possible to provide answer to such questions in this research due to lack of data pertaining to cash-flows.

Table 6.11 Significant differences between D and ND airlines

	Past		Present		Future	
Statement	*Group*	*Mean*	*Group*	*Mean*	*Group*	*Mean*
Operations						
Aircraft utilisation			D (20)	7,950 Ψ		
			ND (20)	8,850		
Hub and spoke	D (20)	6,000 ***	D (20)	5,400 *		
operation	ND (17)	1,412	ND (19)	2,895		
Management						
Decentralised			D (20)	6,250 *		
organisation struct.			ND (19)	4,263		
Job rotation	D (19)	5,158 *	D (20)	5,800 ***	D (22)	5,773 **
	ND (17)	2,706	ND (19)	3,158	ND (19)	3,579
Marketing						
Media advertising			D (20)	5,500 **		
			ND (20)	7,300		
Brand image	D (19)	5,895 Ψ				
	ND (18)	7,333				
Service quality	D (20)	6,350 *				
	ND (18)	8,167				
Merger/acq. to gain	D (19)	3,947 *				
market-share	ND (17)	1,941				
Alliance with the	D (20)	4,167 *	D (18)	5,278 *	D (20)	6,350 Ψ
incumbents	ND (17)	2,353	ND (19)	3,474	ND (19)	4,684
Expansion into new			D (20)	6,450 Ψ	D (22)	6,818 **
markets			ND (20)	7,550	ND (20)	8,250
Finance						
Achieving critical	D (20)	6,850 Ψ				
mass	ND (17)	4,824				
Off-balance sheet	D(20)	6,650 Ψ				
financing of aircraft	ND (17)	4,765				
Cost reduction			D (20)	7,500 *	D (22)	8,136 *
			ND (20)	8,700	ND (20)	9,100
Information						
Computer reservation	D (20)	6,600 *				
system	ND (18)	5,167				
Yield management	D (20)	5,600 Ψ				
system	ND (18)	3,667				
Market-intellig.					D (22)	8,045 *
inform.- and comm.					ND (20)	6,889
Environment						
Investors' attitude	D (20)	7,100 *				
towards the NE	ND (17)	4,710				
Favourable attitude of			D (20)	8,300 Ψ	D (22)	9,000 *
travel agents			ND (20)	7,250	ND (20)	7,900

Note: *** = $p<.001$; ** = $p<.01$; * = $p<.05$; Ψ = $p<.1$. The mean for italicised statements is significantly different for both failed and non-failed, and distressed and non-distressed carriers. Note that only Part II, past was tested for the failed/non-failed group.

Cost reduction was significantly different between the two groups at the *present* (7.5 vs. 8.7, $p<.05$) and in the *future* (8.1 vs. 9.1, $p<.05$), with non-distressed carriers placing more importance on the factor. Understandably, the factor was highly important during the period in which the survey was conducted, due to a recession in air transport. Thus, it is no surprise that high emphasis on cost reduction and non-distress go hand in hand.

Information factors. Distressed carriers placed more importance on *computer reservation system* (CRS) in the *past* (6.6 vs. 5.2, $p<.05$), and *yield management system* (YMS) also in the past (5.6 vs. 3.7, $p<.1$). This emphasis on systems in the past reinforces the notion that new-entrants were at an disadvantage if poorly represented in a CRS or not having a YMS. The future dimension shows one new item that occurred neither in the past nor in the present dimension, namely *market intelligent information and communication system*, emphasised more by distressed carriers (8.0 vs. 6.9, $p<.05$). Thus, poor information systems may play a role at distressed carriers, making lack of market information an important source of difference in profitability and a driving force to change as this factor indicates with higher emphasis at distressed carriers.

Environment factors. As expected the distressed carriers placed significantly more importance on *investor's attitude towards the new-entrant* (7.1 vs. 4.7, $p<.05$). Understandably this factor is going to play a major role on the survivability of the carrier under distress, making persuasive selling of future plans and turnaround important. The same applies to *favourable attitude of travel agents* (TA) as they play no less significant role in the survivability of a distressed carrier due to the risk of sell away if confidence is lost among TA. This factor was rated significantly higher by distressed carriers at the present (8.3 vs. 7.3, $p<.1$) and in the future (9.0 vs. 7.9, $p<.05$).

Summary

Statements differentiating between both failed and non-failed carriers and distressed and non-distressed carriers for Part I of the questionnaire, were: *the airline's success is largely dependent on factors out of its control, everyone in our airline understands our long term aims and objectives, we plan and allocate sufficient resources to developing new markets, lack of capital will not limit our growth, we fulfil our customers' needs well,* and *we are innovators in customer service.* Non-failed and non-distressed carriers had higher means for all the named statements except the first one.

Statements showing significant difference ($p<.05$) between both failed and non-failed carriers and distressed and non-distressed carriers were: *hub and spoke operations, yield management system, achieving critical mass, job rotation and computer reservation system.* One more statement showed significant ($p<.001$) difference between failed and non-failed carriers, *Delegation* and *operations without unionised staff.* No highly significant ($p<.001$) difference appeared between distressed and non-distressed, except: *Hub and spoke operations* and *Job rotation.* However, statements showing significant ($p<.05$) difference were: *service quality (past), merger/acquisition to gain market-share (past), investor's attitudes towards the new-entrant, Alliance with the incumbents, decentralised organisation structure* (present) *and market-intelligent information- and communication system* (future).

Distressed airlines show slightly less emphasis on *cost reduction*, while the statement is highly emphasised by both groups. Distressed airlines show more emphasis on *favourable attitude of travel agents* showing a need for increased emphasis on the distribution system, probably in order to rectify past defects. Results for respondents of non-distressed carriers show increasing importance in the future of factors such as *expansion into new markets, media advertising* and *aircraft utilisation.*

---

116 This belief of managers' willingness to justify their actions or seek explanations from the environment for losses or failure, is clearly apparent from the literature.

117 This criteria of jet-operating new-entrants was to ensure comparability and to exclude plain feeder and commuter airlines which operate under different philosophy than new-entrants serving general markets (general markets being interstate and international markets in particular). The comparability requirement is necessary to exclude financial structures and operating characteristics of smaller turboprop carriers that are quite different from jet carriers. First of all sector distances are shorter for turboprop carriers in general, direct costs are higher, indirect costs are lower due to simpler overhead structure and tie-ins with trunk carriers, usually by feeder agreements or plain ownership.

118 This actually supports the view that attitudes are too imprecise to be rated on wide scales that imply more accuracy than they actually provide.

119 These ideas of wider definition of business areas were first initiated by Theodore Levitt in his landmark article Marketing Myopia in *Harvard Business Review*, July - August, 1960.

120 The mean showed is an aggregated average for time dimensions showing significant difference between the means for distressed and non-distressed carriers.

7 Looking into the crystal ball

Introduction

A failure or distress prediction model can be used by financial institutions to assess the financial health of a company in order to calculate the likelihood of recovering a loan or an investment. Such models can also be used as a early warning system in order to initiate change or proactive turnaround. However, problems are associated to prediction models that must be made clear. For example, if a failure prediction model based on financial ratios indicates that a company is highly likely to fail, the very same model does not indicate in any way 'what' has gone wrong, because financial ratios are symptomatic rather than causal by nature. Examples are known were managers with such knowledge have tried to improve the ratios in various ways without addressing the real problems. There are also examples of the use of failure prediction models to focus managers' attention on the real problems (Altman, 1993). As a result, it is of much interest whether models can be developed that are based on variables that are more indicative as to the cause of firms' problems or well-being.

Theory formulation

Failure prediction models are in most cases purely empirical and lack theory on which the selection of predictive variables is based. Robertson (1984) suggested anterior determinants of failure: trading stability, declining profits, declining working capital and increase in borrowings. He suggested also market share patterns as indicators of company health: market size, market share variance and market share in relation to growing, stagnant or shrinking market.

An econometric model containing only financial statement information would not provide highly accurate classification of failed and non-failed firms. Martin, (1977, p.257) discussing bank failure, recognised this fact,

> These excluded variables (most of which can not be directly observed) determine how vulnerable, in terms of the included variables, a bank would have to be in order to fail'.

Zavgren (1983, p.25) supports Martin's conclusion in her research

> These factors determine for each firm a critical level of vulnerability, or a 'tolerance for vulnerability,' above which the firm will fail.

The classification error of failure prediction models can be explained partially by the fact that companies are dynamic entities that can at any time return to profitability due to management change process or extraordinary circumstances. In view of that fact there will always be misclassification. This is not pertinent to the statistical process as it takes into account only misclassification of companies that are actually non-failed and failed.

Menard (1995) points out that stepwise methods can be used in exploratory analysis for theory development (Menard, p.38) "...when neither theory nor knowledge about correlates of the phenomenon is well developed." Menard further suggests that inclusion and removal of variables under such circumstances is similar as that of theory testing but less stringent. This explains the philosophical stand taken in the approach to this research and supports the suitability of the methodology for the project.

The use of ratios

The financial ratios applied in most of the studies differ as each sample set has different characteristics. However, as suggested by Lev and Sunder (1979, p.187) the use of ratios as such is important to control for the systematic effect of size on the variables under observation. The control of size is for two main reasons; (i) to control for the increased size of individual components of the ratio over the years, such as an increase in equity; and (ii) to fulfil the requirements of the statistical technique employed.

There is relatively little conformity on what ratios are the best indicators of failure as Table 7.1, indicates. The studies cited in the table show that the sample drives the selection of ratios in such a way that only two identical ratios are used in more than two models and six ratios are used in two models. Thus, ratio analysis does have its limitations and pitfalls that are important to address in any research using the methodology. Morley (1984, p.35) discusses five main dangers: (i) ignorance of accounting policies; (ii) disregarding of the unique characteristics of the industry; (iii) improper comparisons; (iv) technical errors in constructing ratios; (v) and relying exclusively on ratios. The first point, ignorance of accounting policies constitutes, for example, comparison of firms: using different accounting policies, from different countries, applying different depreciation schedules and so on. The second point does not apply to this project as the comparison is only on airlines in the USA. The third, point does not apply, as the comparison will only be in terms of probability of failure and not a comparison of the financial ratios themselves.

Table 7.1 Ratios used in failure prediction models of five studies

Ratio	Frequency	Study
Cash flow[a]/total debt	3	Deakin, Beaver, Blum
Quick assets [b] /current liabilities	3	Deakin, Zavgren, Edmister
Cash/total assets	2	Deakin, Zavgren
Current assets [c] /current liabilities [d]	2	Blum, Zavgren
Inventory/sales	2	Zavgren, Edmister
Net income/total assets	2	Ohlson, Deakin
Total debt/total assets	2	Beaver, Deakin
Current assets/total assets	2	Beaver, Ohlson
Working capital [e] /total assets	1	Deakin
Cash/current liabilities	1	Deakin
Cash/sales	1	Deakin
Current assets/sales	1	Deakin
Current liabilities/current assets	1	Ohlson
Current liabilities/equity	1	Edmister
Debt/total capital	1	Zavgren,
Dummy variable for total assets > total liabilities	1	Ohlson
Earnings before interest and taxes/total assets	1	Altman
Equity/sales	1	Edmister
Funds flow/current liabilities	1	Edmister
Funds from operations/total liabilities	1	Ohlson
Log (total assets/GNP price level index)	1	Ohlson
Market value equity/book value of total debt	1	Altman
Net income/total assets	1	Beaver
Net quick assets/inventory	1	Blum
Net working capital/sales	1	Edmister
No credit interval	1	Beaver
Quick assets/sales	1	Deakin
Quick assets/total assets	1	Deakin
Quick flow ratio	1	Blum
Rate of return to equity	1	Blum
Receivables/inventory	1	Zavgren
Retained earnings/total assets	1	Altman
Sales/net plant	1	Zavgren
Sales/total assets	1	Altman
Total income/total capital	1	Zavgren
Total liabilities/total assets	1	Ohlson
Variability and trend of net income	1	Blum
Variability and trend of net quick assets/inventory	1	Blum
Working capital/sales	1	Deakin
Working capital/total assets	1	Deakin

[a] Net cash flow = profit after tax plus depreciation plus increases in deferred tax minus dividends. [b] Quick assets = current assets less stock. [c] Current assets = stock, debtors and cash. [d] Current liabilities = liabilities due for payment within one year following the balance sheet data. [e] Working capital = current assets less current liabilities.

Source: Altman (1968), Deakin (1972), Beaver (1966), Edmister (1972), Blum (1974), Ohlson (1980), Zavgren (1983).

The fourth pitfall is basically not to observe what should be used as numerator and denominator during calculations. The fifth point is not to rely exclusively on ratios but to research the accounts to check for possible 'window dressing', which involves major transactions just before the balance sheet date.

Non-financial ratios have been used in number of failure prediction models but are usually pseudo-financial or accounting procedure linked. Keasey and Watson (1987) tested 18 qualitative variables and found that companies with few directors, longer than average submission lags of financial statements and secured loans held by banks, were more susceptible to failures. Furthermore, companies were more likely to fail if they had received an audit qualification in their last report. On the basis of Keasey and Watson, Innes, Aitken and Mitchell (1991) derived a set of non-financial variables along similar lines. The qualitative variables employed in the above models do not address the underlying causes of failure but address symptoms just as the financial ratios.

There is one question that remains to be answered, why one does not simply refer to analysis of the means of ratios to segregate a sample of firms into two groups failed and non-failed? To answer this can refer to Beaver (1967) and Altman (1968), two of the early researchers in field of bankruptcy prediction. Beaver used Univariate Ratio Analysis (URA) to classify corporations into failed and non-failed groups, but Altman concluded that URA would not provide comprehensive profile of the firm when each individual ratio is assessed independently. Multiple Discrimination Analysis (MDA) on the other hand combined those ratios having optimum discrimination powers into a single formula that could be used to predict bankruptcy of non-sample companies. In that sense MDA and a similar method logistic regression analysis (LRA) are superior to URA. To sum up, MDA and LRA are superior to simple analysis of the means like URA, by taking into account the more complex relationship of the variables and returning this relationship in a near optimum discrimination function.

Statistical methodology

Altman (1968) pioneered the use of MDA to distinguish between failed and non-failed companies in 1968. The variables in his model were based on financial ratios and the sample was composed of 66 manufacturing companies that were segregated into two groups failed and non-failed. The firms in the sample were operating in the US during 1946 to 1965 and half of those had filed for bankruptcy under Chapter 10 of the National Bankruptcy Act and had mean asset size of \$6.4 million. The sample was paired, recognising the differences in asset size and industry, using stratification based on size and industry. The data was derived from financial statements one-year ('reporting period') prior to bankruptcy.

Altman included 22 ratios from which five were finally selected as the greatest discriminators of the dichotomous dependent variable. The model took the form

$$Z = .021X_1 + .014X_2 + .033X_3 + .006X_4 + .999X_5 \qquad (7\text{-}1)$$

Where, Z is the overall index and X_1 is Working Capital/Total Assets, X_2 Retained Earnings/Total Assets, X_3 Earnings Before Interest and Taxes/Total Assets, X_4 Market Value of Equity/Book Value of Total Debt, and X_5 is Sales/Total Assets.

These ratios were empirically selected from the set of 22 as the best discriminators of the dichotomous variable. In evaluating the statistical significance of the discriminant function Altman used (*ctd. in* Zavgren, 1983, p.16) the following methodology: (i) traditional evaluation of the statistical significance; (ii) intercorrelation among the discriminating variables; (iii) predictive accuracy of the discriminant function; and (iv) researcher's judgement.

The principal aim in failure prediction is to reduce the misclassification error of the models in order to increase the predictability of the model. This feature of the models can be tested on a hold out sample that represents similar characteristics as the sample on which the model is based. A summary by Zavgren (1983) shows the classification error of Altman's (1968) model increases three years prior to failure, in comparison to the rest of the models. However, Deakin's (1972) probabilistic model shows better results in terms of misclassification, especially more than one year from failure. Wilcox (1971) reported good results, as well, with his theoretical Gambler-Ruin Model having 24 percent overall error rate five years prior to failure, while Altman's model had 64 percent, Beaver's (1966) 22 percent, Deakin 17 percent and Blum (1974) 17 percent.

In the years following Beaver's and Altman's work, an ongoing process took place where attempts were made to improve the predictability of the models. Altman, Haldeman and Narayanan (1977) published an improvement of Altman's original model, where the new model had 53 bankrupt and 58 non-bankrupt firms. It is important to pay attention to the fact that the model mixes two industries, a practice that must be considered controversial in bankruptcy prediction. Classification accuracy of this new model rose considerably with overall classification error of 7.2 percent one-year prior to failure, 11 percent for the holdout sample two-years prior to failure, 16.5 percent for the holdout sample three-years prior, 20.2 percent for the holdout sample four years prior, and finally 23.2 percent for the holdout sample five-years prior to failure. Edminster (1972) also achieved quite good results in his model that utilised dummy variables to indicate upward or downward trend in ratios, a new methodology he proposed.

The logistic regression methodology

The third frequently used statistical method for failure prediction is logistic regression analysis (LRA). It estimates a logistic regression equation and then uses a critical level of Z to distinguish between the two classes: failed or non-failed. Collins and Green (1982) find the logistic method more theoretically appealing in bankruptcy prediction, than MDA. One of the reasons is that the logistic cumulative distribution function is a 'sigmoid curve' (S-curve) that has the 'threshold' trait that a bankruptcy forecasting problem logically requires. Furthermore, they mention the fact that the LRA formulation is more robust to distribution assumptions due to the possibility of several such assumptions.

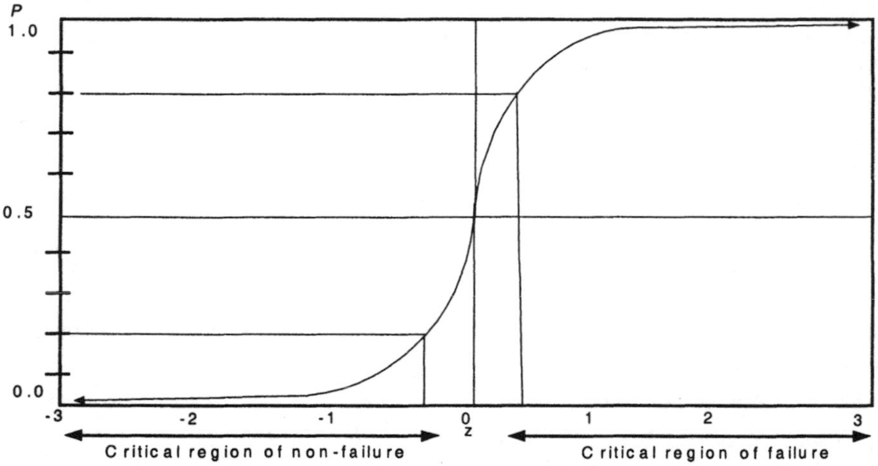

Figure 7.1 The LRA S-Curve

The determination of the 'threshold' is important because if the probability score falls along the lower bend of the curve, *p*(0 to .2) the probability of failure is practically 0. However, if the score passes the bend and falls along the growth section of the curve, *p* (0.2 to 0.5), the probability of failure increases dramatically. Hence, there is little increase in the probability of failure as the change in the ratio falls along the upper bend of the curve, *p* (0.8 to 1). Thus, the 'breaking' point falls somewhere in the middle of the growth section of the curve, *p* (0.5), for example. The logistic regression function produces a *Z* value that is transformed by the probability function into a probability. The *Z* is the linear combination of the resulting model, taking the form

$$p(\text{failure}) = \frac{1}{1 + e^{-z}} \tag{7-2}$$

Where, $Z = B_0 + B_1 X_1 + B_2 X_2 + ... + B_p X_p$, e = 2.718 (the base of the natural logarithms)

Logistic regression, applied to failure prediction has the advantage of having few of the problems of MDA analysis. Ohlson (1980) argues, nevertheless, that certain discipline in data collection has to be adhered to. For example, the data has to be available prior to failure so that the model can be evaluated realistically.

Catastrophe theory

An alternative method of bankruptcy prediction is the Catastrophe Theory (CT) which is a mathematical approach modelling a discontinuous behaviour in a system. The theory is an approximation of a situation where a continuous change in independent variables causes a discontinuous change in the dependent variable. CT has been applied to corporate bankruptcies by: Scapens, Ryan and Fletcher (1981); Francis, Hastings and Fabozzi (1983); and Gregory-Allen and Henderson (1991). The first study used CT to show the relationship between accounting data and behavioural responses of creditors. Their results showed CT explanatory ability rather than predictive capacity and that variable identification was crucial but problematic. The second study included exogenous forces on the model and is unlike other CT bankruptcy studies for that sake. In other terms the two studies yield similar models and results. The third study was based on Francis *et al.* (1983) and concluded that there was a strong indication of parameter shift and that the presence of the shifts along with heteroscedasticity is consistent with CT (Gregory-Allen and Henderson, 1991).

All models are composed of one 'state' variable (X), one 'normal' variable (N) and one 'splitting' variable (S). The selection of only three variables is according to the 'cusp' model that requires all selected variables to be collapsed into the three main variables. The three variables define the three dimensional space within which the system behaves.

Neural networks

Neural nets were proposed and researched as early as the 50s and 60s but were at that time found to be limited due to their limited learning ability. Advancement in the field has caused increased interest in the applicability of such networks for number of differing fields, among those is corporate failure prediction.[121]

The neural net is composed of interconnected computation devices that can be represented as mathematical functions. Rumelhart *et al.*, proposed the following function (*ctd. in* Tam and Kiang, 1992, p.929)

$$I_i = \sum_j w_{ij} o_j + \phi_i \qquad (7\text{-}3), \qquad\qquad o_i = \frac{1}{1 + e^{I_i}} \qquad (7\text{-}4)$$

Where,

$I_i =$ input of unit i,

$O_i =$ output of unit i,

$w_{ij} =$ connection weight between unit i and j,

$\phi_i =$ bias of unit i.

The function works as described by Tam and Kiang (p.929): 'A unit i receives input signals from other units, aggregates these signals based on input function I_i , and generates an output signal based on an output function O_i (sometimes called a transfer function). The output signal is then routed to other units as directed by the topology of the network.' Tam and Kiang reported in a misclassification test on a hold-out sample of 44 banks (22 failed and 22 non-failed) in one and two year periods, that the neural net remained the best classifier in terms of low *Type II* error and overall classification. The neural-network representing 10 hidden units achieved the second lowest total error rate of 11.3 percent, compared to a low 7.5 percent of the logistic regression model applied on the same data.

Theoretical failure prediction models

There are a number of simple theoretical models developed to explain corporate failure. A simple model cited by Scott (1981, p.326) assumes that a firm goes bankrupt if its debt exceeds the liquidation value, stated as

$$D_1 > V_1 \qquad (7\text{-}5)$$

Where, D_1 is the debt and V_1 is a random variable of the firm's value at a end of period.

Thus if the bankruptcy is specified on the normal curve the firm will go bankrupt if

$$\frac{D_1 - \mu_v}{\sigma_v} > \frac{V_1 - \mu_v}{\sigma_v} \qquad (7\text{-}6)$$

Where, μ_v is a location parameter, and σ_v as scale parameter.

The gamblers ruin models proposed by Borch (1967), Tinsley (1970), Wilcox (1971), Santomero and Vinso (1977) are based on a capital variable that changes randomly according to positive or negative effects on the firm's cash flow from operations. When the firm encounters negative effect on K it has to liquidate assets until K becomes negative at which stage it goes bankrupt, stated as

$$\frac{\mu_z + K}{\sigma_z} \qquad (7\text{-}7)$$

Where, ***K*** is the stockholder's equity and μ_Z the mean and σ_Z the standard deviation of the next period's change in retained earnings.

Models with perfect access to exogenous capital assume that stockholders do not need to sell assets in order to meet losses but can sell debt or equity instead. Thus stated as

$$\frac{\mu_x + S}{\sigma_x} \qquad (7\text{-}8)$$

Where, ***S*** is the market value of equity and μ_X is the mean, and σ_X the standard deviation of next period's net income.

If the firm has imperfect access to exogenous capital, the model takes the form (Scott, p.336)

$$\frac{\mu_x + \Delta K + S / (1 + c)}{\sigma_x} \qquad (7\text{-}9)$$

Where, ***ΔK*** is the optimal change in stockholders' equity, given that the firm is faced with earnings losses, and ***c*** is the proportional flotation costs.

The hindering of perfect access to capital, according to Scott, may be based on the costs incurred when floated or personal tax system that favours internally funded corporate investments.

As can be detected from the models discussed, theoretical based failure prediction models are based on financial factors exclusively and do not, therefore, address the underlying contributing factors. Such models are apparently less useful than empirically based models to predict bankruptcy.

Discussion

Empirical failure prediction models

The main criticism of Altman's model has been its limitation in terms of prediction ability more than two years before failure. This could be considered limited predictability, in view of the fact that most analysts will already have detected all the signs of imminent failure by then. Furthermore, as is with most failure prediction models it is not based on theory. Therefore, it has limited use in turnaround situations as deterioration in financial ratios represents symptoms rather than causes of decline and failure. In addition, the model is based on published accounts that may have been polished through creative accounting, especially in failing firms. This criticism applies, however, to all models based on financial ratios.

Eisenbeis (1977) identified a number of problems applying failure prediction models. First, the variables used in the model are assumed to be multivariate normally distributed, although, it is more likely that deviations from normality is more frequent than not. Second, group dispersion matrixes have to be equal across all groups and if this assumption is relaxed it will affect the significance test for the difference in group means. Third, the discriminant model does not allow the determination of the relative importance of the variables, as the output is simple ordinal ranking. Fourth, the reduction of dimensions has limitations for the same reasons as stated for the second problem above if the group dispersions are unequal. Thus, it may be unwise to reduce dimensions or variables if classification[122] is the primary goal of the model. The effect must be established and the decision of keeping or dropping variables and dimensions must be related to the efficiency of the classification.

Theoretical causal models

Wilcox abandoned his functional model but constructed an empirical model based on the variables derived from the earlier model. Altman (1993) concluded that the classification accuracy of his empirical model was very promising, but lacked verification, as it was not tested on a hold-out sample. Theoretical models suffer due to their simplicity and use of superficial explanation of business failure, as can be seen through emphasis on financial variables, in lieu of accepted academic view that the change in the financial variables is symptomatic.

Alternative failure prediction models

Catastrophe theory has been criticised (Sussmann and Zahler, 1978) in relation to its application to the social sciences on the basis of lack of understanding of the social phenomena itself rather than the mathematical theory. This criticism has been rebuffed by other researchers (Oliva and Capdevielle, 1981) claiming that the model does apply but subject to weaknesses just as any other mathematical method, requiring caution on behalf of the user.

The Neural Network (NN) methodology has its shortcomings as to identifying the importance of individual variables in segregating the dichotomous variable. In addition the NN does not yield any symbolic formula as to its segregation function. This is not a limitation as to the evaluation of its prediction accuracy but more so if individual inputs need to be tested for significance. Furthermore, there is no method available to derive the network configuration for a classification task.

Summary

Empirical failure prediction models gained acceptance in the 1960's. These models have, however, lacked theoretical foundation. Most empirical failure prediction models are based on financial ratios, but there is little conformity on what ratios to use and each model seems to come up with its own set of empirically selected ratios. The most popular statistical method for failure prediction is Multiple Discriminant Analysis that makes more demand on the sample design than Logistics Regression Analysis, which returns probability of failure instead of a Z value where a cut-off point has to be determined.

Most researchers have emphasised the improvement of the predictability of the models by using increasingly sophisticated statistical methods. It is unlikely that any great advancement will occur in these terms in the future based on the statistical methodology on its own. Further, advancement has to come from theoretical advancement in terms of identifying factors having clear relationship with failure.

A number of alternative methods of failure prediction have been used, such as Catastrophe Theory and Neural Networks. These models show some promise, but do not provide any increase in overall predictability. Furthermore, such models do not provide any advances in terms of identifying causal factors of failure. Simple theoretical models have been developed on corporate failure. These models suffer from too much simplicity and reliance on financial variables.

---

[121] One development was the back propagation learning algorithm to train a multilayered network that can reproduce the XOR function.

[122] Dimension reducing methods have traditionally been concerned with the contribution significance of the variable to the statistic used in testing hypothesis about the equality of group means. *See* Eisenbeis and Avery (1972).

8 Assessing new-entrant airlines

Introduction

Three types of failure prediction models will be presented in this chapter: two based on Part I and Part II of the questionnaire survey and one on quantitative variables. The purpose of developing different models was to test whether there are similarities among the variables selected into the models, and whether other model sources than the traditional financial source can perform as well or better in classifying airlines into the failed and non-failed, and distressed and non-distressed groups.

The stated null hypotheses was that there is no difference in the classification accuracy of models derived from different subsets of variables from the questionnaire and that these do not differ in terms of classification ability. The same hypothesis was tested for the quantitative variables.

Methodology considerations

Multicollinearity is certainly an issue in traditional regression analysis. In logistic regression multicollinearity can be used to enhance the discriminatory power of the regression function. Cochran (1982) showed that a variable that appears unimportant on its own, may in combination with other variables be highly important and enhance classification ability of the model. In general one must assume that the same relationship exists between the independent variables and the dependent variable when the function is used to predict failure and non-failure. As discussed in Zavgren (1983, p.15), if multicollinearity is present, another assumption must be added, namely that of a stability between intercorrelations of the group on which the model is based and the group on which the function will be used to predict. If this latter assumption does not hold the results will be sample specific and predictability will be poorer than for the original group from which the function is derived.

Zavgren (p.17) also notes that another function based on the variables excluded in the model may be as good in predicting bankruptcies due to correlation with the variables included. Thus, it is not appropriate to assume that any one function derived from the sample data to be unique information.

One more important issue in failure prediction is the potential cost of errors. Such costs are, of course, relative according to who is using the results of prediction model. For example, from the standpoint of investors the cost of *Type I*[123] error would be more costly. Conversely from the standpoint of managers of firms the cost of *Type II* error would be more costly raising creditors alarm unnecessarily.[124]

Bankruptcy prediction models have sometimes been developed separately for each year prior to failure, often up to five years. This practice is highly questionable,[125] since the practitioner can not determine accurately which model to use for prediction on non-sample data, the one year, the second year or the third year model if we assume a three year data-set. However, there is a difference if the models are presented as base models,[126] whereas their predictability is then tested on the other years.[127,128] Under such circumstances the use of a model based on the year prior to failure and another based on the third year prior to failure could enhance bankruptcy and distress prediction.

The application of the logistic regression methodology

Model construction

As the logistic model is non-linear an iteration algorithm is used for parameter estimation. In logistics regression a number of specific terms and concepts are used. The *likelihood* is the probability of the observed result given the parameter estimates. It is represented by -2 times the *log* of the *likelihood* (-2LL) and represents how well the model fits the data. Thus, a good model has a high likelihood of the observed results, translated into small value for -2LL (Norusis, 1990). The model's improvement is the change in the -2LL as each successive variable is entered or excluded from the model. Thus, a large difference between the initial -2LL with only the constant included and the final model with one or more variables indicates high probability of observed result given the parameter estimates. Thus, a model classifying the sample perfectly into two groups failed and non-failed, will have -2LL of 0.

Interpretation of the logistic coefficients is meaningful, unlike in Multiple Discrimination Analysis. If we write the logistic model in terms of the log of odds, or logit, we find

$$\ln\left(\frac{\text{Prob (event)}}{\text{Prob (no event)}}\right) = B_0 + B_1X_1 + \ldots + B_pX_p \qquad (8.1)$$

Thus, the logistic coefficient can be interpreted as change in log odds as the independent variable changes by one unit. Thus, a coefficient of .5 in a failure prediction model will with one unit change in the independent variable increase the log odds of failure by .5. If we rewrite the formula to represent odds only, instead of log odds, it takes the form

$$\frac{\text{Prob(event)}}{\text{Prob(no event)}}) = e^{B_0+B_1X_1+...+B_pX_p} = e^{B_0}e^{B_1X_1}...e^{B_pX_p} \qquad (8.2)$$

Thus, e raised to B_i will result in a factor that determines the odds change when the ith independent variable increases by one unit. As a result, if the estimator B_i is positive the factor will be grater than 1, leading to an increase in the odds; if the B_i is negative it leads to a factor of less than 1, that reduces the odds. Thus, if B_i is 0 the factor becomes 1 and the odds are left unchanged. This leads to the third equation used to estimate the probability of failure in our case (Norusis, p. B-43)

$$\text{Estimated prob (failure)} = \frac{1}{1+e^{-z}} \qquad (8.3)$$

Where, e is the natural logarithm and z the log-odds.

In the model construction both *forward stepwise* (FSTEP) variable entry and *backward stepwise* (BSTEP) was used. FSTEP was only used on the variables in Part I of the questionnaire survey, because BSTEP led to a large set of non-significant coefficients. Using FSTEP this problem was resolved although classification property and uniformity of significant coefficients was preserved. In the former method an independent variable is entered based on the significance level of the score statistic. Thus, the variable with highest significance level (p<.05) is entered and variables already in the model are tested for removal based on the significance of the likelihood-ratio[129] (LR) statistic (p>.1).[130] The backward stepwise methodology enters all variables at the first step and then proceeds to eliminate variables from the model as in FSTEP. The significance level for variable entry was set at .05 and .1 for variable elimination. A relaxation of significance levels lead to an increase in the inclusion of non-significant coefficients in the models, which was found unacceptable.

It is important in the interpretation of the model coefficients to analyse the reasons behind reverse signs to what was expected. The apparent relationship of the means with the signs of the coefficients appears to be in the direction of the difference of the means. Thus, if the mean is greater for non-distressed (ND) than distressed (D) the sign is positive, conversely if the mean is lower the sign is negative. Furthermore, interpretation of coefficient signs has to take into account that the representative variable may be highly emphasised or agreed to by both groups, regardless of its classification properties. Thus, one must be careful to interpret a variable as a *failure factor* or *success* factor, one can state that the intensity of its rating differs between the two groups under observation, and that these factors as critical.

Qualitative models

Model derived from questionnaire Part I

Model Q1, is based on the variables from questionnaire *Part I.* Using logistic regression to classify the cases into two groups, distressed (D) airlines and non-distressed (ND), 91.11 percent overall classification was attained. Two coefficients were significant and one highly significant. Some multicollinearity was present, which implies that the resulting model may be sample specific.

Table 8.1 Results of logistic regression for Part I

Model 1.1	Statement	β	
SUCC	The airline's success is largely dependent on factors out of its control	-1.0158	
CUST	We fulfil our customer' needs well	1.4569	
MARK	Our marketing is aggressive	-1.1002	
CAPI	Lack of capital will not limit our growth	1.7224	**
AIMS	Everyone in our airline understands our long term aims and objectives	1.1385	*
REWA	Employees are rewarded for taking actions that benefit our customers	-1.4643	*
CONS	Group consensus is the usual way we make decisions	-.7493	
	Constant	-.9600	
-2 Log Likelihood	30.159		
Goodness of fit	30.810		
D ND	95.83 85.71		
Overall	91.11		
Model Chi-Square	32.024***		
Pseudo R	.51		
n	D24 ND21		

Note: *** = p<.001; ** = p<.01; * = p< 05; Ψ = p<.1.

The *Type I* error was 4.17 percent, while the *Type II* error was 14.29 percent. The model chi-square was significant (p<.001), while the pseudo-R squared[131] was satisfactory at .51. Two coefficients were significant, *everyone in our airline understands our long term aims and objectives* (***AIMS***, p<.05) and *employees are rewarded for taking actions that benefit our customers* (***REWA***, *p*<.05), while the coefficient representing *lack of capital will not limit our growth* (***CAPI***, *p*<.01) was highly significant.

The statement *employees are rewarded for taking actions that benefit the customer,* receives higher mean for distressed carriers (3.5, vs. 3.0). One could presume that this should be a positive coefficient, but the reason for greater agreement among respondents of distressed carriers is probably due to their attempt to turn-around (*see* discussion on Increased Activity in Chapter 9).

Models derived from questionnaire Part II

For *Part II* of the questionnaire the variable set was divided into six sub-groups, then a separate model was made for each sub-group in the three time intervals *past*, *present* and *future*. Table 8.2 shows the resulting models for the *past*, while Table 8.3 and Table 8.4 show models constructed for the *present* and the *future.*[132]

Models based on the past (*see* Table 8.2). Model construction was successful for all sub-groups except *financial*, that yielded no result and is omitted from the table. Other models were significant, with highly significant model Chi-Square (*p*<.01 or better) for the *operations* (***Q4a***), *management* (***Q5a***) and the *marketing* (***Q6a***) models. While the *environment* (***Q2a***) and *information* (***Q3a***) models had significant Chi-Square (*p*<.05). Examining only the three best models, the pseudo-R squared shows satisfactory models for *operations* and *marketing* but poorer model for *management*. The best classifying result was obtained from the *marketing* model or 87.5 percent overall classification. The *Type I* error was 11.76 percent and *Type II* error 13.33 percent. The second best performing model was that of *operations* with 84.85 percent overall classification capability. That model has considerable poorer result on *Type I* error or 16.67 percent, while *Type II* error was the same as that of the *marketing* model.

All coefficients were significant (*p*<.05 or better), except *alliance with the incumbents* (***ALLI***), in the *marketing* model. In the *operations* model two coefficients were significant: *hub and spoke operations* (***HUB1***, *p*<.01) and *freight operations* (***OPS1***, p<.05). In the *management* model significant coefficients were *job rotation* (***JOB1***, *p*<.01) and *decentralised organisation structure* (***ORGA***, *p*<.05) In the *marketing* model it was *service quality* (***QUAL***, *p*<.01) and *market-share* (***MASH***, *p*<.05). The *environment* model had one significant coefficient, *investor attitudes towards the airline* (***INVE***, *p*<.01). The *information* model had also only one significant coefficient, *yield management system* (***YIEL***, *p*<.01). The surprising result was that logistic regression on the financial variables produced no model given the same constraints on variable entry as for other models. As a result it appears that the qualitative financial variables applied are poorer predictors of financial distress for this population than presumed.

Table 8.2 Results of logistic regression by variable sub-group: Part II, past

	Environment Model *Q2a*	Information Model *Q3a*	Operations Model *Q4a*	Management Model *Q5a*	Marketing Model *Q6a*
	Investor attitudes towards the airline -0.2553** (***INVE***)	Yield management system -0.2776** (***YIEL***)	Hub and spoke operations -.8010** (***HUB1***)	Job rotation -.7925** (***JOB1***)	Alliance with the incumbents -.4157 $^{\Psi}$ (***ALLI***)
	Constant 1.5113$^{\Psi}$	Constant .9083	Freight operations .6450* (***OPS1***)	Decentralised organisation structure .5362* (***ORGA***)	Market-share -.6874* (***MASH***)
			Constant .5926	Constant .7047	Service quality 1.0123** (***QUAL***)
					Constant -2.6641
-2 Log Likelihood	39.594	40.946	25.122	33.104	24.114
Goodness of fit	32.320	33.665	25.266	39.612	27.902
D ND	76.47 56.25	73.68 60.00	83.33 86.67	78.95 80.0	88.24 86.67
Overall	66.67	67.65	84.85	79.41	87.50
Model Chi-Square	6.123*	5.716*	20.353***	13.558**	20.122***
Pseudo R	0.13	0.12	0.45	0.29	0.45
n	D17 ND16	D19 ND15	D18 ND15	D19 ND15	D17 ND15

Note: *** = $p<.001$; ** = $p<.01$; * = $p<.05$; $^{\Psi}$ = $p<.1$.

Models based on the present (*see* Table 8.3). Regression on the *present* part of the questionnaire resulted in only three usable models, all showing similar classification accuracy. The sub-groups of variables that did not produce models were the same sub-groups that produced the poorest models in the *past*. The pseudo R^2 was .39 for the *management* (***Q5b***) model .32 for the *operations* (***Q4b***) and .30 for the *marketing* (***Q6b***) models. The *operations* model outperformed the *marketing* model producing the highest overall classification or 78.4 percent. However, this is a considerable poorer performance compared to 84.9 percent for the *operations* model in the *past*. Model *Q6b* provided much poorer result in the 'present' variable set or 76.5 percent overall classification. The *Type I* and *Type II* errors differed much between the three models. For model *Q4b* the *Type I* error was 21.05 percent, while models *Q5b* and *Q6b* had 20.0 and 29.41 percent, respectively. *Type II* error was 22.22 percent for Q4b, 29.41 percent for *Q6b* and 17.65 percent for model *Q6b*.

Table 8.3 Results of logistic regression by variable sub-group: Part II, present

	Operations Model *Q4b*	Management Model *Q5b*	Marketing Model *Q6b*
	Aircraft utilisation .5887$^{\Psi}$ (***UTIL***)	Flexible job descriptions .5311* (***FLEX***)	Market research -.9361* (***MARK***)
	Hub and spoke operations -.4684* (***HUB2***)	Job rotation -.8461** (***JOB2***)	Media advertising .8910* (***MEAD***)
	Freight operations .4138* (***OPS2***)	Constant -.1557	Constant .5289
	Constant -4.8343$^{\Psi}$		
-2 Log Likelihood	35.083	31.194	32.907
Goodness of fit	30.697	28.297	48.363
D ND	78.95 77.78	80.00 70.59	70.59 82.35
Overall	78.38	75.68	76.47
Model Chi-Square	16.183***	19.855***	14.227***
Pseudo R^2	0.32	0.39	0.30
n	D19 ND18	D20 ND17	D17 ND17

Note: *** = *p*<.001; ** = *p*<.01; * = *p*< .05; $^{\Psi}$ = *p*<.1.

All the coefficients are significant (*p*<.05 or better), with the exception of *aircraft utilisation* (***UTIL***, *p*<.1) in model *Q4b*, that had two other coefficients that were significant, *hub and spoke operations* (***HUB2***, *p*<.05) and *freight operations* (***OPS2***, *p*<.05). The only highly significant coefficient *was job rotation* (***JOB2***, *p*<.001) in model *Q5b*, which had also another significant coefficient, *flexible job descriptions* (***FLEX***, *p*<.05). Model *Q6b* had two significant coefficients, market research (***MARK***, $p<.05$) and media advertising (***MEAD***, $p<.05$).

Models based on the future (see Table 8.4). The *future* part of the questionnaire survey produced as before a *marketing* (***Q6c***) and *management* (***Q5c***) model, while the *operations* (***Q4c***) variable sub-set produced no model. However, the *information* (***Q3c***) sub-set produced a poor one variable model. Model Q5c has pseudo R^2 of 0.35, while the other models *Q3c* and *Q6c* had .10 and .25, respectively.

Table 8.4 Results of logistic regression by variable sub-group: Part II, future

	Information Model *Q3c*	Management Model *Q5c*	Marketing Model *Q6c*
	Market-intel. Inform.- and communic. system -.4793* (***INTEL***)	Employees productivity 1.0119* (***PROD***)	Frequent flyer programs -.2585* (***FREQ***)
	Constant 3.3324^{Ψ}	Job rotation -.7903** (***JOB3***)	Expansion into new markets .7555** (***EXPA***)
		Constant -5.6825	Constant -4.4099*
-2 Log Likelihood	48.168	40.250	37.506
Goodness of fit	37.828	35.080	37.637
D ND	90.91 29.41	71.43 64.71	73.68 70.59
Overall	64.10	68.42	72.22
Model Chi-Square	5.255*	12.007***	12.289**
Pseudo R^2	0.10	.35	.25
n	D22 ND17	D21 ND17	D19 ND17

Note: *** = $p<.001$; ** = $p<.01$; * = $p<.05$; $^{\Psi}$ = $p<.1$.

The surprising aspect of model *Q3c* is the low *Type I* error of only 9.09 percent, while the *Type II* error was very high, or 70.59 percent. This means that the model is good in classifying failed firms as failed, but poor at classifying non-failed airlines as non-failed. The reason behind this is not clear. Model *Q6c* has 72.2 percent overall classification, while model *Q5c* yields 68.48 percent. Both models have lower *Type I*, compared to *Type II* errors, 28.57 and 26.32 percent for *Type I*, and 35.29 and 29.41 percent for

Type II, for models *Q5c* and *Q6c*, respectively. The distribution traits are especially important to identify extreme outliers[133] that are common to all models due to carriers that are operationally, strategically or financially very different from the rest, causing different responses to the statements compared to the majority of cases in the same group.

Model *Q3c* had one significant coefficient *market intelligent information and communication system* (***INTEL***, $p<.05$). Model *Q5c* had two significant coefficients *employees' productivity* (***PROD***, $p<.05$) and *job rotation* (***JOB3***, $p<.01$). Model *Q6c* had also two significant coefficients *frequent flyer programs* (***FREQ***, $p<.05$) and *expansion into new markets* (***EXPA***, $p<.01$).

Conclusion. The overall conclusion is that the *operations*, *marketing* and *management* models yield the best[134] results in terms of distribution traits. Of these three, the *marketing* model (*Q6a*) shows apparently better overall distribution traits than the rest of the models.

Quantitative models

The airline database[135] was constructed for the purpose of producing a variable set for discrimination between failed and non-failed new-entrant airlines in the United States from 1978 until 1992. The selection of new-entrants for inclusion in the quantitative analysis was based on same principles as the selection of new-entrants for the questionnaire survey.

The Phase-In Algorithm for the small population case

The population of jet-operating new-entrants posed a number of practical problems. One was the establishment of adequate number of carriers in the two groups of the dichotomous observed variable due to the small population. Another was the large proportion of failed carriers. Based on the data presented in previous chapters, one can easily infer that many jet-operating new-entrants were quite successful for a period in their life-cycle, making it appropriate to divide their life-cycle into phases of three years and handle each phase as a separate module for entry as failed or non-failed. The following discussion will provide detailed analogy of the method developed and applied in the study.

The first phase is when the carrier has operated for three complete years, which was the minimum operating life for inclusion. The second phase includes carriers that have operated for at least seven years.[136] However, carriers failing anytime during year t+5 to t+7, will be included only as failed counting from the last full financial year and backwards three years. For example, a carrier failing in the middle of year t+6, is included as failed and years t+5, t+4 and t+3 are included in the database.

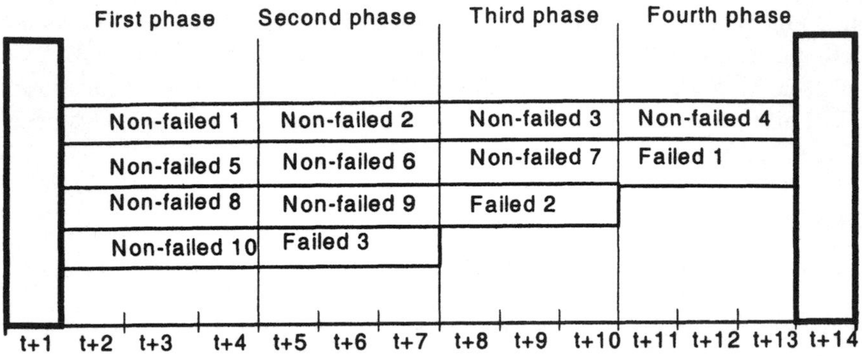

Note: non-failed = nf; failed = f.

Figure 8.1 Life-Cycle Phase-In group inclusion[137]

If a carrier fails, however, in year t+8, it will be included twice, first as non-failed by including years t+2, t+3 and t+4 and then as failed counting year t+5, t+6 and t+7. Year t+1 is then counted as slack for a partial year of operations.

Table 8.5 Dataset selection rules for inclusion in the analysis

Non-failed	Failed
nf1, nf5, nf8	nf10 - f3
nf2, nf6	nf9 - f2
nf3, nf4	nf7 - f1

A carrier operating successfully through all four phases will be included four times in the database as successful, thus, providing a contrast to carriers that fail during each of its successful phases. Table 8.5 derived from Figure 8.1 shows clearly the decision rule for determining whether or not the period should be included as failed or non-failed.

Selection of ratios

Selection of ratios and other measurement variables in the analysis was divided into three distinctive parts: (i) financial ratios; (ii) non-financial ratios; and (iii) ratios composed of one financial and one non-financial element, termed as mixed (*see* descriptive of quantitative data in Appendix C).

The construction of mixed ratios was based partially on the assumptions put forth by Doganis (1986), namely that a cost unit should be part of a ratio supposed to measure efficiency. In addition, the factor of stage length and aircraft size was observed as important. Doganis makes the use of available tonne kilometres (ATK) rather than available seat kilometres (ASK). As the ATK was not readily available to the researcher, the alternative to ATK, ASK was used. This alternative was further reinforced on the basis of the tendency of US airlines to base most of their income on the carriage of passengers rather than cargo.

Table 8.6 Ratios and variables derived from the database

Financial variables	Non-financial variables	Mixed variables
	Industry-specific	
Net Worth/Total Debt	Load-factor	Yield
EBIT/Sales	% Non-scheduled	Fuel Cost/ASK
Net Income/Net Worth	Average stage length	Dir. Op. Exp./ASK
Long Term Debt/Total	Aircraft Dep./Total Personnel	Ind. Op. Exp./ASK
Total Debt/Total Assets	Aircraft Hours/Total Personnel	Maintenance/ASK
Current Assets/Total Revenue	Weight Load-factor	Tot. Op. Exp./ASK
ADV/Fixed	Average no. of seats per dep.	Depreciation/ASK
Labour Cost/ADV	Average daily rev. hours	Operating Rev./Employee
ADV/Working Capital	Distance per hour flown	Tot. Op. Exp./Employee
Depreciation/ADV	Average passenger haul	ASK/$1000 Wages
Current Assets/Total Assets		ASK/$1000 Op. Exp.
	Environment	Pax rev./RPK (Pax yield)
		Revenue/Passenger
	Percent change in GDP	Operating profit/ASK
	Change in consumer prices	
	Change in crude oil prices	
	Change in spot fuel prices	
	Spot fuel rate (Jet A/Jet A1)	
	Interest rate	
	Change in interest rate	

Selection of financial ratios was based primarily on previous studies of effective financial ratios for failure prediction primarily derived from Chen and Shimerda (1981) and Davis and Kay (1990) for variables related to *added value*. No attempt was made to produce a larger set of financial variables than presented in the two named studies. The non-financial variables have no cost or revenue element associated with the exception of *% non-scheduled*, that is calculated on the basis non-scheduled revenues as a percentage of total revenues. Non-financial variables can be divided into two parts *industry-specific* and *environment* related. The industry-specific variables were based on a proposed practice on measuring performance of airlines as reported by Doganis (1986).

Table 8.7 Significant differences between failed and non-failed carriers

Ratio/Variable	Population	Mean
Net-worth/Total debt	Failed	-.0056***
	Non-failed	.5719
Ebit/Sales	Failed	-.1082***
	Non-failed	.0558
Total debt/Fixed assets	Failed	1.2285**
	Non-failed	.6693
Revex	Failed	.9037***
	Non-failed	1.0486
Depreciation/ASK	Failed	.0028*
	Non-failed	.0044
Operating expense/ASK	Failed	-.0067***
	Non-failed	.0036
Long term debt/Total assets	Failed	.5592Ψ
	Non-failed	.3875

Note: *** = $p<.001$; ** = $p<.01$; * = $p<.05$; $^{\Psi}$ = $p<.1$.

The environment variables were based on a forecasting model of the influences of the economic environment on air transport demand (Gudmundsson, 1986). *A priori* assumption was that disposable income, interest rates and fuel costs would represent this influence adequately in the study. These were represented with changes in GDP, consumer prices, crude oil prices, spot fuel rates and interest rates. The rate of change was considered to represent the influence of the variable under consideration more clearly than if the actual value would be used.

Significant differences between groups

Of the 48 ratios and variables tested (*see* Table 8.7) only six showed significant difference between failed and non-failed carriers. All of these ratios are highly significant ($p<.001$) with the exception of *depreciation to ASK* that was significant ($p<.05$) and *long-term debt/total assets* ($p< .1$).

Models derived from database variables

Database models one year prior. All five models presented in Table 8.8, provide high overall classification except the *non-financial* model (DB5-1) and the *financial* model (DB1-1) having slightly higher *Type I* error than the other models. Model DB5 had highly significant model *Chi-Square*, while the other models had highly significant ($p<.001$) model chi-squares. The *pseudo*-R^2 ranged from .48 for model DB5 to .84 for the *mixed2* model (DB4-1).

Significant coefficients included *aircraft hours per employee* (***Aircraf1***, $p<.05$), *aircraft departures/total personnel* (***Aircraft***, $p<.05$), *average no of seats per departure* (***Average1***, $p<.05$) and *load factor* (***Load_fac***, $p<.05$) in model *DB5-1*. *Added value/fixed assets* (***ADV_Fixe***, *p*<.05), *total debt/total assets* (***Total_De***, *p*<.05) and *long term debt/total assets* (***Long_ter***, *p*<.05) in model *DB2-1*. *Earnings before interest and taxes/sales* (***Ebit_sal***, *p*<.01) was significant in model *DB-1* and *operating profit/ASK* (***Operatin***, *p*<.05) in model *DB3-1*. There was no significant coefficient in the *DB4-1* model.

Table 8.8 Classification result one year prior

	Financial1	Financial2	Mixed1	Mixed2	Non-financial
	Model *DB1-1*	Model *DB2-1*	Model *DB3-1*	Model *DB4-1*	Model *DB5-1*
	Ebit_Sal	***Revex***	***Maintena***	***Operatin***	***Average1***
	-49.0844**	-13.8773	.-310.362	-2053.89	-.0396*
	Constant	***ADV_Fixe***	***Operatin***	***ASK_$101***	***Aircraft***
	-.0386	-8.7176*	-1223.04*	0.000054	-.3580*
		Total_De	Constant	***Tot._Rev***	***Distance***
		21.4537*	1.8685	-.0406	-.0231$^{\Psi}$
		Long_Ter		Constant	***Aircrafl***
		-22.4908$^{\Psi}$		-4.1067	.2345*
		Constant			***Average3***
		10.7039			.0020
					Load_Fac
					-20.096*
					@_Non_Sc
					-12.9935$^{\Psi}$
					Change_2
					-9.1595$^{\Psi}$
					Constant
					30.9817*
-2 Log Likelihood	15.309	14.098	9.915	7.802	25.779
Goodness of Fit	29.201	20.428	10.310	6.753	25.846
Classification					
F NF	94.44 88.89	94.44 94.44	94.44 94.44	94.44 94.44	83.33 83.33
Total	91.67	94.44	94.44	94.44	83.33
Model Chi-Square	34.60***	35.809***	39.992***	42.105***	24.128**
Pseudo R^2	.69	.72	.80	.84	.48
n	f 18 nf 18	f 18 nf 18	f 18 nf 18	f 18 nf 18	f 18 nf 18

Note: *** = *p*<.001; ** = *p*<.01; * = *p*<.05; $^{\Psi}$ = *p*<.1. *Variable key*: ***Maintena*** = maintenance costs/ASK; ***ADV_Fixe*** = Added value/fixed assets; ***Total_De*** = Total debt/Fixed assets; ***Long_ter*** = long-term debt/total assets; ***operatin*** = operating profit/ASK; ***ASK_$101***=ASK/$1000 in wages; ***Tot._Rev*** = Total revenue/Pax; ***Aircraft*** = aircraft departures/total personnel; ***Distance*** = distance per hour flown; ***Aircrafl*** = aircraft hours/total personnel; ***average3*** = average passenger haul; ***@_Non_Sc*** = percent total ASK non-sheduled; ***Change2*** = change in spot fuel prices; ***Ebit_Sal*** = Earnings before interest and taxes/Sales; ***Revex*** = Revenues/Expenses; ***Load_fac*** = load factor; ***Average1*** = average no of seats per departure.

The one year prior model is the base-model on which the two year and three year data is tested. The reason being there is no point in specifying separate base models for each year, as the practitioner can not know which model to use as date of bankruptcy is unknown.

Database models two years prior. Two years prior to failure the overall classification declined for all models (*see* Table 8.9), while the *financial2* and *non-financial* models gave the best results,[138] 75.0 and 69.44 percent overall classification, respectively. *Type I* error was quite different between the two, or 22.2 and 33.3 percent and *Type II* error was 27.8 in both models.

Table 8.9 Classification result two years prior

	Financial1 Model *DB1-2*	Financial2 Model *DB2-2*	Mixed1 Model *DB3-2*	Mixed2 Model *DB4-2*	Non-financial Model *DB5-2*
	Ebit_Sal	***Revex***	***Maintena***	***Operatin***	***Average1***
	-9.8130*	-3.2898	-.0000032	-.0000753	.0043
	Constant	***ADV_Fixe***	***Operatin***	***ASK_$101***	***Aircraft***
	-.0517	-.0747	-31.5307	.000047	-.1456*
		Total_De	Constant	***Tot._Rev***	***Distance***
		4.8552	.7216	-.0056	-.0086
		Long_Ter		Constant	***Aircraf1***
		-3.8757		-.3986	.1419$^{\Psi}$
		Constant			***Average3***
		1.3234			.0003
					Load_Fac
					-8.1492
					@_Non_Sc
					-1.4555
					Change_2
					4.5861
					Constant
					9.8932
-2 Log Likelihood	44.265	38.907	49.049	7.802	34.621
Goodness of Fit	34.987	30.848	35.934	6.753	30.552
Classification F NF	61.11 66.67	66.67 72.22	77.78 44.44	61.11 50.00	77.78 72.22
Total	63.89	69.44	61.11	55.56	75.00
Model Chi-Square	5.642*	11.00*	.858	1.525	15.286$^{\Psi}$
Pseudo R^2	.11	.22	.02	.03	.31
n	f 18 nf 18	f 18 nf 18	f 18 nf 18	f 18 nf 18	f 18 nf 18

Refer to Table 8.8 for the key to variable names.

It is surprising how poorly the *financial* model performs in view of the emphasis placed on good performance of such models in prior research. Thus, it must be concluded that non-financial variables do provide better classification results for this sample further away from bankruptcy than one year, than financial variables. One possible explanation of this discrepancy, is 'window dressing' of financial results. Such actions on traffic data are not as readily practised or possible.[139] The pseudo-R^2 is adequate for the *DB5-2* model, but the model yields non-significant model Chi-Square, while the *DB2-2* model had significant Chi-Square but low pseudo-R^2. Significant coefficients were *Ebit_Sal* in the *financial1* model, *operatin* in the *DB4-2* model and *aircraft* in the *DB5-2* model.

Database models three years prior. Three years prior (*see* Table 8.10) the *non-financial* model is still providing better results than the *financial2* model, producing 72.2 percent overall classification compared to 66.67 percent for the latter model.

Table 8.10 Classification result three years prior

	Financial1 Model *DB1-3*	Financial2 Model *DB2-3*	Mixed1 Model *DB3-3*	Mixed2 Model *DB4-3*	Non-financial Model *DB5-3*
	Ebit_Sal	***Revex***	***Maintena***	***Operatin***	***Average1***
	-4.0177	2.5342	-23.5084	-.00000408	-.0143
	Constant	***ADV_Fixe***	***Operatin***	***ASK_$101***	***Aircraft***
	-.0125	-2.1062*	-.00000177	.00006554	-.1034*
		Total_De	Constant	***Tot._Rev***	***Distance***
		11.6443*	.4535	.0062	.0002
		Long_Ter		Constant	***Aircraf1***
		-11.819*		-1.2543	.1297*
		Constant			***Average3***
		-4.5059			.0008
					Load_Fac
					-14.0717
					@_Non_Sc
					1.1717
					Change_2
					2.7637
					Constant
					7.9386
-2 Log Likelihood	47.239	39.730	49.512	47.135	36.593
Goodness of Fit	34.854	32.026	36.013	35.735	31.440
Classification F NF	44.44 77.78	61.11 72.22	77.78 44.44	61.11 66.67	72.22 72.22
Total	61.11	66.67	61.11	63.89	72.22
Model Chi-Square	2.667	10.176*	.395	2.772	13.314
Pseudo R^2	.05	.20	.01	.06	.27
n	f 18 nf 18	f 18 nf 18	f 18 nf 18	f 18 nf 18	f 18 nf 18

Refer to Table 8.8 for the key to variable names.

The model Chi-Square is not significant although the classification result was superior to other models presented, including the significant financial2 model. The pseudo-R^2 indicates that the models *DB5-3* and *DB2-3* are performing much better than the rest, although, the values are not particularly good, as expected.

Practical application of the models

Prediction enhancement through model comparison

The best performing models presented so far for the qualitative and quantitative sections were tested on those airlines that participated in the questionnaire survey and were included in the quantitative section, thirteen airlines in total. The results are presented as predicted probabilities (*see* Table 8.11). Perfect probability of $p = 1$ denotes failure and $p = 0$ non-failure, and $p = 0.5$ is the cut-off point for the two states. On the basis of the cut-off point the conformity of models was calculated, meaning that a probability of $p > .5$ renders the airline distressed or failed and $p < .5$ counts as non-distressed or non-failed. So if an airline is considered distressed or failed in all four models and is in such a state (status) the conformity of models is 100%. If only three models return the actual status the conformity is 75% and so forth.

The main conclusion from the table is that the comparison of models from varying sources enhances the information content, as there is usually conformity of predicted probabilities between individual respondents in the questionnaire survey and the predicted probabilities for the associated airline derived from the database models. In the few cases where there is not conformity, such as case 108, there is conformity, however, of the two database models. In the cases where there is large difference between the financial and non-financial model, such as cases 115, 122, 301 and 304, the explanation can be sought in the type of route strategy adopted by the respective airlines. Airlines 301 and 304 had highly efficient route systems, while airlines 301 and 304 had services heavily geared to business travellers with the cost structure associated with such strategy. As a result, these will be predicted as bankrupt if the *non-financial* model is considered in isolation.

The predicted probabilities of financial distress depicted for model *Q1* at airline 122, imply different views of the management, although the operation seem to be in good condition. Such an airline should be analysed carefully to clarify the reasons behind the differing attitudes and emphasis. Actual research on the airline involved confirms the findings. A reverse situation occurs for case 108, where predicted probabilities for *Q1* and *Q6a* imply management characteristics and emphasis of a non-distressed firm, although both the *financial* (*DB2*) and *non-financial* (*DB5*) models classify the carrier as failed. In reality this finding is confirmed by research, as the carrier was presenting poor financial results at the time and operating an inefficient route system. Apparently, the management aspect of the airline is non-characteristic of distressed firms, meaning that the firm is either exceptional or about to turn-around.

Table 8.11 Prediction enhancement through model comparison

Airline#, Status / Case #	Questionnaire attitude model *Q1*	Questionnaire emphasis model *Q6a*	Database financial model *DB2-1*	Database non-financial model *DB5-1*	Conformity of all four models
109 Non-distressed	**0.00**	**0.06**	**0.03**	**0.33**	100%
115 Non-distressed	**0.01**	**0.06**	**0.01**	**1.00**	75%
118 Non-distressed	***mean* = 0.37**	**0.00**	**0.00**	**0.20**	100%
Subject a	0.02	0.00			
- b	*0.83*	0.00			
- c	0.27	0.00			
120 Non-distressed	**0.08**	**0.00**	**0.19**	**0.01**	100%
122 Non-distressed	***mean* = 0.53**	**0.03**	**0.01**	**0.99**	50%
Subject a	0.80	0.00			
- b	0.31	0.00			
- c	0.49	0.08			
104 Distressed	***mean* = 0.71**	**0.99**	**0.99**	**1.00**	100%
Subject a	0.70	0.99			
- b	0.65	1.00			
- c	0.90	0.98			
- d	0.59	1.00			
105 Distressed	***mean = 0.92***	***0.79***	**0.69**	**0.96**	100%
Subject a	0.88	0.92			
- b	1.00	0.63			
- c	0.75	0.60			
- d	0.99	0.82			
- e	0.99	1.00			
108 Distressed	***mean* = 0.01**	**0.29**	**0.94**	**1.00**	50%
Subject a	0.01	0.01			
- b	0.03	*0.87*			
- c	0.00	0.01			
301 Failed	**1.00**	**0.82**	**0.63**	**0.08**	75%
304 Failed	**1.00**	**1.00**	**1.00**	**0.28**	75%
306 Failed	**1.00**	**0.93**	**0.94**	**1.00**	100%
307 Failed	**0.93**	**0.99**	**1.00**	**1.00**	100%
313 Failed	**0.84**	**1.00**	**0.98**	**0.57**	100%
Overall classification	93%	97%	100%	70%	86.5%

1 = failure/distress, 0 = non-failure/non-distress. The determination of the dichotomous state non-failure/failure and non-distress/distress is based on financial data until 1993. Financial status applies to 1994 in the case of existing airlines. Predicted probabilities italicised can be regarded as extreme outliers.

The comparison of the four models can also warn the practitioner of possible conflict among top managers as can be seen for subject 6 of airline 108 and subject 6 of airline 118. Such cases indicate highly differing views on the airline's management reality, necessitating further research into the possible cause. Furthermore, the use of the four distinctive models will reduce the possibility of misclassification of extreme outliers of a single model, that are uniformly classified by the other three models. Furthermore, such combination of models will indicate if management problems are present although still not affecting financial performance or operating efficiency.

Comparison of classification accuracy

Table 8.12 shows a comparison of the models derived from the database source and models following from other research. What is apparent, as mentioned before, is that the non-financial model *DB5-1* has much better traits further away from bankruptcy than the financial model *DB2-1*. Both models perform better than the Altman model in the third year. The models are, however, non-spectacular in terms of classification accuracy but do give strong indications on the potential of future research of airline distress and failure prediction with regard to non-financial data.

Table 8.12 Misclassification rates of bankruptcy prediction studies

	Altman (1968)			Deakin (1972)			Blum (1974)			DB2-1 Financial			DB5-1 Non-fin.		
Meth.	MDA			Prob. MDA			MDA[140]			LR			LR		
Years		(2) (3)		(4)				(1) (5)							
prior to	Overall	Type		Overall	Type		Overall	Type		Overall	Type		Overall	Type	
failure		I	II		I	II		I	II		I	II		I	II
		%						%							
	(27 %)	(4)	(21)	(22 %)			(5 %)	(4)	(7)	5.5 %	5.5	5.5	16.7 %	17	17
1	5 %	6	3	3 %	3	3	7 %								
				(6 %)			(20 %)	(16)	(24)	30.6 %	33	28	25.0 %	22	28
2	18 %	28	6	4½ %	3	6	12%								
				(12 %)			(30 %)	(29)	(32)	33.3%	39	28	27.8 %	28	28
3	52 %	-	-	4½ %	6	3	20 %								
				(23 %)			(20 %)	(12)	(26)						
4	71 %	-	-	21 %	16	25	14 %								
				(15 %)			(31 %)	(33)	(29)						
5	64 %	-	-	17 %	25	9	17 %								

(1) Figures in parentheses test against holdout sample. Figures not in parentheses are tested against same sample from which dichotomous classification test was estimated. (2) *Type I* error is misclassifying a failed firm. *Type II* error is misclassifying a non-failed firm. (3) *Type I* and *II* errors are shown for the first two years. (4) Figures in parentheses represent test against randomly selected sample. Figures not in parentheses represent test against sample from which the discriminant function was estimated. (5) Error rates based on discriminant function for four years of data.

The better trait of the non-financial model is probably due to the fact, that it is much harder to 'window dress' airline traffic data, than financial data. Furthermore, the non-financial data is more clearly influenced by the quality of management, strategy and the environment, than financial data. Thus, it is clear that the combination of the financial and non-financial models is a highly recommended practice in the case of airline failure and distress prediction.

The models could not be tested on a hold-out sample due to the small population, as a result they can not be compared to the other models in the table in that respect. There is, however, every reason to believe that the models will show poorer results under such circumstances, as the models usually do so. However, as the population of new-entrants increases, there is every reason to believe that hold-out tests could be carried out and, what is more, a new more reliable model developed with greater number of airlines in each group.

Summary

The null hypotheses, that all the sub-sets of variables would provide the same classification, can be rejected on the basis of the varying classification ability of the models. This result is valid for the past, present and future variable sub-sets of the questionnaire survey Part II. The same conclusion was obtained for the sub-sets *financial, mixed* and *non-financial* in the database models.

The best predictor variables based on model *Q1* are the attitude statements: *lack of capital will not limit our growth, everyone in our airline understands our long term aims and objectives* and *employees are rewarded for taking actions that benefit our customers*. For the importance models $Q2_i$ to $O6_i$ (for i {a,b,c} = past, present, future), the best predictors were: *yield management system, hub and spoke operations, investor' attitudes towards the airline* and *service quality*. Turning to the present and the future emphasis models the best predictors are *job rotation*, while *expansion into new markets* and *cost reduction* perform well in the latter time period only. Other significant factors in the past were *freight operations, decentralised organisation structure* and *market-share*.

The models from the present subset of variables yielded as best predictors: *flexible job descriptions, freight operations, market-research* and *media advertising*. Finally, in the future it was *market-intelligent information* and *communication system, employees' productivity* and *frequent flyer programs*. The factor that appeared in all three periods was *job rotation*, while *freight operations* and *hub and spoke operations* appear in models of two time dimensions.

Looking at the database models, the best predictors are Earnings before tax and interest divided by sales. This variable had very high discrimination ability of the dichotomous variable. Other significant variables where added value divided by fixed assets; total debt divided by fixed assets; operating profit per available seat kilometre; aircraft departures per employee, distance per hour flown, aircraft hours per employee and load factor. Qualitative financial variables are poor predictors of financial distress and airline failure.

Respondents of qualitative statements show dissipating reliability from the past (experience) into the future (projection). This is due to reduced information and the uncertainty associated with the unknown. This phenomenon appears in less variation in responses of the two groups under observation. The shift in emphasis on individual variables should, however, not be undermined as an indicator of future trends in management emphasis, given large enough sample of respondents. The comparison of three model sources: financial database, non-financial database and questionnaire survey; improves the information content and poses a possibility to improve the accuracy of failure and distress prediction.

---

123 *Type I* error is to predict a failed firm as non-failed; *Type II* error is to predict a non-failed firm as failed.

124 In the case of airlines the cost of *type 2* error can in fact be detrimental for the airline, due to the travel agency dependency, whose bookings usually are dramatically reduced as rumours of imminent failure occur.

125 See discussion in: Keasey and McGuinnes (1990) and Robertson and Mills (1991).

126 A base model means that the formula is based on that years data. This means that one can produce a base model from data three years prior to failure and test its classification ability on data one and two years prior. This alternative raises the practitioners' ability to predict failure of companies that might not be classified as prone to failure according to a model based on first year prior to failure. In fact one can suggest an algorithm where the practitioner starts out with a model based on one year prior, then with a two year prior model and lastly with a three year prior model. If there is a discrepancy between the three base models there is a reason to research the company more thoroughly.

127 Such methodology was used by: Innes, *et al.*, (1991).

128 In fact the practitioner can not, based on the statistical model, infer how far from bankruptcy a given case is.

129 The likelihood-ratio test estimates the model with each variable eliminated and looks at the change in the log-likelihood.

130 Variable entry was limited to alpha level 0.05 and variable exclusion to alpha level 0.1. This led to fewer variables being included in the model and increased the number of significant coefficients.

131 The pseudo R squared is an attempt to produce a measurement device of the adequacy of the model, such as that used in multiple linear regression. The underlying principle is the 'proportion of variation explained by the model' or R^2 in multiple linear regression, simulated as pseudo-R^2 in logistic regression:

$$R^2 = 1 - \frac{\text{Residual sum of squares}}{\text{Total sum of square}} \qquad \text{Pseudo } R^2 = \frac{\text{Initial -2 LL - model -2 LL}}{\text{Initial -2 LL}}$$

132 One model for each time period had to be constructed rather than to test a base model on the data sets of the other periods. The reason is that one can not assume that the same variables are as important in the future as in the past, due to the inherent dynamism of the qualitative variables.

133 Extreme outlier is a case that has high predicted probability in the opposite direction to observed classification.

134 A 'best' model in this context, is a model producing predicted probabilities much to the expected extremes, 1 for failed and 0 for non-failed.

---

135 The database was constructed by the researcher directly from filings at the US DoT. The data was validated thoroughly, discounting errors in filings on behalf of the airlines themselves.

136 These phases are constructed for convenience in building the model and do not have theoretical basis. In fact it can be alleged that there are actually four phases of failure; initiation failure phase - when the airline never gets off the ground; start-up failure phase - when the airline is undercapitalised and fails within few years; growth failure phase - when the airline grows too fast or too slow; and mature failure phase - when the airline has reached large size and starts to expand into riskier markets to sustain growth or decline.

137 This selection algorithm is only pertinent to the database analysis, not the questionnaire survey.

138 Unlike the questionnaire based models, the variables obtained from the empirical selection into the one year prior models are tested two and three years prior, rather than having new variables entering.

139 U.S. airlines are required by law to file financial, personnel and traffic data with the D.o.T. In some cases, however, airlines become delinquent in such filing, which in it self could be an indication of financial distress.

140 Blum did not utilise searching to determine the ratios for the prediction model. He used a concept of ratio selection as Beaver did based on the firm being ‘a reservoir of financial resources with the probability of failure being expressed in terms of expected cash flows’ (*Source:* Altman 1993, p. 224.).

9 Critical factors

Introduction

In this chapter *critical factors* are identified and discussed. It is important to note that the critical factors identified on the basis of the failure prediction models in previous chapters are not altogether unique as there could be other factors that are just as good or almost as good predictors of failure or non-failure. This fact does, however, not reduce the importance of the critical factors identified here.

Management and organisation factors

The fundamental conclusion of the book is that any firm's success or failure is determined by the quality of management. Management as such is subject to various constraints that limit alternatives, however, it is the management of these constraints and the ability to overcome those that distinguishes the good performers from the poor performers in the long-term. The key to that ability is careful planning, analysis (research), information gathering and exceptional ability to motivate employees. The founders of new-entrant airlines have in almost all cases had extensive experience in the airlines before starting their own, in that sense the initial risk has been less than if the founder was entering an entirely new industry. Thus, the alternative operating formats compared to that of the incumbents has usually been based on prior experience within other airlines, rather than being thought out by a complete outsider. The most important aspect of these alternative methods has been better *utilisation of employees* through cross-utilisation programs, given that such programs do not go to the extreme. Furthermore, the *division of the workforce* into smaller units of responsibility that allows for comparison between units, enhances performance at larger airlines and permits the retention of some of the motivating characteristics of smaller organisations.

To make the airline's *long term aims and objectives* clear to the employees is important to stimulate success, due to the motivation it provides and concentration of efforts. Furthermore, to manage, select and motivate staff is important part of achieving a success. The staff function must approach an exceptional level in order to distinguish between the non-distressed and the distressed.

Comparatively much *decentralisation* and *job rotation* is apparently not beneficial at the new-entrant airlines, as it characterises distressed new-entrant airlines to a greater extent than non-distressed. Too frequent changes in employees' job responsibilities are probably causing lack of quality due to the employee's constant process of getting familiar with new tasks leading to reduced productivity. Furthermore, decentralisation without very clear objectives and vision can not yield what it is supposed to achieve, thus, leading to chaos. These two factors, decentralisation and job rotation, proved to distinguish well between the two groups of carriers in the failure prediction models presented. The third and fourth factors that appeared in the models were *flexible job descriptions* and *employee's productivity* both highly related as one is the function of the other.

Marketing and strategy factors

Controlled growth is an important ingredient for non-failure of new-entrants. Extremely fast growth places great demand on the airline's resources that eventually leads to inefficiencies, as well as strategic alterations that cause serious adjustment problems for the airline. *Market-share* is important, but only on the micro-level, meaning that overall market-share is not important for survival, but high market-share on individual airports and routes is important. Large market-share at airports is especially important trait of a new-entrant in order to be able to fend off competition of the larger carriers.

Comparatively *low-fares* are important during entry, but they have to be backed up by *comparatively high service quality* (but not necessarily service features) in order to maintain an advantage when the incumbent matches or beats the fares offered by the new-entrant. Extreme emphasis on *low-costs* and therefore cost control is a fundamental trait of a new-entrant. This control has to be achieved, however, without sacrificing quality. The non-failed and non-distressed new-entrants are comparatively more customer orientated both in terms of *fulfilling customer needs* and provide *innovative features* in their service. Through this ability, non-distressed carriers achieve comparatively greater customer loyalty that reinforces their non-distressed status. The non-distressed carriers spend *more resources on planning* new markets, thus, reducing the risks involved. Non-distressed carriers are more marketing orientated and utilise the tools of marketing to a comparatively larger degree than distressed carriers. Such tools being: *media advertising, brand image* and *service quality*. Furthermore, non-distressed carriers are more prone to *expand into new markets* than distressed carriers, but such entry is based on careful analysis and planning that *distressed* carriers emphasise to a lesser degree. Finally, non-distressed carriers stay independent as they emphasise *alliances* and *merger and acquisition to gain market-share* much less than distressed carriers. This indicates that such programs affect the longevity and financial wellbeing of new-entrants negatively in the long-run.

The questionnaire based failure prediction models came up with seven marketing related critical factors: *alliance with the incumbents*, *market-share*, *market research, frequent flyer programs*, *service quality*, *media advertising* and *expansion into new markets*. The first four are negatively related to success while the remaining three are positively related. Although the first two factors listed above are good in segregating the two groups of carriers it does not indicate that these aspects should be de-emphasised by the airlines, rather it is an indication that distressed carriers emphasise those more regardless of the factors relationship to the distress present. This means that these factors are critical, but the questionnaire findings do not imply how or why.

The database failure prediction models came up with four critical factors associated with marketing: *load-factor*, *average passenger haul, percent ASK non-scheduled* and *average seats per departure*. The load-factor coefficient in the model has negative sign meaning that there is negative relationship with non-failure. This is because many of the failed carriers had relatively high load-factors, achieved through too low fares. Average passenger haul is positive, however, meaning that the longer the distance each passenger is carried the better for the airline's results. The third factor, *level of non-scheduled operations*, is negatively related to non-failure. This means that the less the carrier is involved in charter operations the better. The relationship is only to an extent, as charter operations as pure by-product can not harm the profitability of the carrier, but scheduled operations as a by-product, probably does harm the carrier involved. The last factor, *average seats per departure*, is negatively related, indicating that carriers operating smaller equipment fared better than those operating larger equipment. The influence of the former charter-based new-entrants is probably reflected in this finding, due to their very poor results.

Financial factors

Lack of capital is a greater limiting factor of growth for distressed carriers than non-distressed, although both groups seem to have problems raising capital to a sufficient degree. Distressed carriers emphasise *critical mass* more than non-distressed carriers. This implies that the resulting market-share building is based on lack of the necessary product traits that are the fundamental prerequisite of successful and profitable market-share building. As a result, these carriers enter too costly strategies aimed at market-share building primarily. In order to grow faster than their balance sheet may allow, distressed carriers are more prone to use off-balance sheet financing of aircraft than non-distressed carriers. Perhaps the most important difference of the two groups of carriers is that non-distressed carriers emphasise *cost reduction* comparatively more than distressed carriers. This finding is striking in the light of the greater incentive of the distressed carriers to practice cost reduction, a classical cause and effect problem.

Financial variables derived from the database failure prediction models, were in all cases ratios: *EBIT/sales*, *operating profit/ASK*, *revenue/expenses*, *added value/fixed assets*, *total debt/fixed assets*, *long-term debt/total assets*, *maintenance costs/ASK*, *ASK/$1000 in wages* and *total revenue/passenger*. Here we can see that the four first ratios are related to earnings, while the next two are related to debt. This means that the proportional earning capability of a new-entrant in relation to sales, expenses, fixed assets and output is critical for the airline in terms of survivability. The other two ratios have conflicting signs that might indicate co-linearity. That does, however, not change their status as being critical ratios. The general conclusion is therefore that gearing and revenue as a proportion of resources applied are critical factors. The critical ratio, *maintenance costs*, has a negative sign indicating inverse relationship with non-failure. The sign could be wrong, or that maintenance costs are lower for distressed carriers. The latter relationship would therefore reinforce the critics of deregulation that have maintained that maintenance would suffer as a result of increased competition. Unfortunately, this relationship can not be proved here, but further research on this issue is necessary. Available seat kilometres as a ratio to $1000 in wages gives an indication of productivity in terms of employee costs. The sign is positive indicating a positive relationship with non-failure. The last ratio divides total revenues with the total number of passengers. This relationship is negative meaning that the higher the average income per passenger the less the survivability of the carrier. The relationship seems far-fetched but it is not so as one can point to the premium-service new-entrants and the long-haul new-entrants to support the relationship, but these had high revenue per passenger, but failed anyway.

The ratio *net worth/total debt* did not appear in one of the failure prediction models, but the difference in this ratio between the two groups is highly significant. The direction of the difference is in the order of smaller value for failed new-entrants. The same applies to *depreciation/ASK* that is significantly higher for non-failed carriers. The relationship is probably due to greater assets per operating unit (ASK) than that of failed carriers, sometimes referred to as critical mass.

Operations

Much emphasis on *aircraft utilisation* is characteristic of non-distressed carriers. The result of this emphasis is lower cost structure as high aircraft utilisation affects costs in almost all aspects of the airline. Conversely the non-distressed carriers emphasised *hub and spoke operations* to a much lesser degree than distressed carriers. That finding reinforces the importance of aircraft utilisation as hub and spoke operations lead to less aircraft utilisation than direct-service does.

The failure prediction models provided one more critical factor, *freight operations* in addition to the factors already mentioned. That factor is positively related to non-distress, implying that freight operations are an important operating feature of non-distressed carriers. This implies that greater utilisation of the aircraft by carrying freight is an important additional revenue source for new-entrant airlines, reinforcing non-distress.

The database failure prediction models came up with number of operations related ratios and factors: *aircraft departures/total personnel*, *aircraft hours/total personnel* and *distance per hour flown*. The first two are efficiency ratios of operations in terms of employee input. This aspect comes up again and again showing that aircraft utilisation is important in running a successful airline. However, the previous ratio has negative sign indicating that a high ratio of aircraft departures per employee is negatively related to non-failure. Carriers having relatively many departures per employee have therefore been more prone to bankruptcy compared with those having a lower ratio. It is possible that this inverse relationship is caused by poorer service quality of such carriers. Further research must be carried out to establish such relationship. The latter ratio *aircraft hours per employee* has, however, positive sign. That indicates, as expected, that an aircraft in the air is more productive than an aircraft on the ramp. However, one can expect airlines having longer average sector lengths to have more flight hours per employee than short-haul carriers.

Information- and communication factors

Strangely enough, the distressed carriers emphasised information and communication more than non-distressed carriers. This could indicate the inadequacy of the information function at the distressed carriers. The following factors yielded difference between the two groups: *computer reservation systems*, *yield management systems* and *market-intelligent information- and communication system*. As these factors imply, any disadvantage pertaining to these areas would cause the disadvantaged airline to emphasise the factor more until such disadvantage was eliminated. The two latter factors appeared as critical in the failure prediction models, both negatively related to success.

Environment

As expected *investors' attitudes towards the new-entrant* is emphasised to a greater extent by distressed carriers. This implies that the airline will be more careful about information released to stakeholders and the media in order not to harm its outside financial resources unnecessarily. The same goes for *favourable attitude of travel agents* for the reason that if travel agents alarm is raised regarding the financial health of the airline, there will be a substantial drop in bookings. Managers at distressed carriers are more prone to *feel out of control* in terms of shaping their airline's destiny. Such attitude leads to less motivation and consequently poorer results for the affected carrier.

There was only one critical environment factor derived from the database models: *Change in spot fuel prices.* The negative sign shows that as spot aviation fuel prices increase, the worse off the airline is.

The Increased Activity phenomenon

It is apparent from the questionnaire that the respondents of the failed airlines rate the importance of the factors in Part II, higher for those factors that are significantly different between the two groups. There are two possible explanations to this phenomenon. First, the respondents could be concerned about their own performance prior to the airline's failure, thus, overrating the importance placed on the various factors. Second, the respondents may actually be rating the importance placed on the factors during the trouble period just prior to failure. The latter explanation is more likely in the case of failed firms. This is due to the fact that all activity in the airline increases during the problem period in an attempt to rectify the 'causes' of the airline's problems. The actual reason is in many cases the previous inactivity of the management in terms of these factors that suddenly gain so much importance when the airline is facing failure. Therefore, one can infer that the responses for the failed airlines on Part II are accurate for the failed airline just prior to failure but do not indicate clearly, which factors where neglected before the increased activity.

Figure 9.1 shows a situation where an airline has been indifferent to its environment both internally and externally until a 'catastrophe' occurs, causing a sudden increase in activity. The catastrophe can be caused by a year of a very large loss, losses for period of years causing a reaction of creditors or shareholders, or a market entry of a more efficient competitor. As a long period of inactivity and ignorance of external and internal developments has weakened the airline, the increased activity will not necessarily save the airline. That depends on the access to capital as it will take considerable time to make the carrier fit again to reach profitability. In either case the period before failure or successful turn-around will be characterised by increased activity in the organisation, sometimes termed and well described as 'fire-fighting'.

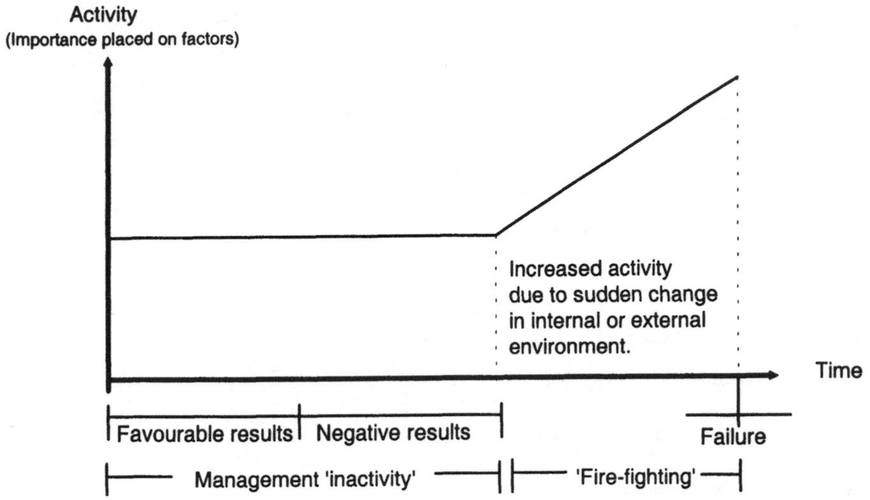

Figure 9.1 Increased Activity prior to failure

Critical Performance Factors

Argenti's hypothesis, discussed previously, was that corporate failure has two distinctive components, namely *symptoms* and *causes*. Based on that analogy, we can presume that management's decision-making determines a company's fate, making it the primary causal factor. However, in order to apply its decision-making function, management can apply many 'tools' that directly affect the company's performance. As a result, it is logical to look upon these tools as causal by nature. For example the management of an airline can increase flight frequency (tool) in an attempt to improve an airline's performance. Such change in the causal factor (tool) 'flight frequency' can affect the airline in a number of ways that appear as 'symptoms'. The symptoms in this case could be, if we examine the negative effects, deteriorating load-factor and deteriorating *Revex* ratio, just to name two. From the example one can determine quite clearly the distinction between causal and symptomatic factors. It is enough to recognise that the load-factor can not be applied as a tool and is therefore not causal. Frequency, on the other hand, can be changed directly by the management and is therefore a causal factor.

Having made this conclusion one needs to decide whether the environment is causal or symptomatic. In fact the conclusion is that it is neither. First, the management has no control over the environment variables (generally speaking) and can therefore not apply environment factors as tools. If environment factors cannot be adjusted by management there is not going to be any symptoms. Therefore, one must look upon environment factors as exogenous influence, which the management can either decide to adjust to by applying its tools or not to do so.

Empirical identification of Critical Performance Factors

In Table 9.1 and Table 9.2 we can see factors that showed significant ($p<.1$ or better) difference of the means for distressed and non-distressed carriers. Based on the analogy of causes and symptoms the former table shows *Critical Performance Factors* (CPF), while the latter *Performance Indicators* (PI).

Table 9.1 Critical Performance Factors for airlines

Type	Statement	Group	Mean
CPF +	Expansion into new markets	Distressed (20)	6,450 Ψ
		Non-distressed (20)	7,550
CPF +	Media advertising	Distressed (20)	5,500 **
		Non-distressed (20)	7,300
CPF +	Cost reduction	Distressed (20)	7,500 *
		Non-distressed (20)	8,700
CPF -	Hub and spoke operation	Distressed (20)	5,400 *
		Non-distressed (19)	2,895
CPF -	Job rotation	Distressed (20)	5,800 ***
		Non-distressed (19)	3,158
CPF -	Alliance with the incumbents	Distressed (18)	5,278 *
		Non-distressed (19)	3,474
CPF -	Computer reservation system	Distressed (20)	6,600 *
		Non-distressed (18)	5,167
CPF -	Yield management system	Distressed (20)	5,600 Ψ
		Non-distressed (18)	3,667
CPF -	Merger/acquisition to gain market-share	Distressed (19)	3,947 *
		Non-distressed (17)	1,941
CPF -	Market-intelligent information- and communication system	Distressed (22)	8,045 *
		Non-distressed (20)	6,889
CPF -	Off-balance sheet financing of aircraft	Distressed (20)	6,650 Ψ
		Non-distressed (17)	4,765

Note: *** = $p<.001$; ** = $p<.01$; * = $p<.05$; Ψ = $p<.1$. The factors were rated on a scale from 0 (no importance) to 10 (most important).

The importance of this exertion is to learn first of all whether organisations at different performance levels differ as to the emphasis placed on various factors, and secondly in what direction the difference moves. If there is a statistically significant difference between distressed and non-distressed carriers for that particular factor it can be declared as either CPF or PI, depending on whether the factor can be manipulated or not as discussed before. On the basis of the direction of the difference it is possible to segregate the *CPF* and the *PI* into two groups, i.e., positive or negative difference for non-distressed carriers. According to the approach positive difference would indicate that the CPF is associated with non-distress, and can therefore be classified as *success factor* (*CPF* ⁺), while if the difference is in the other direction it would be classified as *failure factor* (*CPF* ⁻).

It is important to emphasise that the *CPF* whether success or failure orientated does not necessarily mean that when a *CPF* ⁻ is emphasised that particular airline is more prone to failure than an airline not emphasising the factor. It means rather that the airlines observed having financial difficulties are more likely to emphasise this factor than an airline not under distress. This can be interpreted in a number of ways, namely that the airline emphasises this factor in order to turnaround its fortunes, or it is emphasising a factor that does have adverse influence on its well-being. Looking at the *PI* a similar pedagogic applies, namely that negative *PI* are more important to distressed carriers than non-distressed ones.

Table 9.2 Performance Indicators for airlines

Type	Statement	Group	Mean
PI ⁺	Aircraft utilisation	Distressed (20)	7,950 Ψ
		Non-distressed (20)	8,850
PI ⁺	Decentralized organisation structure	Distressed (20)	6,250 *
		Non-distressed (19)	4,263
PI ⁺	Brand image	Distressed (19)	5,895 Ψ
		Non-distressed (18)	7,333
PI ⁺	Service quality	Distressed (20)	6,350 *
		Non-distressed (18)	8,167
PI ⁻	Achieving critical mass	Distressed (20)	6,850 Ψ
		Non-distressed (17)	4,824
PI ⁻	Investors' attitudes towards the new-entrant	Distressed (20)	7,100 *
		Non-distressed (17)	4,710
PI ⁻	Favourable attitude of travel agents	Distressed (20)	8,300 Ψ
		Non-distressed (20)	7,250

Note: *** = $p<.001$; ** = $p<.01$; * = $p<.05$; Ψ = $p<.1$.

Critical Performance Factors and causal analysis

Taking the concept further it can be demonstrated how the factors correlate to each other, as the causality of each CPF can be complex and linked to adjustment in other CPF. Furthermore, in causal analysis decision rules can be derived from the concept to make correlation charts in a specific way. Figure 9.2 shows a correlation chart for the factors presented in the tables, factors in bold are CPF, while other factors are PI. All the factors, were tested for correlation and the chart shows significant correlations ($p<.05$). To guide the development of a correlation chart for causal analysis the following propositions were made

(i) A CPF can be correlated with another CPF, because a change sought in an airlines' performance may be a function of more than one CPF (combined causality).
(ii) A CPF can 'cause' change in a PI, but not directly the other way around (*see* iii).
(iii) All PI have feedback loop to the 'human factor' or management that uses information as one input element when taking action on the CPF.
(iv) PI can have relationships with other PI in both directions.

It is apparent from the analysis that a relationship can be straightforward like *service quality* influencing *brand image*. Service quality and brand image are both intangible factors that can not be directly manipulated and are therefore PI that have an apparent one way relationship.

Conclusion

As with any instrument of some complication instructions have to be issued to the user. The use of a failure prediction model is no different in this aspect. In fact one can allege that a failure prediction model can be of a great harm if improperly administered. In view of that the following should be observed carefully by the potential user of the models presented here

(i) The models must be used on the same type of companies as were included in the original sample. To use a model specified for new-entrant airlines on a large airline such as American would be an unacceptable use of the model, giving a potentially unreliable result.
(ii) The models must only be used on airlines in the same geographical region as those airlines in which the original sample airlines operate. To use a model based on US carriers on UK carriers will lead to unreliable results.[141]

Much had been written about the new-entrant airlines in the United States during the early years of success, some were praised as marvels of business management others were criticised, but most felt that the new-entrants proved that deregulation was working. However, as the new-entrants disappeared one after another those that praised got silent and the sceptics named a thousand and one reasons for the new-entrant airlines' failures.

It is hoped that this book will be of some value to those that want to ask questions such as why and how, in this respect. Those are the ones that will be able to understand that the basis of success is knowledge on the reasons behind previous failures.

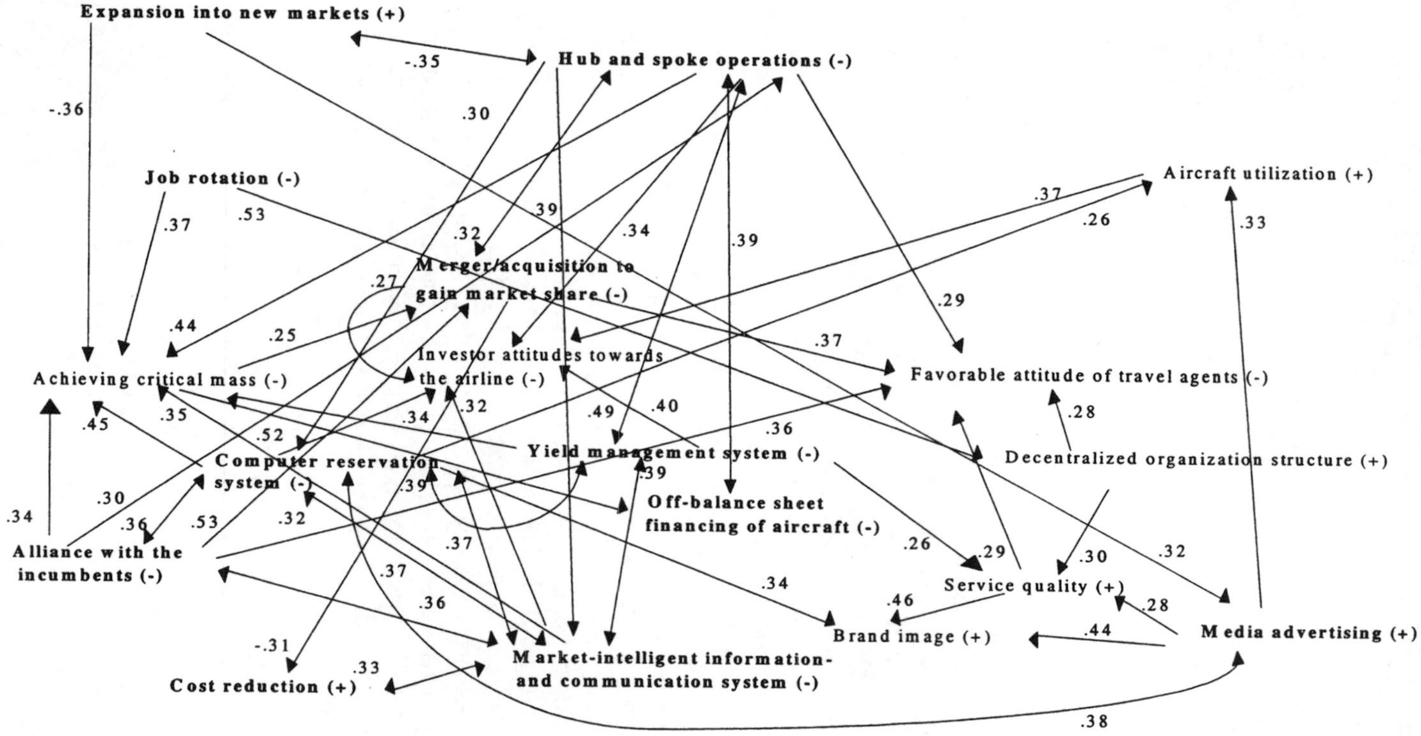

Figure 9.2 Correlation between CPF and PI

An important distinction between environment influence, causal factors and symptoms has been pointed out as a concept of *Critical Performance Factors* and *Performance Indicators*. Many of the findings in the book are related to the symptoms that result from the application of the Critical Performance Factors. Thus, one must make it clear that managers should not attempt to forge changes in the symptomatic factors in isolation but emphasise changes in the Critical Performance Factors according to concrete analysis as to the impact that such change will have on the organisation. For example, if the load-factor (symptomatic) has deteriorated it makes no sense to reduce flight frequency (causal factor) as an isolated attempt to raise it. Such move could in fact cause serious harm, as frequency is related to service quality and aircraft utilisation, to name just two factors. Thus, an attempt to increase the passenger load-factor, or any other symptomatic factor for that matter, is a complex feat that involves many aspects of airline management.

Regardless of the barriers discussed in the previous sections, it is believed that the research is important, given its limitations. First, by introducing an important methodology (Phase-in) of failure prediction for the small population case. Second, by introducing various sources of models that can be utilised together in order to enhance prediction quality. Third, by introducing thoroughly the industry, the environment and characteristics of the population from which the models were derived. Fourth, by focusing the research on a segment of the airline industry, a practice that is in many aspects uncommon compared to other research in this field that is usually quite general in terms of inclusion of many diverse industry sectors (all manufacturing firms, all service firms, etc.). In fact failure prediction has been criticised by laymen on the basis of its inaccuracy when general models are applied to various industry sub-segments. The answer to such problems is apparently to focus the research more into the various sub-segments and produce separate models for those. This research is an attempt at that and is important as such.

If one wanted to give a prescription for success or avoidance of failure it would naturally appear here. However, the general conclusion of the book must be that no such prescription exists due to the dynamism of the airlines' interaction with its environment. Nevertheless, it is difficult not to mention six critical factors or strategies worth emphasising for new-entrant airlines: (i) high relative quality; (ii) dominant market-share on routes and airports (usually only achievable on secondary routes and airports); (iii) high relative aircraft utilisation; (iv) high relative employee utilisation with *care*; (v) controlled growth in terms of maintaining item *(ii)*; low costs in terms of achieving items *(iii)* and *(iv)*; and (vi) resourceful innovation without going into the extremities.

---

141 This is a fully acceptable statement for financial data due to differing accounting standards, but less so for models based on non-financial data and qualitative assessment such as questionnaire surveys. The researcher found that operating strategy will have the greatest impact on extreme outliers of non-financial models.

APPENDICES

Appendix A

Table A.1 Questionnaire Part I - descriptives

N = 45 Questionnaire indicator	Mean	St.D.	S.E.	95% C.I. Lower	Upper
Our organisational structure was decentralised	2.78	1.52	.23	2.32	3.23
Our financial control system was efficient	3.96	1.19	.18	3.60	4.31
The airline had a vision of the future shared by all the employees	3.53	1.31	.19	3.14	3.93
We surrounded ourselves with staff who promoted different orientations and points of view	3.80	1.06	.16	3.48	4.12
Group consensus was the usual way we made decisions	3.29	1.38	.21	2.88	3.70
The airline's success was largely dependent on factors out of its control	2.44	1.29	.19	2.06	2.83
The number of serious problems we were faced with increased constantly	3.02	1.13	.17	2.68	3.37
Our staff was encouraged to have open discussion about the airline's problems	4.16	1.04	.16	3.84	4.47
We did detailed analysis before taking any major decision	3.89	1.34	.20	3.49	4.29
We made changes in our service quite frequently	3.02	1.47	.22	2.58	3.47
We usually had enough resources to plan for the future	3.02	1.41	.21	2.60	3.44
Our customer loyalty was strong	4.07	1.18	.18	3.71	4.42
We fulfilled our customers' needs well	4.42	.58	.08	4.25	4.60
We acted immediately upon customer complaints	4.00	1.09	.16	3.67	4.33
Our marketing performance was good	3.93	.96	.14	3.64	4.22
Our long term aims and objectives were easily achievable	2.66	1.20	.18	2.29	3.02
Our marketing was aggressive	3.80	1.01	.15	3.50	4.10
We usually received many useful suggestions from our employees	3.71	1.04	.15	3.40	4.02
We were more efficient than most of our competitors	4.31	1.10	.16	3.98	4.64
We tried to avoid head to head competition with our larger competitors	3.42	1.56	.23	2.95	3.89
Our long term aims and objectives guided our business decisions	3.78	1.15	.17	3.43	4.12
Our airline was flexible enough to respond immediately to major opportunities	4.62	.81	.12	4.38	4.86
We were pleased with the performance of our distribution outlets	3.55	.87	.13	3.28	3.81
We were innovators in customer service compared to our competitors	3.91	1.24	.19	3.53	4.28
Lack of capital did not limit our growth	2.60	1.40	.21	2.18	3.02
Everyone in our airline understood our long term aims and objectives	3.16	1.36	.20	2.75	3.57
We were constantly identifying threats and opportunities to our business	4.20	1.04	.15	3.89	4.51
The improvement of the airline's market-share was our number one priority	3.05	1.49	.23	2.59	3.50
We were rarely taken by surprise by our business environment	3.25	1.22	.18	2.88	3.62
We emphasised planning for the future	3.56	1.29	.19	3.17	3.94
We grew by selling our services to more customers	4.38	.91	.14	4.10	4.65
We allocated major resources for diversification into other industries	1.39	.87	.13	1.12	1.65

We planned for and allocated sufficient resources to developing new markets	3.33	1.40	.21	2.91	3.75
Long-term prospects in our primary markets were excellent	3.93	1.18	.18	3.58	4.29
We had customer-oriented front-line people	4.36	.98	.15	4.06	4.65
Our service had a range of features that made it distinctive	4.11	1.11	.17	3.78	4.45
Quality was our major competitive advantage	3.82	1.15	.17	3.48	4.17
Everyone in our airline understood how they could improve quality	3.40	1.25	.19	3.02	3.78
We were effective in monitoring our customers' expectation of quality	3.77	1.21	.18	3.39	4.14
Our internal social and political system supported our business aims	3.50	1.21	.18	3.13	3.87
We were good at changing our staff's beliefs and values	3.13	.89	.13	2.86	3.40
Our staff provided us with a competitive advantage	4.18	.89	.13	3.91	4.44
We had incentives for our staff that encouraged extra commitment	3.09	1.26	.19	2.71	3.47
We had all the information we needed on our customers. markets and opportunities	2.69	1.04	.16	2.38	3.00
Employees were rewarded for taking actions that benefited our customers	3.24	1.21	.18	2.88	3.61
Our information system provided us with a clear competitive advantage	2.60	1.05	.16	2.28	2.92
We were constantly upgrading and improving our information system	3.84	1.07	.16	3.52	4.16
We would create the same organisation structure as we had. if given the opportunity	3.38	1.40	.21	2.96	3.80
We made effective cash-flow forecasts	4.29	1.01	.15	3.98	4.59
We were good at stimulating demand for our services	4.14	.88	.13	3.87	4.40
We were effective in monitoring important cost areas	4.16	1.15	.17	3.81	4.50
Important information was communicated to employees to enable effective decision-making	3.82	1.15	.17	3.48	4.17
The board of directors was highly involved in the airline's affairs	3.89	1.32	.20	3.49	4.28
The atmosphere among employees was very good	3.87	1.14	.17	3.52	4.21
Our information systems provided quick, accurate and relevant information	3.36	1.16	.18	3.01	3.72

Appendix B

Table B.1 Questionnaire Part II - descriptives

N = 43 to 51.

Construct	Questionnaire indicator	Mean	St.D.	S.E.	95% C.I. Lower	95% C.I. Upper
Influence of external environment	Investors' attitudes towards the airline (Investment bankers, stockholders, etc.)	6.02	3.42	.48	5.05	6.99
	Reduction of CRS bias affecting the airline	6.01	2.28	.32	5.37	6.65
	Influencing government policy on aviation	5.92	2.62	.37	5.18	6.66
Scale reliability = 0.76	Forecasting adverse effects of the economy on the airline	5.73	2.20	.31	5.10	6.37
	Favourable attitude of travel agents	5.69	3.12	.45	4.78	6.59
	Competitor analysis	5.64	3.13	.44	4.75	6.53
Information- and communication system	Computer reservation system	6.16	2.21	.31	5.53	6.78
	Interdepartmental communication	5.88	2.28	.32	5.24	6.52
	Market-intelligent information- and communication system	5.79	2.39	.35	5.09	6.49
Scale reliability = 0.85	Control systems (monitoring the work of the organisation)	5.70	2.38	.34	5.02	6.38
	Planning systems (integration of information to prepare business action plans)	5.69	2.54	.36	4.96	6.42
	Motivation systems (targets and objectives for staff involvement and motivation)	5.56	2.57	.36	4.83	6.29
	Logistics systems (linking of different parts of the organisation)	5.16	2.00	.29	4.59	5.74
	Yield management system	5.02	3.19	.45	4.12	5.92
	Simplification of information- and communication systems	4.80	2.20	.31	4.17	5.43
Operations management	Aircraft utilisation	7.78	1.88	.27	7.35	8.41
	Matching of aircraft size with route requirement	6.64	2.58	.36	5.91	7.37
Scale reliability = 0.83	Homogeneous aircraft fleet	6.43	2.56	.36	5.71	7.15
	Frequency in served markets	6.35	3.05	.43	5.49	7.21
	Acquisition of airport slots	6.02	3.26	.46	5.10	6.94
	Acquisition of new aircraft	5.98	2.94	.41	5.15	6.81
	Quality of terminal space and ground facilities	5.55	2.35	.33	4.89	6.21
	Operation on trunk routes	5.10	3.20	.46	4.18	6.03
	Interlining agreements	5.06	3.03	.42	4.21	5.91
	Hub and spoke operations	3.98	3.54	.51	2.96	5.00
	Long haul routes	3.90	3.75	.53	2.83	4.97
	Freight operations	3.08	2.45	.35	2.38	3.78
	Feeder airline agreements	2.84	2.55	.36	2.12	3.56
	Code sharing	2.62	2.83	.40	1.82	3.42

General management and organisation	Employees' productivity	7.80	2.21	.31	7.18	8.43
	Employee relations	7.20	2.38	.33	6.53	7.87
	Flexible job descriptions	7.00	2.45	.34	6.31	7.69
	Operations without unionised staff (where possible)	6.90	3.19	.46	5.98	7.81
Scale reliability = 0.84	Company culture (shared attitudes, beliefs, norms)	6.80	2.73	.38	6.04	7.57
	Business strategy	6.66	2.50	.35	5.95	7.37
	Management's external contacts (Government, etc.)	6.10	3.00	.42	5.25	6.94
	Shared company vision (the future 'we' want)	6.08	2.84	.40	5.28	6.88
	Company mission (Long-term aims and objectives)	5.76	2.93	.41	4.93	6.59
	Management teams (interdepartmental teams)	5.53	2.40	.34	4.84	6.22
	Delegation	5.45	2.50	.36	4.73	6.17
	Employees' autonomy to take decisions	5.32	2.27	.32	4.67	5.97
	Managers' incentive program	5.18	3.09	.43	4.31	6.05
	Employees' incentive program	5.00	3.16	.44	4.11	5.89
	Union relations	4.20	3.62	.51	3.17	5.23
	Job rotation	4.20	2.99	.43	3.35	5.06
	Staff reduction	3.81	2.86	.41	2.98	4.64
	Decentralised organisation structure	3.72	3.01	.43	2.86	4.58
Marketing management	Passenger load factors	7.06	2.12	.30	6.46	7.66
	Expansion into new markets	7.04	2.57	.36	6.31	7.77
	Price leadership in served markets	6.86	3.09	.44	5.98	7.74
Scale reliability = 0.86	Service quality	6.73	2.68	.38	5.97	7.48
	Brand image	6.50	2.72	.38	5.73	7.27
	Media advertising	6.20	2.61	.37	5.46	6.94
	Promotion	6.12	2.30	.33	5.47	6.77
	Distribution network	5.76	2.27	.32	5.10	6.41
	Business passengers	5.75	3.19	.45	4.85	6.64
	Market research	5.74	2.40	.34	5.06	6.42
	Avoidance of price wars	5.00	3.22	.46	4.08	5.92
	Market share	4.94	3.04	.43	4.09	5.80
	Weight load factor	4.81	2.81	.43	3.95	5.68
	Commission overrides	4.43	2.52	.36	3.70	5.14
	Frequent flyer programs	3.59	3.33	.47	2.65	4.52
	Alliance with the incumbents	3.17	2.63	.38	2.40	3.93
	Merger/acquisition to gain market share	2.84	3.00	.43	1.98	3.70
	Diversification into other industries	1.49	2.54	.36	.76	2.22
Financial management	Cost control	7.73	2.41	.34	7.05	8.40
	Cost reduction	6.71	2.86	.40	5.90	7.51
	Fuel costs (fuel efficient aircraft, etc.)	6.68	2.20	.31	6.06	7.30
Scale reliability = 0.76	Increase margins	6.59	2.49	.35	5.89	7.29
	Turnover growth	5.75	2.56	.37	5.01	6.49
	Off balance-sheet financing of aircraft	5.66	3.09	.44	4.78	6.54
	Achieving critical mass (investment necessary before profits will be made)	5.56	3.23	.46	4.64	6.48
	Long-term rather than short-term profits	5.49	3.06	.43	4.63	6.35
	Debt reduction	5.43	3.04	.43	4.55	6.30
	Reduction of labour costs	5.34	2.75	.39	4.56	6.12

Appendix C

Table C.1 Quantitative ratios and variables – one year prior

Ratio/Variable		Mean	S.E.	S.D.
ADDED_VA	Added value	81992434	23674390	142046340
@_NON_SC	% non-scheduled	0.08	0.03	0.16
ADV_FIXE	ADV/fixed assets	0.33	0.10	0.62
ADV_WORK	ADV/Working capital	-1.92	2.44	14.64
AIRCRAF1	Aircraft dep./total personnel	34.54	2.14	12.85
AIRCRAFT	Aircraft hours/total personnel	33.46	3.66	21.96
ASK_$100	ASK/$1000 operating expense	17775	1430	8579
ASK_$101	ASK/$1000 wages	107000	11944	71667
AVERAGE_	Average daily rev. hours	1116.94	197.95	1187.69
AVERAGE1	Average no of seats per dep.	113.59	12.19	73.16
AVERAGE2	Average passenger haul	6.32	0.36	2.17
AVERAGE3	Average stage length	1496.23	319.27	1915.61
CHANGE_1	Change in consumer prices USA	-0.09	0.03	0.21
CHANGE_2	Change in interest rate USA	-0.14	0.03	0.18
CHANGE_I	Change in spot fuel prices USA	0.03	0.00	0.01
CURRENT_	Current assets/total assets	0.25	0.03	0.15
CURRENT1	Current assets/Total revenue	0.19	0.01	0.08
DEPRECI1	Depreciation/ADV	0.0038	0.00045	0.0027
DEPRECIA	Depreciation/ASK	0.10	0.18	1.09
DIRECT_O	Direct op. Exp./ASK	0.03	0.00	0.02
DISTANCE	Distance per hour flown (km)	597	22	135
EBIT_SAL	EBIT/sales	-0.03	0.02	0.13
FUEL_ASK	Fuel/ASK	0.013	0.002	0.014
INDIRECT	Indirect op. exp./ASK	0.05	0.01	0.03
INTEREST	Interest rate USA (money market)	0.074	0.003	0.018
LABOUR_C	Labour cost/ADV	0.74	0.50	3.00
LOAD_FAC	Load-factor	0.60	0.01	0.09
LONG_TER	Long term debt/total assets	0.50	0.06	0.34
MAINTENA	Maintenance/ASK	0.011	0.002	0.018
NET_INCO	Net income/net worth	0.11	0.27	1.61
NET_WORT	Net worth/total debt	0.26	0.10	0.58
OPERATI1	Operating rev./employee	145027	12765	76591
OPERATIN	Operating profit/ASK	- 0.0014	0.0015	0.0087
PAX_REVE	Pax revenues/RPK (passenger yield)	0.11	0.02	0.09
PERCENT_	Percent change in crude oil prices (US$/barrel)	0.0346	0.0017	0.0101
PERCENT1	Percent change in GDP USA	-0.10	0.04	0.26
REVEX	Revex	0.98	0.02	0.13
SCHED._R	Total revenue scheduled ops.	95.81	11.74	70.46
SPOT_FUE	Spot fuel $ (Jet A/Jet A1)	61.00	2.39	14.34
TOT._REV	Total revenue	148043	12756	76535
TOT.OP.E	Total op. Exp./employee	115	20	121
TOT._OP.	Total operating expense/ASK	0.08	0.01	0.05
TOTAL_DE	Total debt/total assets	0.98	0.10	0.61
WEIGHT_L	Weight load factor	0.52	0.01	0.09
YIELD	Yield	0.0748	0.0086	0.0516

N = 36. Numbers are rounded to two digits or less, unless it leads to a 0, in which case rounding was to three or four digits.

Appendix D

Table D.1 Airlines included in quantitative models

		Status
1	Carnival	0
2	Air California	0
3	Air Wisconsin 1	0
4	Air Wisconsin 2	0
5	America West 1	0
6	Horizon Air 1	0
7	Horizon Air 2	0
8	Midway Airlines 1	0
9	Midwest Express	0
10	New York Air	0
11	PSA-Pacific Southwest	0
12	People Express 1	0
13	Southwest Airlines 1	0
14	Southwest Airlines 2	0
15	Southwest Airlines 3	0
16	Tower Air 1	0
17	Tower Air 2	0
18	World Airways 1	0
19	Air Atlanta	1
20	Air Florida	1
21	Air Wisconsin 3	1
22	America West 2	1
23	Arrow Airways	1
24	Aspen	1
25	Braniff II	1
26	Capitol Air	1
27	Empire Airlines	1
28	Florida Express	1
29	Jet America	1
30	Midway Airlines 2	1
31	Muse Air	1
32	New York Air 2	1
33	People Express 2	1
34	Presidential Airways	1
35	Sunworld International Airway	1
36	World Airways 2	1

0 = non-failed, 1 = failed. Numbers following airline name denote Phase-In period, i.e. the airline's life-cycle was divided into non-failed and failed phases and included twice or more in the non-failed group and once in the failed group (*see* The Phase-In Algorithm for the small population case, 210).

References

Air Transport World (1982a), September, pp. 79-82.

Air Transport World (1982b), Some said 'It can't be done,' but Empire is doing it, p. 94.

Air Transport World (1982c), Special Report: Interlining an institution in transition, April, pp. 17 - 24.

Air Transport World (1982d), August, p. 44.

Air Transport World (1983a), Jet America is beginning to see daylight, October, pp. 49-50.

Air Transport World (1983b), People Express earns profit in first full year, April.

Air Transport World (1984a), Air 1 expansion planned to attain profits, August, pp. 47-48.

Air Transport World (1984b), Braniff Changes Strategy, October, p. 42.

Air Transport World (1984c), February, p. 61.

Air Transport World (1984d), October, pp. 83-86

Air Transport World (1985a), Northwest/America West combination strengthens position, July, pp. 54-55.

Air Transport World (1985b), Air Atlanta works toward strengthening its position, June, p. 44.

Air Transport World (1985c), Air Wisconsin survives the CRS blues, September, p.34.

Air Transport World (1985d), Regional international services are Air UK's specialty, September, pp. 83-86.

Air Transport World (1986a), Horizon refining management to hold Northwest domination, October, p. 113.

Air Transport World (1986b), Talking to employees: airlines discover internal communications, August, p. 25.

Air Transport World (1987), Southwest Airlines: Different but very much the same, May, p. 51.

Air Transport World (1988), Air UK sees strong growth this year, June, pp. 184-185.

Air Transport World (1989a), June, p. 60.

Air Transport World (1989b), December, p. 30.

Air Transport World (1989c), The (New) Philadelphia, December, p.87.

Air Transport World (1990), More Than a Toe in the Water Now, June, p. 19

Air Transport World (1991a), July, pp. 33-36

Air Transport World (1991b), November, pp. 117-119.

Air Transport World (1991c), Coddling the Rich and Famous, April, p. 54.

Air Transport World (1993), June, p. 110.

Air Transport World (1994), October, pp. 102-105.

Airfinance Journal (1984), Fit to survive, April, p. 18.

Airfinance Journal (1993), Southwest Stays in shape, 150, May, pp. 10-12.

Airfinance Journal (1994), Fit to survive, April, p. 18.

Airline Advertising Reform Act (1991) (H.R.5124), Hearing before the Subcommittee on Aviation of the Comm. on Publ. Works and Transp., House of Representatives, 102nd Congr., 2nd session, Government Printing Office.

Airline Business (1986), PeoplExpress: Time for Caution, July, p. 23.

Airline Business (1989), Emerging Rules, September.

Airline Business (1990a), North American Niches, May, p. 58.

Airline Business (1990b), Independent Lessons, April, pp. 50-55.

Airline Business (1991a), Too Close To The Sun, May, pp. 24-26.

Airline Business (1991b), Under Doctor's Orders, June, p. 56.

Airline Business (1993), Hub hubbub, August, p. 26.

Airline Business (1994), The Skies in 1994: The Growth Virus, p. 29.

Airline Competition Enhancement Act (1992), hearing before the Subcommittee on Aviation of the Committee on Public Works and Transportation House of Representatives, June 18.

Airline Executive International (1990a), America West Leaders Learn from Lorenzo's, June.

Airline Executive International (1990b), Could Presidential Have Survived?, September, pp. 32-34.

Airliners (1993), Class Act: The Muse Air/TranStar Story, No. 21, Spring, p. 26.

Alamdari, F. and Morrell, P. (1997), Airline labour cost reduction: post-liberalisation experience in the USA and Europe, *Journal of Air Transport Management*, Vol 3, pp. 53-66.

Altman, Edward I. (1968), Financial Ratios, Discriminant Analysis and The Prediction of Corporate Bankruptcy, *The Journal of Finance*, vol. 23, no. 4, Sept., pp.589-609.

Altman, Edward I. (1971), *Corporate Bankruptcy in America*, Heath-Lexington Books, Toronto-London .

Altman, Edward I. (1993), *Corporate Financial Distress and Bankruptcy*, 2nd ed., John Wiley & Sons.

Altman, Edward I., Haldeman, Robert G. and Narayanan, P. (1977), ZETA ANALYSIS: A new model to identify bankruptcy risk of corporations, *Journal of Banking and Finance*, 1, pp.29-54.

Anderson, John H. (1992), prepared statement in: *Hearing on the Airline Competition Enhancement Act of 1992*, Before the Subcommittee on Aviation of the Committee on Public Works and Transportation House of Representatives, U.S. Government Printing Office, Washington, June 18, pp. 139-167.

Ansoff, Igor (1987), *Corporate Strategy*, (revised ed.) Penguin Business, London.

Argenti, John (1973), *Corporate Collapse: The Causes and Symptoms*, McGraw-Hill, New York.

Aviation Week & Space Technology (AW&ST, 1994), May 9, p. 33.

Avmark Aviation Economist (1986), Charter versus scheduled in a liberalised Europe, October, p. 20.

Avmark Aviation Economist (1987a), Braniff Airlines: Expansion - without repeating history? November, p. 16.

Avmark Aviation Economist (1987b), Changing fortunes of Dallas star, August, p. 19.

Avmark Aviation Economist (1987c), Computer Reservation Systems: More international, more complex, more intense debate, May, p.19.

Avmark Aviation Economist (1989), Refuting the 'nowhere to nowhere' jibe, October, pp.16-20.

Avmark Aviation Economist (1990), Airline expansion on an IT base, February/March, pp. 15 - 21.

Avmark Aviation Economist (1993a), March.

Avmark Aviation Economist (1993b), The silent conversation issue: farce or tragedy?, May, pp. 2-4

Avmark Aviation Economist (1994), Do airlines still need to own CRSs, April, pp. 17-18.

Bailey, Elizabeth and Williams, Jeffrey R. (1988), Sources of economic rent in the deregulated airline industry, *Journal of Law & Economics*, 33, pp. 173 - 202.

Bailey, Elizabeth E., Graham, David, R., Kaplan, Daniel P. (1985), *Deregulating the Airlines*, MIT Press.

Bain, Joe S. (1949), A Note on Pricing in Monopoly and Oligopoly, *American Economic Review*, No. 448, 452 & no.7.

Barker, Julie (1990), Super Savers, *Successful Meetings*, vol. 39, iss. 10, Sep. 1990, pp. 152-154.

Barrett, Sean D. (1990), Deregulating European aviation - A case study, *Transportation*, vol. 16, pp. 311-327.

Baumol, Panzar and Willing (1983), Contestable Markets: An Uprising in the Theory of Industrial Structure, *American Economic Review*.

Baumol, W.J., Panzar, J.C. and Willing, R. (1982). *Contestable Markets and The Theory of Industry Structure*, Harcourt Brace Jovanovich, Sandiago.

Beauvais, G. A. (1992), In: *Hearing on the Airline Competition Enhancement Act of 1992*, Before the Subcommittee on Aviation of the Committee on Public Works and Transportation House of Representatives. U.S. Government Printing Office, Washington, June 18.

Beaver, W. (1967), Financial Ratios as Predictors of Failure, Journal of Accounting Research, vol. 5, pp. 71-111.

Berg, Deanna (1991), In Defence of Disorder, Discomfort and Discontent, Journal for Quality & Participation, vol. 14, iss. 5.

Bernstein, Aaron (1991), *Grounded: Frank Lorenzo and the Destruction of Eastern Airlines*, Touchstone, 1991.

Blum, M. (1974), Failing Company Discriminant Analysis, *Journal of Accounting Research*, Spring, pp. 1-25.

Borch, K. (1967), The theory of risk, *Journal of the Royal Statistical Society*, Series B.

Brander, James A., and Zhang, Anming (1990) Market conduct in the airline industry; an empirical investigation, Rand Journal of Economics, Vol. 21, No. 4, Winter.

Briggs, Martin (1991), The English Summer of 1990 - Further Progress Towards Deregulation of the Aviation and Travel Industry, Air Law, Vol. 16, No. 2, pp. 52-55.

Business Week (1981), Upstarts in the Sky: Here comes a new kind of airline, June 15, p. 89

Business Week (1985), Up, Up and Away?, November 25, p.64.

Business Week, Upstarts in the Sky: Here comes a new kind of airline, June 15, 1981, p. 89.

Button, Kenneth (1989a), The deregulation of U.S. interstate aviation: an assessment of causes and consequences (Part 1), *Transport Reviews*, Vol. 9, No. 1, pp. 99-118.

Button, Kenneth (1989b), The deregulation of U.S. interstate aviation: an assessment of causes and consequences (Part 2), *Transport Reviews*, Vol. 9, No. 2, pp.189-215.

Button, Kenneth (1991), *Airline Deregulation: International Experiences*, David Foulton Pub., London.

Buzzell, Robert D. and Gale, Bradley T. (1987), *The PIMS Principles: Linking Strategy to Performance*, The Free Press, Macmillan.

Carlson, Edward E. (1976), statement in: *Regulatory Reform in Air Transportation*, Hearings before Subcomm. on Aviation of Sen. Committee on Commerce on S.2551, S.3364, and S.3536, 94th Cong. 2nd Sess., pp. 532 and 534.

Carolyn Y Woo. and Arnold C. Cooper (1982), The Surprising Case for Low Market Share, *Harvard Business Review*, November-December 1982, pp. 106-113.

Chen, Kung H. and Shimerda, Thomas A. (1981), An Empirical Analysis of Useful Financial Ratios, *Financial Management*,Spring, pp. 51-60.

Chow, G., Gritta, R. D. and Hockstein, R. (1988), Airline Financing Policies in a Deregulated Environment, *Transportation Journal*, Spring, pp. 40-42

CIO (1989), Cancelled Flights, April, 1989, pp. 48-54.

Civil Aviation Authority (CAA 1993a), *Civil Aviation Act 1982: Statement of Policies on Route and Air Transport Licensing* - extract from Official Record Series 2, 25 May, London.

Civil Aviation Authority (CAA, 1993b), *Airline Competition in The Single European Market*, London, November (Report CAP 623).

Clutterbuck, D. and Kernaghan, S. (1990), *The Phoenix Factor: Lessons for Success from Management Failure*, Weidenfield & Nicolson.

Cochran, R. and Green, R. (1982), Statistical Methods for Bankruptcy Forecasting, *Journal of Economics and Business*, March, pp. 349-354.

Collins, Robert A. and Green, Richard D. (1982), Statistical Methods for Bankruptcy Forecasting, *Journal of Economics and Business*, vol. 34, pp.349-354.

Commission of the European Communities (EC, 1988), Press release 9 March.

Commuter Air International (1992), September, p. 13.

Conley, G. A. (1992), Statement in: *Hearing on the Airline Competition Enhancement Act of 1992*, Before the Subcommittee on Aviation of the Committee on Public Works and Transportation House of Representatives. U.S. Government Printing Office, Washington, June 18, pp. 168-200.

Conway, M. J. (1993), Statement in: Financial Condition of The Airline Industry: Hearings Before the Subcommittee on Aviation of the Committee on Public Works and Transportation, Government Printing Office, Washington, February 1993, pp. 640-653.

Cowan, David A. (1990), Developing A Classification Structure of Organisational Problems: An Empirical Investigation, *Academy of Management Journal*, vol.33, no.2, pp. 366-390.

Cras, Bernhard J.H. and Cras, Steven P. (1994), EC Aviation Scene, *Air & Space Law*, vol. XIX, no. 1.

D'Aveni, Richard A. (1989), The Aftermath of Organisational Decline: A Longitudinal Study of the Strategic and Managerial Characteristics of Declining Firms, *Academy of Management Journal*, vol. 32, iss. 3, pp.577-605.

Dahl, Dan and Sykes, Randolph (1989), Life Goals=Self Motivation=Business Success, Manage, vol. 41, iss. 2.

Davidow, William H. and Uttal, Bro (1989), *Harvard Business Review*, July-August.

Davis, Evan and Kay, John (1990), Assessing corporate performance, *Business Strategy Review*, Summer, pp. 1-16.

Deakin, Edward B. (1972), A Discriminant Analysis of Predictors of Business Failure, *Journal of Accounting Research*, Spring, pp. 167-179

Department of Transportation (DoT, 1988), *Study of Airline Computer Reservation Systems* (DOT-P-37-88-2), May.

Desai, M. and Montes, A (1982), A macroeconomic model of bankruptcies in the British economy, 1945-1980, *British Review of Economic Issues*, Vol. 4, pp. 1-14.

DeVany, A. S. (1975), The Effect of Price and Entry Regulation on Airline Output, Capacity and Efficiency, *Bell Journal of Economics*, 6, pp. 327-345.

Director (1991), How not to go bust, April, pp. 46-52.

Doganis, R. , Measure for Measure, *Airline Business*, May 1986, pp. 16-20.

Doganis, Rigas (1992), *The Airport Business*, Routledge 1992.

Doganis, Rigas (1993), *The Importance of the Competition Rules for Fair Competition – An Economist's View*, an unpublished paper given at the Royal Aeronautical Society, 1993.

Doganis, Rigas, *Flying Off Course*, Routledge, 2nd ed. 1991.

DoT (1992). In: *Hearing on the Airline Competition Enhancement Act of 1992*, Before the Subcommittee on Aviation of the Committee on Public Works and Transportation House of Representatives, U.S. Government Printing Office, Washington, June 18, p XL.

DoT (1993), *Change, Challenge and Competition*, The National Commission to Ensure a Strong Competitive Airline Industry: A report to the President and Congress, August 1993.

Douglas, G. W., and Miller, J. C. (1974), *Economic Regulation of Domestic Air Transport: Theory and Policy*, Brookings Institution.

Duchesneau, Donald and Gartner, William B. (1990), A profile of New Venture Success and Failure in Emerging Industry, *Journal of Business Venturing*, Vol 5, pp. 297-311.

Edmister, R. (1972), An Empirical Test of Financial Ratio Analysis for Small Business Failure Prediction, *Journal of Financial and Quantitative Analysis*, March, pp. 1477-1493.

Eisenbeis, Robert A. (1977), Pitfalls in The Application of Discriminant Analysis in Business, Finance, and Economics, *The Journal of Finance*, June 1977, pp. 875-900.

Eisenbeis, Robert A. and Avery, Robert B. (1972), *Discriminant Analysis and Classification Procedures: Theory and Applications*, Lexington, Mass., D.C. Heath and Co.

Eisenberg, J.F. and Dillon, Wilton S. (1971), Selection of selfish and altruistic behaviour in some extreme models, in:, eds., *Man and beast: Comparative social behaviour*, Smithsonian Institution, Washington, D.C., pp. 57-91.

European Commission (1990), Press Release IP (90) 870.

European Commission (1992), Decision no: 213/92/EEC, published in OJ 1992 L 96.

European Commission (1993), Press Release: IP/93/521, June 25.

Farrar, Clarence (1990), Early Warning Signals: Symptoms of a Troubled Company, *Retail Control*, March, pp. 10-13.

Fawcett, Stanley E., Farris, Martin T. (1989), Contestable Markets and Airline Adaptability Under Deregulation, *Transportation Journal*, Fall.

Feger, Helena (1987), America West Sets a Risky New Course, *Arizona Trend*, vol. 1, iss. 5, January, p.54.

Feldman, Joan (1987), *Regional airlines in the USA*, Travel & Tourism Analyst, The Economist Pub. Ltd..

Financial Condition of the Airline Industry (1993), Hearings Before the Subcommittee on Aviation of the Committee on Public Works and Transportation House of Representatives, One Hundred and Third Congress, First Session, February 17- 24.

Flamholtz, Eric G. (1990), *Growing Pains: How to Make the Transition from an Entrepreneurship to a Professionally Managed Firm*, Jossey – Bass Publishers, San Francisco.

Flight International (1993), EC Ministers Approve Slot Allocation Rules – Airspace Allocation Legislation, 27 January, p. 6.

Flight International (1994a), 3 – 9 August, p. 4.

Flight International (1994b), 31 August – 6 September, p. 11.

Francis, Jack C., Hastings, Harold M. and Fabozzi, Frank J. (1983), Bankruptcy as a Mathematical Catastrophe, Research in Finance, vol. 4, pp. 63-89.

Friedman, Milton (1962), Capitalism and Freedom.

General Accounting Office (GAO, 1990*), Airline Competition: Industry Operating and Marketing Practices Limit Market Entry*, report RCED-90-147.

General Accounting Office (GAO, 1991), *Airfare Econometric Model*, April, report GAO/RCED-91-101

Ginsberg, Ari and Buchholtz, Ann (1989), Are Entrepreneurs a breed apart? A look at the evidence, *Journal of General Management*, vol. 15, no. 2, pp. 32 – 40.

Goldsmith, Walter and Clutterbuck, David (1985), *The Winning Streak: Britain's top companies reveal their formula for success*, Penguin Business, 1985.

Gorman, Michael and Sahlman, William A. (1989), What do Venture Capitalists Do?, *Journal of Business Venturing*, vol. 4, pp. 231-248.

Goudie, A. and Meeks, G. (1991), The Exchange Rate and Company Failure in Macro-Micro Model of The UK Company Sector, *Economic Journal (UK)*, vol. 1001, iss. 406, May.

Graham, John R. (1991), What's Essential to a Five-Year Plan for Business Success?, Managers Magazine, vol. 66, iss. 7.

Gregory-Allen, Russell B. and Henderson, Glenn V. Jr. (1991), A Brief Review of Catastrophe Theory and a Test in a Corporate Failure Context, *The Financial Review*, vol. 26, no.2, May, pp. 127-155.

Gudmundsson, Sveinn V. (1986), In: *Skýrsla flugmálanefndar* (*transl.* Aviation Committee Report), The Ministry of Transport, Iceland, October, Part V, p. 3.

Gudmundsson, Sveinn V. (1997), The difference between European and US airline management practice: the case of new-entrant airlines, *Journal of Air Transport Management*, vol. 3, no. 2, pp. 75-82.

Gudmundsson, Sveinn V. (1998), New-entrant Airlines' Life-cycle Analysis: Growth, Collapse and Decline, *Journal of Air Transport Management*, vol. 4, no. 4, pp. 217-228.

Gupta, L.C. (1989), *Corporate Boards and Nominee Directors*, Oxford University Press, Delhi.

Hall, David (1992), *The Hallmarks for Successful Business: Survival-Change-Growth*, Mercury Books.

Hall, Richard (1991), The Contribution of Intangible Resources to Business Success, *Journal of General Management*, vol. 16, iss. 4, Summer.

Hamilton, William D. (1970), Selfish and spiteful behaviour in an evolutionary model, *Nature* 228, pp. 1218-1220.

Hampton, David R., Summer, Charles E. and Webber, Ross A. (1982), *Organisational Behavior and the Practice of Management*, 4th. ed., Scott, Foresman and Co.

Harvard Business School (HBS, 1974), Southwest, Case No. 574-060.

Harvard Business School (HBS, 1983), People Express (A), Case No. 483-103.

Harvard Business School (HBS, 1990), People Express, Case No. 490-012.

Hayek, Friedrich (1944). The Road to Serfdom.

Hickey, Denis (1991), Look Beyond the Balance Sheet: Behavioural Warnings of Troubled Businesses, *Commercial Lending Review*, vol. 6, no. 4, pp. 54-59.

Hintz, H. (1993), Statement in: *The Financial Condition of The Airline Industry*, Hearings Before the Subcommittee on Aviation of the Committee on Public Works and Transportation. Government Printing Office, Washington, February 1993, pp. 413-428.

Hoinville, Gerald and Jowell, Roger (1989), *Survey Research Practice*, Gower Pub. Co.

Houtte, Ben Van (1993), Community Competition Law in the Air Transport Sector (I): A Survey of the First Five Years, *Air & Space Law*, vol. 18, no. 2, p. 69.

Independent, The (1991), Virgin Atlantic - Branson's Favourite Baby Grows Up, November 25, p. 26.

Innes, John., Colin Aitken and Falconer Mitchell (1991), Prediction of Small Company Failure, *Credit Management*, September, pp. 37-42.

Jenks, Craig (1986), *US airlines hubs and spokes*, Travel and Tourism Analyst, The Economist Publications Ltd., August.

Jennings, Kenneth M. (1989), Union-Management Tumult at Eastern Airlines: From Borman to Lorenzo, *Transportation Journal*, Summer, pp. 13-27

Jordan, W. A (1970)., *Airline Regulation in America: Effects and Imperfections*, Johns Hopkins Press.

Kahn, A.E. (1978), Deregulation of Air Transportation-Getting from Here to There, In: *Regulating Business: The Search for an Optimum*, San Francisco: Institute for Contemporary Studies.

Keasey and Watson (1987), Non-Financial Symptoms and the Prediction of Small Company Failure: A Test of Argenti's Hypotheses, *Journal of Business Finance and Accounting*, Autumn, pp. 335-354.

Keeler, T.E.(1978), Domestic Trunk Airline Regulation: An Economic Evaluation, *Studies on Federal Regulation*, U.S. Senate Committee on Government Affairs, Washington.

Keeler, T.E., (1972), Airline regulation and market performance, *Bell Journal of Economics*, vol. 3, 1978, pp. 399-424.

Kotler, Philip (1988), *Marketing Management: Analysis Planning, Implementation, and Control*, Sixth Ed, Prentice-Hall, Englewood Cliffs, New Jersey.

Krüger, Wilfried (1989, Patterns of Success in German Businesses, *Long Range Planning*, vol. 22, no. 2, 1989.

Lane, Sarah J. and Schary Martha (1991), Understanding the Business Failure Rate, *Contemporary Policy Issues*, vol. 9, October, pp. 93-105.

Lev, Baruch and Sunder, Shyam (1979), Methodological Issues in The Use of Financial Ratios, *Journal of Accounting and Economics*, vol. 1, pp. 187-210.

Levine, Michael (1965), Is Regulation Necessary? California Air Transportation and National Regulatory Policy, *The Yale Law Journal*, vol. 74, pp. 1416-1447.

Levine, Michael E. (1987), Airline Competition in Deregulated Markets: Theory, Firm Strategy and Public Policy, *Yale Journal on Regulation*, vol 4, no. 2, pp. 392-494.

Lloyd's Aviation Economist (1984a), Southwest Airlines: the alternative route to low costs, October, p. 28-29.

Lloyd's Aviation Economist (1984b), Why Air Florida Failed, August, p.22.

Lloyd's Aviation Economist (1986a), Pushing Back the Final Frontier, May, pp. 23-24.

Lloyd's Aviation Economist (1986b), February/March.

Lowenfeld, Andreas F.(1981), *Aviation Law*, 2nd ed., Matthew Bender Pub.

Maldutis, John, (1993), Additions to the record: *Financial Condition of the Airline Industry* Committee on Public Works and Transportation, February.

Marcus, Alfred A., Airline Deregulation: Why the Supporters Lost Out, *Long Range Planning*, vol. 20, no. 1, p. 97.

Maren, Michael and Rose, Ronit A. (1991), Skinflint Strategies: By Slashing Waste, These Trailblaizers Turn Their Companies into Profit Juggernauts, *Success*, vol. 38, iss 5.

Martin, Daniel (1977), Early Warning of Bank Failure, *Journal of Banking and Finance*, vol. 1, pp. 247-276.

McNamara, Anne H. (1992), Statement in: *Airline Competition Enhancement Act of 1992*, Before the Subcommittee on Aviation of the Committee on Public Works and Transportation House of Representatives. U.S. Government Printing Office, Washington, June 18, pp. 253-278.

Menard, S. (1995). *Applied Logistic Regression Analysis*. Sage University Paper Series on Quantitative Applications in the Social Sciences, 07-106. Thousand Oaks, CA: Sage.

Meyer, J. R., Clinton, V. and Oster, C.V. (1984), *Deregulation and the New Airline Entrepreneurs*, MIT Press.

Meyer, J.R. and Oster, C.V. (1987), *Deregulation and the Future of Intercity Passenger Travel*, Cambridge MIT press.

Miller, A. and Dess, G. G. (1993), Assessing Porter's (1980) Model In Terms of Its Generalizability, Accuracy and Simplicity, *Journal of Management Studies*, vol. 30, no. 4, pp. 553-585.

Miller, Danny (1990), *The Icarus Paradox: How Exceptional Companies Bring About Their Own Downfall*, HarperBusiness.

Miller, Danny and Friesen, Peter H. (1983), Successful and Unsuccessful Phases of the Corporate Life Cycle, *Organisational Studies*, vol. 4, pp. 235-236.

Mises, Ludwig von (1980), *Planning for Freedom*, Libertarian Press.

Morley, Michael F. (1984), *Ratio Analysis*, Gee & Co Ltd.

Morrison, Steven and Winston, Clifford (1987), Empirical Implications and Tests of Contestability Hypothesis, *Journal of Law and Economics*, vol. XXX.

Nahavandi, Afsaneh (1993), Leader Style in Strategy and Organisational Performance: An Integrative Framework, *Journal of Management Studies*, vol. 30, no. 3, May.

Norusis, Marija J. (1990), SPSS/PC+ Statistics 4.0.

Nyathi, M., Hooper, P. and Hensher, D. (1993), Compass Airlines: 1 December 1990 to 20 December 1991: What went wrong?-Part 1, *Transport Reviews*, vol. 13, no. 2, pp. 119-149.

Ohlson, James A. (1980), Financial Ratios and the Probabilistic Prediction of Bankruptcy, *Journal of Accounting Research*, vol. 18, no. 1, pp. 109-131.

Oliva, Terence A. and Capdevielle, Christel M.(1981), Critique and Comment: Sussmann and Zahler: Throwing the Baby Out with the Bath Water, *Behavioural Science*, vol. 26, April, pp. 153-162.

Oum, T. H., Stanbury, W. T. and Tretheway (1991), Airline Deregulation in Canada and Its Economic Effects, *Transportation Journal*, Summer.

Owen Richard and Dynes, Michael (1990), *The Times Guide to 1992: Britain in a Europe Without Frontiers*, Times Books, 2nd ed.

Pass, C., Lowes, B., Pendleton, A. and Chadwick, L. (1991), *Collins Dictionary of Business*. Glasgow, Harper Collins.

PeoplExpress Prospectus (1983), April 26, pp. 21-22.

Peters, Tom and Waterman, Robert (1982), *In Search of Excellence*, Lessons from America's Best-Run Companies, New York.

Porter, Michael E. (1980), Competitive Strategy: Techniques for Analysing Industries and Competitors, *The Free Press*.

Porter, Michael E. (1985), *Competitive Advantage: Creating and Sustaining Superior Performance*, The Free Press, New York.

Preisendörfer, Peter and Voss, Thomas (1990), Organisational Mortality of Small Firms: The Effects of Entrepreneurial Age and Human Capital, *Organisation Studies*, vol. 11, no. 1, pp. 107-129.

Ray, Russ (1991), The 21st Century Manager: A Survey of Futuristic Business Studies, *Review of Business*, vol. 13, iss. 1,2.

Robertson, J. (1984), Research Directions in Financial Ratio Analysis, *Management Accounting* .

Sampson, Anthony (1985), *Empires of The Sky*, Coronet Books, London.

Santomero, A and Vinso, J. (1977), Estimating the probability of failure for firms in the banking system, *Journal of Banking and Finance*, Sept.

Sawers, David (1987), *Competition in the Air*, The Institute of Economic Affairs, London.

Scabens, Robert W., Ryan, Robert J., and Fletcher, Leslie (1981), Explaining Corporate Failure: A Catastrophe Theory Approach, *Journal of Business Finance and Accounting*, vol.. 8, Spring, pp. 1-26.

Schmid, Ronald (1992), Air Transport within the European Single Market - how will it look after 1992?, *Air & Space Law*, vol. XVII, no. 4/5, p. 202.

Scott, James (1981), The Probability of Bankruptcy: A Comparison of Empirical Predictions and Theoretical Models, *Journal of Banking and Finance*, vol. 5, pp. 317-344.

Shaffer, Mark E. (1989), Are Profit Maximisers the Best Survivors?, Journal of Economic Behavior and Organisation, vol. 12.

Shane, Jeffrey N. (1992), Prepared statement in: Hearing on the Airline Competition Enhancement Act of 1992, Before the Subcommittee on Aviation of the Committee on Public Works and Transportation House of Representatives, U.S. Government Printing Office, Washington, June 18, pp. 279-290.

Sharlit, Ian, Tobias, Paul and Weinwrum, George F. (1990), Six Early Warnings of Business Failure, *Executive Psychology*, March, pp. 26-30.

Slatter, Stuart (1984), *Corporate Recovery: A Guide to Turnaround Management*, Penguin Books.

Southwest Airlines (1993), *Flight Schedule*, 31 October, 1993.

Staw, Barry M., Sandelands, Lance C. and Button, Jane E., (1981), Threat-Rigidity Effects on Organisational Behavior: A Multilevel Analysis, *Administrative Quarterly*, vol. 26, December.

Stockton, Richard B. (1989), Symptoms of an Ailing Business, The Financial Manager. January/February, pp. 14-21.

Sussmann, Hector J. and Zahler, Raphael S. (1978), A Critique of Applied Catastrophe Theory in the Behavioural Sciences, *Behavioral Science*, vol. 23, Sept., pp. 383-389.

Tam, Kar Yan and Kiang, Melody Y. (1992), Managerial Applications of Neural Networks: The Case of Bank Failure Predictions, *Management Science*, vol. 38, no. 7, July, pp. 926-947.

Taucher, George (1993), After Success, What Next: Success as a Barrier to Change, *European Management Journal*, vol. 11, no. 1, March, pp. 9-17.

The 1987 Travel Agency Market, pp. 28-45

The Age (1991) (Melbourne, Australia), Compass Crashes, 21 December, p. 1.

The Age (1992) (Melbourne, Australia), 15 January, p.11.

The Australian Financial Review (1993), Is Competition Killing Compass, 4 March, p. 12.

The Times (1985), 20 June, p.3.

Tinsley, P. (1970), Capital structure, precautionary balances, and valuation of the firm: The problem of financial risk, *Journal of Financial and Quantitative Analysis*.

Travel & Tourism Analyst (1987), October.

Travel-Trade-Gazette-Europa (1993), April 22, p. 5.

Tregoe, Benjamin B. and Zimmerman, John W. (1979), Strategic Thinking: Key to Corporate Survival, *Management Review*, February, p. 10.

Varadarajan, P. Rajan and Ramanujam, Vasudevan (1990), The Corporate Performance Conundrum: A Synthesis of Contemporary Views and an Extension, *Journal of Management Studies*, Vol. 27, No. 5, pp. 463-483.

Weatcroft, Stephen and Lipman, Geoffrey (1986), *Air Transport in a Competitive European Market: Problems, prospects and strategies*, The Economist Publications Ltd., pp. 57-58.

Weston, J. Fred and Copeland, Thomas E. (1986), *Managerial Finance*, Eight Edition, The Dryden Press.

Wilcox, J. (1971), A Gambler's Ruin Prediction of Business Failure Using Accounting Data. *Sloan Management Review*, vol. 12.

Williams, George (1990), Cranfield Institute of Technology [now Cranfield University], College of Aeronautics, pp. 87-88, Ph.D thesis.

Windle, Robert J. (1991), The World's Airlines: A Cost and Productivity Comparison, *Journal of Transport Economics and Policy*, January, pp. 31 - 49.

Withey, S.B., (1962), *Reaction to Uncertain Threat, in Man and Society in Disaster*, editied by G.W. Baker and D.W. Chapman, New York: Basic Books.

Woo, Carolyn Y. and Cooper, Arnold C. (1982), The Surprising Case for Low Market Share, *Harvard Business Review*, November-December, pp. 106-113.

Zavgren, Christine V. (1983), The Prediction of Corporate Failure: The State of The Art, *Journal of Accounting Literature*, vol. 2, pp. 1-35.

Index